CW00550474

TRUTH
The first casualty

TRUTH

The first casualty

Michael O'Connell

Published in 1993 by
RIVERSTONE LTD.
EIRE

ISBN 0 9521265 0 8

Printed by Bookcraft (Bath) Ltd.

Acknowledgements

I wish to thank my two nephews – Simon Anthony for helping me with the research for this book, and Timothy Andrew for designing the cover.

*This book is dedicated to my mother, Mary O'Connell,
and to the memory of my Father, James O'Connell (1905-1984).*

Contents

Introduction

This is a book about justice and truth.

Or more accurately about injustice and untruth in England and Ireland. Both countries share a system of law and a tradition of a strong, fearless and independent legal profession which were once a source of mutual pride and the envy of the rest of the world. Both countries were accustomed to regard intimidation of witnesses, police brutality, fabricated evidence and forced and false confessions as the speciality of the South American republics and far removed from these Islands. Not any more. Too many innocent people have been convicted as a result of such conduct that to maintain such a position is to invite ridicule and contempt.

In this book I examine six separate cases. In Chapter One there is an analysis of the events of 30 January 1972, universally known as "Bloody Sunday" when a number of soldiers of the Parachute Regiment opened fire on a crowd taking part in a peaceful demonstration in the City of Derry on that day. The Lord Chief Justice, Lord Widgery, was appointed by the Conservative Government to conduct an inquiry into the loss of life. He was a former brigadier in the British Army; as a practitoner his area of interest and expertise lay in the field of town and country planning. He never displayed any great interest in, or enthusiasm for, criminal law. The report of his inquiry was published on 18 April 1972.

It is my view, shared by others, that that report was a calculated and cleverly contrived whitewash. It did immense damage to Britain's reputation throughout the rest of the world which had witnessed on television the coarse and brutal conduct of the army in Derry on that day. Seven Derry priests issued a statement following the shooting. In part of it they said:

" . . . We accuse the soldiers of shooting indiscriminately into a fleeing crowd, of gloating over casualties, of preventing medical and spiritual aid reaching some of the dying . . . We deplore the action of the army and the government in employing a unit such as the paratroopers who were in Derry yesterday. These men are trained criminals. They differ from the terrorists only in the veneer of respectability that a uniform gives them."

Those very strong words and sentiments were met by the propaganda machine in Britain which attempted to show that the army was under fire and only returned fire at aimed targets. It also tried to conceal the truth in a bodyguard of lies.

9

I consider that Lord Widgery did great damage to the reputation of the English judiciary for integrity,fairness and independence. He was selective in the evidence he heard. For example, John O'Kane – who saw his brother-in-law Gerard McKinney shot whilst unarmed and with his hands in the air saying "no, no, don't shoot" – was available as a witness but not called to give evidence before the Tribunal. Nor was the truth told to the Tribunal by the army. In a television documentary – *Remember Bloody Sunday* – broadcast by the BBC, the award-winning journalist Peter Taylor is shown interviewing the sergeant-major of Support Company of I Parachute Regiment, the soldiers of which fired every rifle shot at the crowd that Sunday afternoon. That NCO said that "Soldier H", whose conduct in Glenfada Park is examined in Chapter 1, fired two more bullets than he had been issued with, and thus had extra ammunition, without authority, in his possession. If he did, what about the others? If the purpose of the incursion into the Bogside was to conduct an arrest operation, why did that soldier arm himself with extra ammunition?

The families of the dead remain convinced that murder was done in Derry on that day. What they found totally unacceptable then, and find now, was the smear campaign directed against some the victims that these had fired at the army, and that in one case – that of Gerald Donaghy – he had nail bombs in his possession. Sadly, Lord Widgery, who gave every appearance of not understanding the forensic evidence, seemed to go out of his way to support the army's version of events. That may or may not not have changed over the past twenty years. In 1972 it was said that each of the dead was a gunman or nail bomber. In 1992, according to one individual soldier – the NCO of Support Company – it is substantially different: "I feel in my own heart," he told Peter Taylor, "that a lot of people were innocent. I feel very guilty about the subsequent effect of that day."

Such a statement, late in the day though it is,maybe a step towards establishing the truth of what really happened in Derry on Bloody Sunday.

In Chapter Two I examine the cases of the Maguire Seven and the Guildford Four. I trust that I make clear the view I have always held that these eleven people are totally innocent of the crimes alleged against them.

1974 was a terrible year for the people of both Ireland and England. On Friday, 17 May 1974, car bombs exploded without warning in the centre of Dublin and in the town of Monaghan in the Irish Republic. Twenty seven people died and more than one hundred were injured. The Minister for Justice said that two of the three cars used in the Dublin bombings had been hi-jacked earlier in the day in Belfast. Five months later, on 21 November, the Provisional IRA bombed the Tavern in the Town and the Mulberry Bush public houses in Birmingham, killing a total of twenty-one people and 161 were seriously injured.

The response of the British Government to the Birmingham public houses bombings was to rush through Parliament the Prevention of Terrorism (Temporary Provisions) Act, 1974. The first person to be arrested under that Act was Paul Hill, one of the Guildford Four. On October 5 1974 members of the Provisonal IRA had bombed two public houses used by the army in Guildford, the Horse and Groom and the Seven Stars. The bomb in the first public house exploded at 8. 30 p.m. and killed five people, including four army recruits, and injured many more. By the time the Seven Stars bomb went off, the public house had been cleared, thus avoiding any casualties. A month later, on 7 November, at 10 p.m., a bomb was thrown into the King's Arms public house in Woolwich, opposite the Royal Artillery depot. Two people were killed, and many more were injured.

Another person arrested in respect of the Guildford pub bombings was Gerard Conlon – in Belfast. I deal with the sequence of events in the text. He told the police that he had been shown by his aunt Annie (Mrs Anne Maguire) how to make bombs. As a result, she and others – the Maguire Seven – were arrested at the family home, an alleged bomb factory, at Third Avenue in North London, on December 3, 1974. For many years I attributed the blame for what happened to the Maguires firmly upon Gerard Conlon's shoulders. I now at least understand, if not condone, his conduct while in custody.

Following his release from prison, Gerard gave an interview to the Independent Television programme *First Tuesday*. He described how he was treated in a police station in Britain. There are many who would not have believed him twenty years ago; many might do so now. He said he was stripped, spat upon, beaten and dumped in an unheated cell. "I was absolutely petrified, I was being beaten, I was being degraded, I was being humiliated, I wasn't given any sleep. And then they turned round and said to me: 'We know where your mother works. She works in the Royal Victoria Hospital. She does shift work. Your sister works in the Dublin road which you know is a dodgy area – a lot of sectarian murders have been committed down there.' They told me they could arrange an 'accident'. And then things were taken out of my hands . . . How would you have felt if they put it to you and you didn't sign and they murdered your mother?"

Gerard Conlon's statements implicated Anne Maguire. A telegram sent by solicitors in Belfast from Gerard's father arrived at the Maguire home. The prosecution case against the Seven was that the telegram triggered off a panic. It defies comprehension that, following the arrest of a suspected terrorist, a telegram should be sent, quite openly, to the premises which the prosecution alleged was the training ground and bomb factory used by that very terrorist, and where the bombs that exploded in the Guildford pubs were made. I regret to say that some in England explain that conduct by calling it "The Paddy Factor". There are many people here, in all walks of life, who regard the Irish at large as both naive and stupid, who would do exactly what was done in that case, without regard for the consequences. It is such a misplaced attitude, which has not the slightest contemplation of the dedication and motivation of those who indulge in terrorism, that it ensures that such terrorism will both continue and thrive.

The remaining two of the Guildford Four are Carole Richardon and Patrick Armstrong. Carole is English, from a difficult personal background. She confessed to bombing both public houses in Guildford. She was addicted to drugs at the time of her arrest. While at the police station she was examined by the police surgeon, because she was hyperventilating. It is unclear whether the surgeon now admits giving her a pethidine injection to calm her down. Her subsequent confessions to bombing both public houses could not both be true, because it was proved that on the evening of 5 October she went to a concert in London, and her time of arrival would have precluded her presence in Guilford at the time the bomb was planted in the Seven Stars.

The explanation advanced to the jury by Sir Michael Havers Q.C., who lead the prosecution team in both the Guildford Four and Maguire Seven cases, was that this was a terrorist counter-interrogation technique, designed to cause confusion by combining both true and false statements. Where and when Carole Richardson, who was aged seventeen at the time of her arrest, received such training was not stated. This particular counter-interrogation technique, allegedly used by the IRA, had not surfaced before the trial, and has not surfaced since. Perhaps a more effective and purposeful training would have a suspect staying completely silent and not providing, as happened in this case, the prosecution with the only evidence of guilt in a confession statement.

In the text I deal in some detail with the confession statements of Patrick Armstrong. At the time immediately prior to his arrest he had been taking amphetamines and barbiturates. He, like the three others, alleged police impropriety in the course of the interviews. Sir Michael Havers, never a person to understate a point, told the court that if accusations of the most appalling kind were true, then there must have been a really gigantic conspiracy between two police forces – the Surrey

Police in Guildford and the Bomb Squad – involving officers of all ranks, and culminating in a most appalling perversion of justice. The conspiracy point seems to have disappeared since the release of the Guildford Four, following the quashing of their convictions by the Court of Appeal.

I deal in some detail in the text with the role of counsel for the prosecution in these two cases. Havers and three others were briefed to prosecute both. In February 1975 two of the team went to the then Attorney General to ask him to sign the consent form to prosecute the Maguire Seven. They had been charged with the unlawful possession of nitroglycerine, although none had been found at the family home where they had been arrested. The Attorney General had been reluctant to give his consent which was required by law. Without it there could be no continuance of the prosecution.

I have never known any such delegation to approach the leading Law Officer of the Crown in this way. A legal assistant in his department had expressed disquiet about the forensic evidence from RARDE, the Royal Armament Research and Development Establishment, part of the Ministry of Defence and based in Woolwich in South East London. Roger Maitland, questioned the methods used by RARDE. When the defence solicitors asked for information about how the forensic tests were carried out, as opposed to simply being told what the results of the tests were, the prosecution failed to reply for six months, and then "hedged" about giving this information. The "hedge" took place, according to one of the prosecuting counsel, Mr Paul Oliver Purnell, because he was concerned about security. Sir John May, who has been (and currently is) conducting an inquiry into the Maguire Seven case, and that of the Guildford Four suggested to Mr Purnell that such matters were the concern of the department of the Director of Public Prosecutions, rather than junior counsel for the Crown. Sir John May has made it clear that he believes the failure of the prosecution to make full disclosure of the forensic evidence contributed to a miscarriage of justice in the Maguire Seven case.

Mr Maitland's reservations about RARDE's procedures may now be justified, in the light of what has since been disclosed about the forensic evidence.

When the Maguire house was searched following the arrests there, no bulk of nitroglycerine was found.

Subsequently a police officer took a number of plastic gloves used by Mrs Maguire from the house. I maintain that search and seizure was illegal in English law and, since the only evidence against her was the minute traces of nitroglycerine on one of the gloves, it is my view she was convicted on evidence which was illegally obtained. Such a search, in Irish law, would be a breach of a fundamental constitutional right of the inviolability of a dwelling house. The Irish courts would not, in the absence of special circumstances which are not applicable here, allow the glove and its test results to be admitted in evidence. The Irish courts expect the police and others who administer the law to observe it.

In Chapter Three I deal with the Hackney Arms Trial. The most important point to be made in this case is that if there had been a prosecution against those police officers, presumably from the Birmingham area, who had in some way allowed the hand gun found in Hackney to leave their custody in the Midlands, then such a prosecution to conviction might have persuaded others that planting and fabricating evidence is not worthwhile. Might society have then been spared the activities in the 1970s and 1980s of the West Midland Serious Crimes Squad, who have done so much to damage, almost beyond repair, the reputation of the police in England and Wales?

In Chapter Four I deal with the case of Edward Manning Brophy. He was charged with a number of terrorist offences in Northern Ireland, including the murders of twelve people in a most terrible bombing of the La Mon House hotel. He was acquitted of forty-eight offences, but he confessed, freely and openly in my view, to membership of a proscribed organisation, the Provisional IRA. The House of Lords quashed his conviction for that offence, notwithstanding the fact that it was based on his confession. By coincidence, four of the same Law Lords refused leave to the Birmingham Six to pursue a civil action against the police for damages for assault, on the ground that the same issue had already been decided against them by another court. Four of those six were convicted on the strength of confession evidence which they had not volunteered freely and openly; these confessions had been extracted by brutality and violence. On any view of Mr Brophy's case, truth was a casualty at his trial.

In Chapter Five I describe the deaths of two children, Majella O'Hare and John Boyle. These are two cases which are etched deeply into the conciousness of the people directly concerned in them. They should also stir the consciences of those who stay silent in the face of injustice. The death of a child in such violent circumstances is tragic enough, but when efforts were made to conceal the circumstances of the death by blatant and outright lies the grief is immeasureable. The first reaction of the army when Majella and John were shot dead by soldiers was immediate and instinctive; it was to issue public statements which obliterated any regard for the truth.

Mentioned in this chapter are the savage killings of five members of two separate Catholic families on Sunday, 4 January 1976. Masked gunmen broke into their homes and shot them dead. The following day the Provisional IRA exacted terrible retribution when twelve gunmen stopped a bus at Kingsmills, County Armagh and shot ten workmen in cold blood. All were Protestants. Words are not adequate to describe such pitiless, merciless savagery. No side in Northern Ireland has a monopoloy of shocking, unmitigated terror, and I can only equate the callousness of these dreadful murders with the killing of Miriam Daly on 26 June 1980.

Mrs Daly was a lecturer in political science at Queen's University Belfast. At 3:20 in the afternoon of Thursday, 26 June,Mrs Daly was found, bound hand and foot, shot in the head six times from close range, in the hallway of her home in Andersonstown, West Belfast. She was lying face downwards; a cushion had been used to deaden the sound of the shots. The blood on the floor and on the walls of the hall made it resemble a badly kept abattoir. The person who found the body was Mrs Daly's ten year old daughter, who had just returned home from school. The traumatic effect of that murder on the little girl can only be imagined. The killers were thought to be members of the protestant paramilitary Ulster Freedom Fighters; they have never been brought to justice.

Also in this chapter I mention the book by Brigadier Peter Morton, published in 1989, which describes the incident in which Majella O'Hare died. He commanded a battalion of the Parachute Regiment on a tour of duty in Northern Ireland in 1976. In his diary he noted "What we want is dead terrorists, not empty cartridge cases," and he speaks of being "keen to avenge the deaths" of soldiers killed by the IRA. Majella was shot by a soldier of 3 Parachute Regiment, but that was hardly the revenge he had in mind. However, like so many others he cannot resist the old canard of the drunken Irish, and he describes a husband and wife in Belfast (where they keep coal in the bath, so he says) leaving their six children, in order to spend every night in the public house. This is pretty rich from a person whose fellow patriots, according to the latest statistics of the National Prevention of Cruelty to Children, cause on average the deaths by violence or neglect of three children in Great Britain every week of the year.

Brigadier Morton's book deserves to be read because it is essentially the rattle of a simple man who, like so many of his generation and in his position, blindly, obediently and unquestioningly accepts that charity begins at home, but overlooks the fact that Britain's Empire began in other peoples' homes.

In Chapter Six I examine the case of Stephen McCaul. If any society is judged by the way it treats its children, then this case might cause someone to pause for thought about not only the attitude of society to criminal conduct and its investigation, but to reflect on the whole legal system in Northern Ireland.

In Chapter Seven, I deal with the killing of two unarmed men – Seamus Grew and Roderick Carroll – by members of the security forces in County Armagh on 12 December 1982. This case is frequently linked with two others, the killing on 11 November 1982 of three men and the killing of one youth and the wounding of another on 24 November 1982, also in County Armagh. It was following these three separate shootings that John Stalker, then the Deputy Chief-Constable of the Greater Manchester Police, was appointed to conduct an investigation into the circumstances of the three cases where six people had been shot dead and one grievously wounded, and in which certain members of the Royal Ulster Constabulary, the RUC, provided false or misleading information to members of the Criminal Investigation Branch in connection with the shootings. He had also to investigate the circumstances in which members of the RUC entered the Irish Republic from Northern Ireland on 12 December 1982 while on duty, and to investigate and report on the handling of informants by police officers. He was not asked, as is commonly supposed in some quarters, to decide whether there was evidence that the security forces were operating a policy of "shoot-to-kill" in Northern Ireland.

The three men shot dead in a car at Tullygally East Road – Eugene Toman, Sean Burns and Gervaise McKerr – were killed on 11 November 1982, by officers who belonged to a Special Support Unit of the RUC based at police headquarters in East Belfast

That unit had been trained in methods favouring "speed, power and aggression" the hallmarks of the SAS units of the British Army. Many members of the special support units were themselves former soldiers in the army, and they operated with a secret undercover group known as Echo Four Alpha, E4A, which conducted surveillance often with the equipment and expertise of British Intelligence services, MI5. The three deceased men were alleged by an informer to have been responsible for the murders of three RUC officers who died in a landmine explosion at Kinnego near Lugan on 27 October 1982. That informer was said to have received the sum of £20.000 for that information, which may or may not have been true for no evidence of their involvement in the murders has ever been produced. In the absence of evidence there was then, as there still is now, always the option of an ambush in which the suspects attempt to flee or resist or try to resist arrest by force of arms. In the event it was alleged that these three men did both.

A Ford Escort car driven by Mr McKerr sped away and the RUC officers, believing that they were being fired upon, returned fire. The Escort ran off the road; RUC officers had fired 108 shots at the three occupants. The three deceased were unarmed. The RUC press office said in a statement the following morning that the car had been approaching a vehicle check point, was signalled to stop, appeared to do so but then accelerated away, injuring an officer. In truth there was no road block and no officer was injured in the way described. In fact the three men in the Escort had been under surveillance for many hours and there was a plan to intercept their car, apparently in another area. The police officers waiting for them were armed with a Sterling sub-machine-gun, Ruger rifles and a handgun. They claimed that they had followed the Escort over a distance of some five hundred yards.

When the RUC officers were charged with murder they were acquitted by the late Lord Justice Gibson who said that they were "absolutely blameless". He praised them for their "commendable courage and determination" and for "bringing the three deceased to justice, in this case the final court of justice." His comment caused some unease in England, but in the Republic of Ireland it was regarded as a real gem, so neatly encapsulating the quality of British justice for the Nationalist Community in the North. There was a difficulty in the case that might have troubled some members of the judiciary: after the crash the body of Eugene Toman was found on the ground outside the car; questions might have been asked how that could have happened if he was shot dead during the car chase. The explanation put forward in court was that Mr Toman had fallen against the inside door handle and his dead weight had pushed down that handle, causing the car door to open.

There was no reason at all why the trial judge should not have been invited by the prosecution to inspect the Ford Escort and test the probability of this explanation.Had that happened it would have become clear immediately that such an explanation was worthless, because in the particular model of the Ford Escort involved the door handle was a small plastic lever which was pulled out *towards* the passenger, and not *downwards*, out of a moulded niche. This important rebuttal evidence was never put before the court.

A similar format of events was to be repeated in the killings of Seamus Grow and Roderick Carroll. They also were alleged to have driven through a vehicle check point and injured an officer. An inept and incomplete police investigation by the RUC followed. John Stalker regarded the investigations of the shootings as a "catalogue of ineptitude". My view is that these two were sentenced to death not as part of a deliberate policy to shoot-to-kill but more a policy to kill without question because there was no evidence against them, only suspicion of involvement in terrorist murder. In their case too there was an elaborate cover-up story prepared, so John Stalker considered, even before the shootings had taken place. There was also the use of an RUC officer who may have honestly believed that he was killing an entirely different person, a dangerous terrorist – Dominic McGlinchey.

John Stalker discovered that one of the officers present at the scene of the Tullygally Road East shootings was also present at the killing, in a hayshed at Ballyneary, of Michael Tighe, aged 17. The deceased and his friend Martin McAuley, aged 19, went into the shed where three old rifles with their bolts removed had been left. There was no ammunition in the hayshed. Exactly what happened next has never been fully disclosed;the RUC officers involved lied to the original investigation. When Martin McAuley appeared before Belfast Crown Court charged with the unlawful possession of three rifles with intent to endanger life, the trial judge said of those officers: "I have some reservation about the credibility and accuracy of certain parts of their evidence. Unfortunately, they enter the arena of credibility under a cloud; the cloud that initially each of them knowingly made a false allegation in their first written statements to the effect that Sergeant X had seen a man armed with a rifle enter the hayshed and that on seeing this, had said so to Constables Y and Z. There was not a word of truth in this- It was invented, not by them, but regrettably by one or more of their superiors who told them that there were obliged to say it and under orders they did say it."

Is there not something extremely distasteful about the sight of the occupiers of the high moral ground in a fight for the principles of law and order against terrorism indulging in the dissembling of the truth and the purveying of false information with such regularity? One question the RUC ought to be asked, and perhaps more importantly their press officers ought to answer, is why is it better to lie than to tell the truth?

In his defence evidence at his trial, Martin McAuley described the events at the hayshed. He said the police officers had opened fire without warning. Then he had been called on to come out of the shed, but before he could move he was hit by another burst of gunfire which was rapidly followed by a second burst. He was dragged out of the shed and an officer held a gun against his head and spoke of finishing him off. In his inquiry, John Stalker discovered that, unknown to anyone at the trial, there had been placed inside the hayshed an MI5 listening device. This was apparently being monitored by a joint RUC/British Army team nearby, and the events at the hayshed had been recorded on tape. That tape would have disclosed whether the RUC officers had, as they claimed, called out two warnings outside the hayshed before opening fire, and might have recorded and thereby destroyed the allegation about "finishing off" Martin McAuley. On the other hand, it might have proved that he was telling the entire truth.

In the event, Mr Stalker's efforts to obtain that tape were not successful. He regarded the obtaining of it as an issue that transcended all others in his inquiry in Northern Ireland. In his autobiography published in 1988 he set out his reasons for strongly pursuing that tape: "As an individual, I also passionately believed that if a police force of the United Kingdom could, in cold blood, kill a seventeen year old youth with no terrorist or criminal convictions, and then plot to hide the evidence from a senior police officer deputed to investigate it, then the shame belongs to us all . . . The cover stories, the lies, the obstruction were insignificant when placed alongside State murder."

He was up against formidable opposition. Rather than let him have that tape, the political/police legal establishment in Northern Ireland and in Great Britain were prepared to sacrifice him and his entire career as a police officer. The plain people of England are only allowed to know what those in positions of authority consider they can safely be told, and Mr Stalker might have discovered facts which were not suitable for public consumption. Better to resort to a bodyguard of lies rather than admit to the existence of prime facie evidence of unlawful killing in the name of the security of the State.

Mr Stalker, a rising star within the police establishment destined for the highest offices in the police service, might have been regarded by those responsible for his appointment to this inquiry as a "safe pair of hands", who would put self-interest before truth. As it turned out they could not have been more wrong. John Stalker would settle for nothing less than the full unvarnished truth about the events he was asked to investigate; he was not to be allowed to tell it. He was removed from the inquiry before he delivered his final report to the Chief Constable of the RUC.

For my part – and I may not be alone in this – I would welcome a clear unequivocal condemnation of unlawful State violence in Northern Ireland from the Cardinal Archbishop of Westminster and the Catholic Archbishops and Bishops of England and Wales. Too often in the past the Catholic Church in the United Kingdom of Great Britain and Northern Ireland has been a Church of Silence in the face of such institutional violence. It is of course right to condemn the vicious brutality of the Provisional IRA, but the violence is no less vicious, or brutal or more lawful because it is carried out by those wearing the uniform of the State and who acted in the way John Stalker described. There can be no compromise on truth. No one should be above the law, but accountable to it.

Finally, I wish to pay tribute to, and to thank, a Catholic priest whose courage and integrity I admire greatly. Father Raymond Murray, Administrator of St. Patrick's Cathedral in Armagh, has helped and encouraged me in my writing for a number of years. He has been, and continues to be, a tireless worker – together with Father Denis Faul – in the cause of justice and truth. He is an implacable opponent of terrorism, and he is unequivocal in his condemnation of the Provisional IRA. I share those values and support his statements of condemnation. But like him I also condemn all forms of terrorism, from whatever side, and in whatever guise, whether it is the protestant paramilitaries or the death squads of the security forces, especially the SAS, as well as the IRA.

It has always been my view that Ireland may be worth living for, but it is not worth dying for. Moreoever, the cause of Ireland cannot in any circumstances justify the taking of the life of another. I have known many people in Ireland who shared that sentiment.

It is only the truth that will defeat terrorists and their tactics. Truth is a very fragile commodity, especially in the mouths of the politicians, who seem to approach every problem about Ireland with mouths that are so frequently open and minds that are so firmly shut. I hope that this book will encourage people to think and to talk of all the things that are done in all our names. Anyone who reads this book might not be much wiser after doing so, but at least they will be better informed. Those who do not learn from the mistakes of the past are destined to repeat them in the future.

Chapter 1

BLOODY SUNDAY – A JOLLY GOOD SHOW?

In January 1972 the Northern Ireland Civil Rights Association informed the then Minister for Home Affairs of the Stormont Government in Belfast that it proposed to hold a protest march in the City of Derry on Sunday, 30 January 1972. All marches had been banned in Northern Ireland since 9 August 1971, under the Civil Authorities (Special Powers) Act (Northern Ireland) 1922, when internment without trial was introduced.

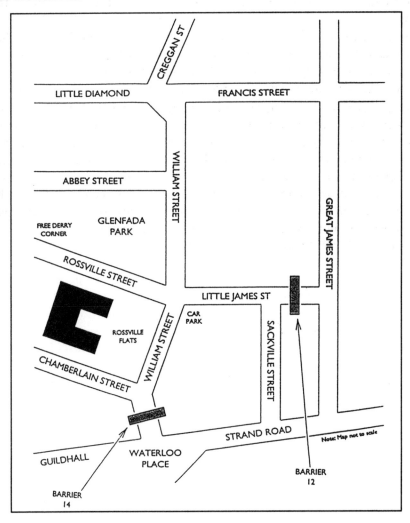

The purpose of the march was to protest not only against internment but also against the physical brutality inflicted upon internees, especially at the Interrogation Centre at Ballykinler in County Down. One man, James Auld, was alleged to have been forced to stand facing a wall, hands overhead against it, with his legs spread apart for a total of forty-three hours. He, and others, were fully hooded – navy or black coloured bags of tightly woven or hessian cloth were place over their heads. They were subjected, pending interrogation or between interrogations, to a continuous hissing noise, or electronic "mush".[1] Internees who attempted to rest or sleep by propping their heads against the wall were prevented from doing so. If one collapsed on the floor he was picked up by the armpits and placed against the wall to resume the approved posture.

Sir Edmund Compton, who conducted an inquiry into allegations against the security forces of brutality, refers to the case of Patrick Joseph McClean who, he says, "persisted" in collapsing from the start. Mr McClean, a schoolteacher, was somewhat overweight. After a short time he "was not forcibly held up but allowed to lie on the floor." [2] In Compton's view this was a magnanimous gesture on the part of the supervising staff (as they are referred to in his Report). The reaction in the rest of the United Kingdom to this unlawful and brutal treatment of innocent men, in what was an information gathering exercise, was extremely muted.

Meanwhile, the response of the Security Forces in Northern Ireland to the proposed illegal march, following a "final decision taken by higher authority"[3] was that the Civil Rights march in Derry would be allowed to begin, but that it should be contained within the general area of the Bogside and the Creggan Estate, so as to prevent rioting in the City Centre and damage to commercial premises and shops[4]. Twenty six barriers were erected in the streets. A total of 1800 troops assembled at the borders of the Bogside in support of the Royal Ulster Constabulary[5]. Amongst the soldiers was the First Parachute Regiment (1 Para).

In the afternoon of Sunday,30 January 1972, twenty-one soldiers from 1 Para fired 107 rifle shots in the Bogside at the crowd of marchers. Thirteen civilians were shot dead and another thirteen were wounded. One journalist, Simon Winchester, then of *The Guardian*, reports another journalist as saying it had been "a jolly good show."[6]

The marchers had assembled on the Creggan Estate "in a carnival mood". They included many women and some children and were orderly and good humoured.[7] They reached the outskirts of the Bogside at the west end of William Street. Ahead and to the right was Rossville Street leading to Free Derry Corner; beyond and just past the junction of

William Street and Chamberlain Street was barrier 14, manned by soldiers of the Royal Green Jackets and C Company of 1 Para. That barrier prevented the marchers from proceeding on to Guildhall Square. The march stewards, acting in accordance with the prior decision of the organisers[8] turned the procession to the right along Rossville Street, thus avoiding a head-on confrontation with the army at barrier 14.

A substantial number of the marchers, however, approached barrier 14 and threw stones and heavy objects at the soldiers. No soldiers were injured. But that did not stop the army from responding with rubber bullets and CS gas. A water cannon which had been held in reserve behind the barrier was brought up; the soldiers proceeded to drench the crowd with water coloured with a purple die.

In the words of Lord Widgery, the Lord Chief Justice – and a former British Army officer – who had been appointed by the Government to inquire into the Events of 30 January 1972: "At about 15:55 hours the troops appeared to be reaching a position in which they might disperse the rioters and relieve the pressure upon themselves."[9] That being so, there was no need and no justification for launching the arrest operation which followed shortly afterwards. Even Lord Widgery was forced to recognise that, for he says in his Summary of Conclusions at number 3: "If the army had persisted in its 'low key' attitude and had not launched a large scale operation to arrest hooligans the day might have passed off without serious incident."

It was about 15:55 that the first gun shots, five in all, were fired by the army. This was during an incident separate and apart from the central incident beginning after 16:05, when the majority of the casualties were caused. It began in this way:

A number of soldiers of Support Company of 1 Para were providing cover for a wire-cutting party which was clearing a route into the Bogside over a wall at the side of a Presbyterian church. The main body of Support Company was assembled behind barrier 12 on Little James Street – the street which bisects William Street. When the presence of the cover party was noticed by those throwing stones in Little James Street, " . . . a hail of missiles was thrown at these soldiers. After a time Soldier A fired two rounds and Soldier B fired three rounds."[10] The soldiers shot a teenager – Damian Donaghy – and a middle-aged man – John Johnson. The victims were treated for their injuries by a local doctor, Raymond McClean, who puts the time of treatment at approximately fifteen minutes before the shooting from the direction of Glenfada Park[11].

Lord Widgery accepts that "Having seen and heard Mr Johnson I have no doubt that he was telling the truth as he saw it. He was obviously an innocent passer-by going about his own business in Londonderry that afternoon and was *almost certainly* [emphasis added] shot by accident."[12]

Damien Donaghy was still detained in hospital and did not give evidence to Lord Widgery's Tribunal. However, Lord Widgery was content to say he "was satisfied that had he [Donaghy] given evidence it would have been in the same sense as that given by Mr Johnson."[13] Thus it was accepted that he too was an unarmed innocent person;was he too *almost certainly* shot by accident? Soldier A told the Tribunal he fired two shots at a man who appeared to be lighting a nail bomb. The first shot missed.The second hit the bomber. Soldier B fired three shots at a man who appeared to be lighting a nail bomb. The first shot had no effect, so he fired two more, "whereupon the man fell back and was dragged away by two of his comrades."[14]

The difficulty with the soldiers' explanation may be that none of the numerous photographs or reels of television film show any civilian holding or throwing a nail bomb; no casualties were suffered by the army as a result of the explosion of a nail bomb; no trace of gelignite was found under forensic examination on any civilian, living or dead, on that Sunday or any subsequent day.

Apart from a brief undetailed reference by Lord Widgery to a rifle shot, the available evidence is that the first gun shots of Bloody Sunday, five in all, on their own admission, and on their own evidence, were fired by members of Support Company of 1 Para. This fact, which cannot now be contested, is irreconcilable with the statement of Mr Harold Wilson in the House of Commons on Monday, 31 January 1972 when he said: " . . . we have had the categorical statements of the Commander, Land Forces, to the effect that no shots were fired until sniping began, and that shots were fired *only at snipers* [emphasis added]."[15]

Lord Widgery accepts that "By 16:00 hours the pressure on barrier 14 had relaxed. There were still 100 to 200 hooligans in the William Street area but most of the non-violent marchers had either turned for home or were making their way down Rossville Street to attend a meeting at Free Derry Corner where about 500 were already assembled."[16] This is confirmation that there was no need to launch an arrest operation.

A detailed plan – 8 Infantry Brigade Operation Order No. 2/72, dated 27 January – had been prepared by Brigadier MacLellan. That Order "provided that the march should be dealt with in as low a key as possible and indeed that if it took place entirely within the Bogside and Creggan it should go unchallenged. No action was to be taken against the marchers, unless they tried to breach the barriers or used violence against the security forces."[17]

24

No barriers were breached and no soldier had been injured by 16:00. Lord Widgery says: "In the light of events the wisdom of carrying out the arrest operation is debatable. The army had achieved its main purpose of containing the march and, although some rioters were still active in William Street, *they could have been dispersed without difficulty* [emphasis added]."[18] However, the Operation Order had allotted a specific task to 1 Para. It was as follows:

"1. Maintain a Brigade Arrest Force to conduct a scoop-up operation of as many hooligans and rioters as possible. (a) This operation will only be launched either in whole or in part on the orders of the Brigade Commander." Sub-paragraphs (b) and (c) are coyly omitted by Lord Widgery's Report, but he sets out the terms and effect of (c) on page 11 because he appreciates its importance. "(d) It is expected that the arrest operation will be conducted on foot."

On page 11 Lord Widgery incorporates sub-paragraphs (d) and (c) together in that reverse order. "Further, the Brigade Order said it was expected that the arrest operation would be conducted on foot and that the two axes of advance were likely to be towards the areas of William Street/Little Diamond and William Street/Little James Street i.e. the Order did not contemplate the use of Rossville Street as an axis of advance." It was clearly not intended that the army should advance into the Bogside towards free Derry Corner which lay at the end of Rossville Street. Yet that is exactly what some soldiers of 1 Para did. It was argued before Lord Widgery that in so doing those soldiers had acted without orders or in defiance of orders. In spite of the written documentary evidence which supported it, and which was compiled by the army in the form of a contemporaneous record, he rejected that argument.

The Brigade Log, maintained in the Brigade Operations Room during the course of that Sunday afternoon, is a minute by minute record of events and messages. There are two significant entries. First, "Serial 147, 15:55 hours from I Para. Would like to deploy sub-unit through barricade 14 to pick up yobbos in William Street/Little James Street." (It is important to know that the paratroopers at barricade 14 were from C Company, and that a sub-unit is a Company.) There was no apparent response at that time to that request, perhaps because as Lord Widgery records, "by 16:00 hours the pressure on barrier 14 had relaxed."[19] Second, "Serial 159, 16:09 hours from Brigade Major. Orders given to 1 Para at 16:07 for *one sub-unit* [emphasis added] of 1 Para to do scoop-up through barrier 14. Not [and this word is underscored] to conduct running battle down Rossville Street."

The reason for the prohibition was obvious: the Civil Rights marchers who had peacefully walked from the Creggan towards Free Derry Corner were still on Rossville Street, and only, a limited number of stone throwers were between them and the army. These orders are clear and unequivocal and addressed only to C Company. Yet as Lord Widgery records[20], after indicating that three Companies – A, C and Support Company – were available for the arrest operation; "In the event all three Companies *moved forward at the same time* [emphasis added]." A Company operated in the Little Diamond area; no paratrooper of that Company fired a single rifle shot and not one was injured in any way. C Company went forward on foot through barrier 14 (as it had been specifically ordered so to do according to serial 159). No trooper of that Company fired a single rifle shot and not one was injured in any way. Support Company drove in vehicles (ten in all), in spite of the intention that the arrest operation should be conducted on foot, through barrier 12 into Rossville Street Their purpose, so Lord Widgery says[21], was to encircle rioters on the waste ground or pursued by C Company along Chamberlain Street.

Whatever their purpose, paratroopers of Support Company did exactly what was prohibited in Serial 159 and conducted a running battle along Rossville Street. Seven of the dead were shot there. The only Company of 1 Para to open fire that afternoon was Support Company. Two of its soldiers had earlier wounded two pedestrians near William Street shortly before four o'clock that afternoon. Now their tally was thirteen dead and eleven wounded, without a single casualty being inflicted on them by gunfire, stone or any object whatever. On the basis of the Brigade Log they had no orders to proceed through barrier 12 at all; the only order was directed to C Company at barrier 14 with the attached prohibition not to conduct a running battle down Rossville Street.

Just as important, however, is Serial 164 which is properly recorded in the Log, but which Lord Widgery omits completely from his Report. Instead he makes the false and irrelevant point that " . . . when the Brigade Major gave instructions to the log keeper to make the entry which appears as Serial 159 the latter mistakenly thought that the order was a response to the request in Serial 147 and he entered it accordingly."[22] Serial 159, whether standing alone or read in conjunction with another log entry, purports to be the record of an order given by the Brigade Commander to the officer commanding the paratroopers to advance one Company of paratroopers (not three) to carry out an arrest operation through barrier 14, and not to deploy them in a running battle in Rossville Street, as in fact happened. There is no transcript of the order in Serial 159 because, according to the Brigade Major, it was transmitted on a secure wireless link, i.e. one not open to eavesdropping. This link was used because the arrest operation depended on surprise for its success[23].

One might question therefore the wisdom of 1 Para requesting permission to deploy a sub-unit through barrier 14 to pick up yobbos on the normal open link, in serial 147 at 15:55. The Brigade Major told Lord Widgery that he issued the order to 1 Para to begin the scoop-up operation, and although he supervised the entry of the order, serial 159 in the brigade log, that entry does not accurately reflect the order that was given. He said that, although the log entry appeared to authorise only C Company to go in and make arrests, he understood, from the Brigade Commander's plan, that three Companies, including Support Company, were expected to participate in arrest operations[24]. He also denied that any order was given to C Company to return to its original position, despite the clear language of the transcript of the tape recording of the radio message giving this order[25].

Only those messages sent as normal military traffic were recorded on tape; there are no tape recordings of messages transmitted on the secure wireless link. However, every order, regardless of the method of communication used, had to be noted in the Brigade Log. The blame for the alleged wrongful entry in the log as serial 159, in not properly recording the terms of the order issued by the Brigade Major, is firmly placed by Lord Widgery upon the log keeper, in accordance with the long and well established tradition of the buck stopping at the bottom. However, the log keeper's note is supported by the oral evidence of Chief Superintendent Lagan, the senior RUC officer in Derry. He was in the Brigadier's office at the relevant time, and he "formed the impression that 1 Para had acted without authority from the Brigadier." The Brigade Major also tried to contradict the terms of serial 164 as recorded in the Brigade Log, but the log keeper had properly recorded that entry, because it is supported by the transcript of the tape recording. Lord Widgery makes no attempt to resolve the difficulty with the Brigade Major's evidence which conflicts with the Brigade Log; he simply chooses to ignore it. The Brigade Major said that no order to C Company (Brava 3) to return to its original location was ever given; it was merely a suggestion on his part.[26]

Serial 164 is entered in the Brigade Log: "16:13 hours Brava 3 at Aggro Corner ordered to return to initial location."[27] (Brava 3 is C Company; Aggro Corner is William Street and Rossville Street). Thus, according to the army's own written record, at thirteen minutes past four o'clock that company was ordered to return to barrier 14. If three companies of 1 Para had been ordered to advance at the same time one wanders why a subsequent order had been issued to only one company. There can't be any doubt about that because this entry is supported by a tape recording. Of equal importance is the transcript of tape recorded related and relevant radio messages sent and received by Brigade headquarters given in evidence to Lord Widgery. Professor Samuel Dash cites them and summarises them, beginning with the tape recording which corresponds to the Brigade Log entry serial 164 at 16:13 hour[28]:

"[From Brigade Command to 1 Para] During that move through serial 14 did you in fact conduct any scoop-up, over?

"[From 1 Para to Brigade Command] I will get the information for you, over."

"[From Brigade Command to 1 Para] If you have not conducted any scoop-up then you should return your call sign Brava 3 back to its original position for further operation, over."

Then a little later in the transcript there is the following message from brigade command (Zero) to 1 Para[29]:

"Hello, 65, this is Zero. You were *given instructions* [emphasis added] some time ago to move Brava 3 from the area of William Street, Rossville Street, back to its original location, is this now complete, over."

The words "given instructions" are hardly consistent with the Brigade Major's evidence that it was a suggestion he was making to C Company to return to its original location; an instruction is an order, and that is the word recorded in the Brigade Log as representing what was said.

As Professor Dash points out, this transcript tells an extremely important story[30]. It suggests that the Brigade Commander was experiencing anxiety over the activities of C Company, Brava 3. Only six minutes after his order to C Company to move forward through barrier 14, down William Street for a scoop-up operation, his headquarters was inquiring whether C Company had made any arrests, and ordering C Company back to its original position at barrier 14. In the absence of any apparent information or reply from C Company, the Brigade Commander sent a further message referring back to the instructions to return to its original position, and asking whether they have complied. Whatever may be the truth about the number of companies ordered to advance into the Bogside, what is the explanation for repeated messages addressed to one company only? Was there no army interest in the whereabouts and activities of Support Company?

The Support Company of 1 Para killed thirteen men, seven of them under the age of 19 and wounded twelve men and one woman. The soldiers, according to Lord Widgery, escaped injury by reason of their superior field-craft and training[31].

It was the army case that each one of the shots fired was an aimed shot at a civilian holding or using a bomb or firearm[32]. Their superior training seems not to have extended to their marksmanship, because of the 107 shots fired, seventy-nine missed their target completely – only one in every four shots hit the target, intended or otherwise.

After the shooting stopped, the construction of a bodyguard of lies to conceal the truth began. First there was the statement of Colonel Maurice Tugwell, a senior staff officer at Northern Ireland Command and a former parachutist. He said it was "absolute rubbish" for anyone to suggest that IRA gunmen did not fire first. Police investigations had already shown that four of the thirteen men shot were on the security forces "wanted list".[33] That statement could only be an outright lie. On 13 March 1972, E. Brian Gibbons Q.C., Counsel for the army at the Widgery Tribunal, made a public apology on behalf of the Ministry of Defence and said that "none of the deceased was on a wanted list." Colonel Tugwell had also stated that two of the wounded men in hospital had admitted that they had been carrying guns in Londonderry the day before[34].

Those two men were never identified, and the London *Times* which published Tugwell's statements said on 2 February 1972: "Although an army report claimed that two of those detained in hospital had admitted to possessing fire arms at Sunday's demonstration, all who spoke today denied they had been interviewed by either the army or the Special Branch. A hospital spokesman said he was 'not aware' that any approach was made by the security forces to interview the injured in hospital." There can be little doubt that Tugwell's second statement was as false an the first.

There was more to come. Colonel Harry Dalzell Payne, of the Directorate of Military Operations dealing with Northern Ireland, repeated the false statement that four of the dead were an the army's wanted list. He added: "All our shots were fired at identified targets under the rules of the Yellow Card." That document sets out the standing instructions for the army for opening fire. Lord Widgery's Report contradicts Dalzell's assertion, for he says: "There were infringements of the rules of the Yellow Card." [35] He lists four examples of where the rules were breached, notably Lieutenant N, who fired three rounds over the heads of a threatening crowd and dispersed it. Corporal P did likewise. So much for the army's case at the Tribunal that "each of these shots was an aimed shot fired at a civilian holding or using a bomb or firearm."

Indeed, according to the *Sunday Times* Insight Team,which published a map of the Bogside in its report of 23 April 1972:

"Lieutenant N fires three shots, probably first ones." Therefore, within a week of publication of Lord Widgery's Report, at least one journalist was suggesting the army fired first without being fired at. It is a fact that Lieutenant N, who commanded the Mortar Platoon of Support Company, was in the first of the ten vehicles which went throughout barrier 12, and that his armoured personnel carrier turned off Rossville Street and halted on waste ground near to where Eden Place used to be[36].

This is a matter of fundamental importance, because of Lord Widgery's treatment of the incident involving Mortar Platoon in the courtyard of the Rossville Flats. He describes how Mortar Platoon penetrated more deeply than was expected by the crowd, and this caused some panic[37]. Some tried to escape along the alleyways between the blocks of flats. As soon as the vehicles halted, the soldiers began to make arrests. But, says Lord Widgery, "Within a minute or two firing broke out and within about the next ten minutes the soldiers of Mortar Platoon had fired forty-two rounds of 7.62 ammunition and one casualty [John Duddy] lay dead in the courtyard."[38] He says the action in the courtyard is of special importance: "The first shots [other than those in William Street Where Damien Donaghy and John Johnson were injured] were fired here. Their sound must have caused other soldiers to believe that Support Company was under attack and made them more ready than they would otherwise have been to identify gunmen amongst the crowd."

On the sequence of events, as Lord Widgery initially sets them out, it may well be that the sound of shots heard by the other soldiers were those fired over the heads of the crowd by Lieutenant N, whose geographical position was behind them, and they began to fire upon the crowd in the courtyard under the mistaken impression that they were being fired upon.

Lieutenant N was in a difficult position in having to admit that he had failed to observe the rules of the Yellow Card when firing. However, he had no option but to do so, because a photograph (EP2/4) of him doing exactly that was exhibited before the tribunal. He also fired one further round at a man whom he thought was throwing a nail bomb in the direction of another armoured personnel carrier. Whether there was a gap in time between the first three shots and the fourth is not clear. By this time, says Lord Widgery[39], the relevant firing in the courtyard – which another soldier said was continuous for ten minutes – was over and he had seen nothing of it.

It defies belief that the incident involving Lieutenant N took place after, or even during, the episode of ten minutes continuous gun-fire, within a very short distance of where he had emerged from Support Company's first vehicle through barrier 12 and into the Bogside.

The last two vehicles of Support Company that proceeded through barrier 12 were the anti-Tank Platoon which consisted of Lieutenant 119 in command and seventeen other ranks[40]. Initially the platoon deployed in the Kells Walk area was involved in the firing at the Rossville Street barricade. As the army proceeded along Rossville Street, on the left was a mound of rubble across the street near Block 1 of the Rossville Flats; on the right was Glenfada Park. Some of the soldiers of this platoon were to appear later in Glenfada Park.

Of the eighteen soldiers in the Anti-Tank platoon of Support Company, one in particular – Soldier F – deserves special mention. He "probably" shot, so Lord Widgery concludes, Patrick Joseph Doherty aged 31, whose body was found in the area behind Block 2 of the Rossville Flats[41]. Soldier F told the Tribunal that he heard pistol shots and saw a crouching man firing a pistol from the position in which Doherty's body was found. Soldier F said he fired at the man as the latter turned away. Lord Widgery states that: "In the light of all the evidence I conclude that he was not carrying a weapon. If Soldier F shot Doherty in the belief that he had a pistol that belief was mistaken."[42]

Hugh Pius Gilmore, aged 17, was shot near the barricade on Rossville Street by one of the soldiers who fired from Kells Walk – the position where the Anti-Tank Platoon had first been deployed. It was not possible to identify the soldier who shot him.

Another marcher – Geraldine Richmond – saw him shot. She said that as she was running she saw the army vehicles stop, and that the soldiers got out and immediately started to shoot at the running civilians. She and Hugh Pius Gilmore were just past the corner of Block 1 of the Rossville Flats and close to the rubble barricade, when she heard Gilmore say, "I'm hit, I'm hit." As he started to stumble, she grabbed him and helped him towards the barricade, where others assisted Gilmore to get through.

Hugh Pius Gilmore died while Miss Richmond was cradling his head[43]. Lord Widgery accepts that "There is no evidence that he used a weapon."[44] Although Miss Richmond gave oral evidence before Lord Widgery he did not accept it as being entirely accurate. Instead, he chose to rely on the version given in the written statement of Mr Sean McDermott. He " . . . put Gilmore as standing on the barricade in Rossville Street when he was hit and in a position such that his front or side may have been presented to the soldiers."[45]

This approach to the evidence by Lord Widgery is unusual. He had the benefit of observing Miss Richmond as she gave evidence. He saw her being cross-examined. Mr McDermott did not give oral evidence and was not subjected to cross-examination by anyone. No one had the opportunity to observe his demeanour as he gave evidence. When there was a conflict between the written evidence of the brigade log and the oral evidence of three senior army officers, Lord Widgery preferred the evidence he had heard. When there is the conflict between the written statement of Mr McDermott and the live oral statements of Miss Richmond, Lord Widgery accepts as the more accurate the written record. His apparent reason for so doing was the that evidence indicated that the trajectory of the bullet was not consistent with Hugh Pius Gilmore being shot from directly behind, but as he was standing at the barricade. Did Lord Widgery find it more acceptable that the victim was accidentally shot in a stationary position rather than whilst running away from the soldiers who fired?

Shortly after Hugh Pius Gilmore died, Geraldine Richmond heard the voice of another injured person saying, "I don't want to die on me own. Someone please help me." Miss Richmond told Lord Widgery that Bernard McGuigan, carrying a white handkerchief, deliberately left a position of cover to attend to that victim. She said he was shot almost at once[46].

The post-mortem report indicates that the entry wound, some 7mm in diameter, was on the left side of his head approximately 3 inches behind his left ear. There was a gaping laceration in the right orbital space, 5 cm x 3 cm, on the right lower eyelid, which exposed the interior of the skull and the bruised margin of the right upper eyelid, below which the remnants of the collapsed eyeball could be seen[47].

Other civilian witnesses confirm Geraldine Richmond's evidence, and photographs of Mr McGuigan's body show the white handkerchief in question, thus providing the strongest corroborative evidence of what those witnesses say. Lord Widgery considers that the soldier who fired the shot might have been Soldier F, but he could not "form any worthwhile conclusion on this point."[48] If it was indeed Soldier F, then this was the second innocent victim that he had shot; perhaps hs believed that the white handkerchief being waved was either a gun or a nail-bomb, or possibly both?

Michael Kelly, aged 17, was shot dead whilst standing at the Rossville Street barricade. Lord Widgery considers that there was some support for the view that "someone was firing at the soldiers from the barricade, but I do not think that this was Kelly nor am I satisfied that he was throwing a bomb at the time he was shot."[49] The recovered bullet proved that Kelly was shot by Soldier F[50].

Whether this was his first, second or third victim, on any view of the evidence, Soldier F had shot dead an entirely innocent young man. However, Lord Widgery appears to be willing to excuse Soldier F on the grounds that the latter mistakenly believed that Michael Kelly had fired a gun. Widgery does have a mild word of criticism for Soldier F later in his report: "Grounds put forward for identifying gunmen at windows were sometimes flimsy. Thus Soldier F fired three rounds at a window in Rossville Flats after having been told by another soldier that there was a gunman there. He does not seem to have verified the information except by his observation of 'a movement' at the window."[51]

The Anti-Tank Platoon initially deployed in the Kells Walk area was involved in the firing at the Rossville Street barricade. Between thirty and forty people were at the barricade and others were taking cover behind the gable end of the flats in Glenfada Park. Some people were seen moving towards the courtyard of Glenfada Park. Soldiers of the Anti-Tank Platoon followed them. However, there are two conflicting versions of why they did so. Corporal E said he had seen civilians firing from the barricade and he noticed some people moving towards that courtyard. On his own initiative, he told Lord Widgery, he led a small group of soldiers into the courtyard from the northeast corner to cut these people off[52].

Lieutenant 119, the Platoon Commander, gave a different version. He said he had sent Soldiers E and F into the courtyard of Glenfada Park to cut off a particular gunman who had been firing from the barricade[53].

These two do not tally. If Soldier E was acting under orders from his immediate commanding officer he could not have been acting on his own initiative. In the result, however, Soldier E and Soldier F advanced into the courtyard, and Soldiers G and H followed shortly afterwards. With Soldier F on the scene, in the light of his conduct so far, it would not be surprising if casualties were to follow. They did: four men – James Joseph Wray, aged 22, Gerald McKinney, aged 35, Gerald Donaghy, aged 17, and William McKinney, aged 26, were shot dead by the four soldiers.

Soldiers E, F and G gave an account of having been attacked by civilians and having fired in reply. Soldier H gave a version of events which Lord Widgery, even with the best will in the world, was unable to accept as being true.

The killing of Gerald McKinney was witnessed by John O'Kane. He is shown on the television documentary programme *Secret History* (Channel 4) saying: "The brother in law . . . he came out here . . . he was looking to see if there was any soldiers . . . as he turned round I was still standing there . . . he obviously seen a soldier and put his hands up in the air like that and he shouted 'No, no, don't shoot!' and he was shot with his arms in the air, through there and out the back . . . and he fell down on his back; he blessed himself and said 'Jesus, Jesus.' He just happened to be here. It was seen. They would have shot anybody, even anybody that hadn't been on the march; if they had happened to be walking across here they would have been shot too."

If this statement is accepted as true then whoever shot Mr McKinney did so without justification or excuse. It was the shooting down of an unarmed, defenceless man who posed no threat to anyone and who had adopted the posture of surrender; to kill him in such circumstances was nothing less than cold-blooded murder. The post-mortem examination shows that there was entry wound on the left side of the chest and an exit wound on the right. The trajectory line of the bullet was from left to right across the chest, travelling slightly upward and backward[54].

According to Dr Raymond McClean, who had been asked by Cardinal Conway, the Catholic Primate of Ireland, to represent him at the post mortems, "It was very clear from the trajectory line of this bullet that this man must have had both arms raised, otherwise the fatal bullet must have penetrated one or both arms. No reference to this very clear evidence was made anywhere in the Widgery Report." [55]

The day after the shooting, the Catholic priests in Derry accused the British Army of cold-blooded murder. If evidence was needed to support that accusation, it is to be found in this case.

Lord Widgery's findings on these issues are not favourable to the army. He considers it more likely than not that at the time the four men were shot dead "the group of civilians was not acting aggressively and that the shots were fired without justification[56]. He thus rejects the evidence of Soldiers E, F and G that they had been attacked by the civilians in this group. If the shots were fired without justification then the shooting was unlawful. If one looks at Lord Widgery's Summary of Conclusions, at No. 8 he states that "At one end of the scale some soldiers showed a high degree of responsibility; at the other, notably in Glenfada Park, *firing bordered on the reckless"* [emphasis added]. There may be some difficulty in comprehending the distinction between conduct which is reckless, viz. the conscious running of an unjustified risk and conduct which borders on recklessness; whatever Lord Widgery considers it to be, it may be a distinction without a difference. The combination of unlawful shooting by these four soldiers, with the added element of recklessness which endangered the lives of innocent civilians in the courtyard of Glenfada Park, must add up at the very least to the common law offence of manslaughter. No such charge was ever preferred again them.

The case of Soldier H calls for special treatment. He told Lord

Widgery he saw a rifleman firing from the window of a flat on the south side of the Glenfada Park courtyard. "Soldier H said he fired an aimed shot at the man, who withdrew but returned a few moments later, whereupon Soldier H fired again. This process was repeated until Soldier H had fired nineteen shots, with a break for a change of magazine."

That account, as Lord Widgery perhaps reluctantly has to accept, was a lie from beginning to end. Subsequent evidence, supported by photographs, showed that no shot at all had been fired through the window in question. But just as in the same way as the Appeal Court Judges who quashed the convictions in the case of the Birmingham Six, the Guildford Four and the Maguire Family were unable to allow the word "innocent" to pass their lips, so too Lord Widgery is unable to describe Soldier H in the only possible and appropriate term: a liar. Nor did Lord Widgery make the slightest attempt to discover the reason for telling such spectacular lies; he is simply content to make the obvious comment: "So nineteen of the twenty-two shots fired by Soldier H were wholly unaccounted for".[57]

Perhaps worst of all is this episode which utterly discredits Lord Widgery's report for his findings in relation to the quartet of soldiers in the Glenfada Park courtyard, where nineteen shots were unaccounted for, where four men were killed without justification, and where he described the soldiers firing as bordering on the reckless. He nonetheless concludes: "When the shooting began every soldier was looking for a gunman and he was his own judge of whether he had identified one or not. I have the explanation on oath of every soldier who fired for every round for which he was required to account."[58] "With one or two exceptions I accept that they were telling the truth as they remembered it."[59]

Lord Widgery overlooks the fact that he had rejected the explanations of four of the soldiers in the courtyard. He is however critical of another soldier, Soldier S, also a member of the Anti-Tank Platoon: "Even assuming a legitimate target, the number of rounds fired was sometimes excessive. Soldier S's firing of twelve rounds into the alleyway between Blocks 1 and 2 of the Rossville Flats seems to me to have been unjustifiably dangerous for people round about[60]." In the common law tradition, an unjustified act is unlawful; if it is also dangerous and subjects the victim to the risk of harm and death follows, it is manslaughter.

One of the dead found in the Glenfada Park courtyard was seventeen year old Gerald Donaghy. He had been shot in the abdomen by Soldier G. He had been mentioned in the statements published by the London

Times on 1 February 1972, and attributed to Colonel Dalzell Payne. After repeating the false allegation that four of the dead were on the army's wanted list, he said: "One of the dead was found to have four nail bombs in his pocket." This was true. But the circumstances in which the nail bombs came to be in Gerald Donaghy's pockets are still the subject of controversy.

After Gerald was shot he was taken into the home of Mr Raymond Rogan at 10 Abbey Park. Of some importance was the fact that he was wearing a blue denim jacket and trousers with pockets of the kind that open to the front rather than to the side[61]. He was examined by Dr Kevin Swords, an Irish doctor who normally worked at a hospital in Lincoln in England.

Dr Swords told the Widgery Tribunal that he examined every inch of Gerald's body, touching in the course of this examination practically every area of his clothes. He could not have missed observing nail bombs in Donaghy's pockets[62] if they were there. Gerald Donaghy was still alive at that time and, according to Dr Swords, he needed to go to hospital immediately. Mr Rogan volunteered to drive him there in his car. Lord Widgery accepts that at least some of Gerald's pockets were examined for evidence of his identity at some unspecified time. Common sense would seem to indicate that would be done in the house. It is not stated who searched the pockets.

Gerald Donaghy was placed in the back seat of the car and driven by Mr Rogan, who was accompanied by Mr Leo Young. The car was stopped at a military checkpoint; Rogan and Young were made to get out of the car. Presumably, all twenty-six barriers sealing the Bogside, which had been erected earlier that Sunday, were still in place. Mr Rogan's car was then driven by a soldier to the Regimental Aid Post of 1st Battalion Royal Anglian Regiment, where Gerald's body was examined by the Medical Officer (Soldier 138), who pronounced him dead.

The Medical Officer carried out a second examination to discover the nature of the wounds. It was more thorough than the first examination and, because of the abdominal wound, it involved opening of the jeans and adjusting them as well as the jacket[63]. According to his evidence, at no stage during these two examinations did the Medical Officer, a British Army Captain, see a nail bomb in Gerald Donaghy's possession.

Up to this point there had been one search of the pockets – for evidence of identity – and three medical examinations by two doctors, none of which disclosed anything sinister or incriminating or, as Lord Widgery puts it, "unusual" in Gerald's pockets. However, Lord Widgery reports[64]: "After another short interval, and whilst Mr Donaghy's body still lay on the back seat of Mr Rogan's car, it was noticed that he had *a nail bomb* [emphasis added] in *one of his trouser pockets* [emphasis added]." That bomb was actually photographed by the RUC and the photographs were exhibited to the Tribunal as EP 5A/26 and 27. Lord Widgery goes on to state: "An Ammunition Technical Officer (Bomb Disposal Officer, soldier 127) was sent for and found *four nail bombs* [emphasis added] in Donaghy's pockets."

Here was an opportunity for Lord Widgery to demonstrate that he was conducting an inquiry which was impartial and independent of the Government that appointed him and of the army in which he had served, and to establish the truth about at least one event of Sunday, 30 January 1972. He failed to do so. He had the evidence of two doctors who had examined Gerald Donaghy and who had not seen anything unusual in his pockets.

There was the evidence of the search by someone to establish Donaghy's, identify and that person had either failed to see the bomb or bombs or, having seen it or them, disregarded their presence and simply left them there to be found by the army. That almost defies belief. Neither Mr Rogan, who drove the car, nor Mr Young, who accompanied him in the car, had seen the nail bomb(s). However, most surprisingly of all is the fact that the photographer who took the two photographs of the nail bomb in the trouser pocket also seems to have missed the existence of the other three. Or does the absence of a photograph indicate that the other pockets were empty, at that time?

It is not unusual in Northern Ireland for suggestions to be made that when a gun is fired or a bomb is about to be thrown, and the gunman or bomber is shot by the army, that no gun or bomb is subsequently found because it has been removed from the scene before the army could search for it.

That suggestion was certainly made (by the trial judge) in the case of Kevin Heatley who was shot dead by a corporal in the Royal Hampshire Regiment, in Newry, late on the night of 27 February 1973. Kevin Heatley was alleged to have fired a low velocity firearm, probably a pistol, at a heavily armed seven man patrol led by the corporal, from a distance of 390 feet. If that happened it was certainly an ambitious undertaking, in the hope that such a firearm would be accurate and effective over a distance longer than an average football pitch. The corporal fired one shot from his SL rifle and hit Kevin Heatley in the upper part of the forehead, killing him. At such a distance and in such circumstances of poor visibility, it must have taken a crack shot to have hit him with such ferocious accuracy, especially since Kevin was only 4 feet 10 inches tall. His height was hardly surprising, since this alleged gunman was only twelve years old.

The trial judge, Mr Justice Kelly, said: "No pistol or low velocity firearm was found about the body of the deceased or at the scene by the army who searched shortly after the shooting or by the police who searched the next morning in daylight. But of course, it is possible that a firearm might have been secreted away before either search commenced."[65]

Let's suppose the four nail bombs were in Gerald Donaghy's pockets throughout the afternoon. There had been the opportunity, especially in the safety of the house, for someone to hide the bombs away from the body. But this was apparently not done. Lord Widgery heard the evidence of two journalists, Brian Cashinella and John Chartres, both of the London *Times*. In *The Times* dated 31 January 1972, under the by-line of these two journalists is this report: "The body of another man was found on the back seat of a car which wan stopped at a road block on one of the roads leading from Londonderry into the Irish Republic. He had an unexploded *nail bomb* [emphasis added] in his pocket. Reporters were shown *the bomb* [emphasis added] protruding from *his jacket pocket* [emphasis added] before the car was driven off by soldiers so that *the bomb* [emphasis added] could be defused on open ground."

If the two journalists gave evidence to Lord Widgery in accordance with their report, he makes no comment on it. One wonders why the journalists were shown the body at all, and at what stage, and why the newspaper report mentions only *one* bomb in the *jacket* pocket. Was this before or after the RUC photographer has seen the *one* bomb in the *trouser* pocket? Was the car driven off before the examination of the body in the back seat by the Bomb Disposal Officer? Certainly Lord Widgery conveys the impression that the examination took place at the Regimental Aid Post, whereas the journalists indicate that the car was driven off from the place where it was seen so that *the bomb* could be defused on open ground. That seems to point to the four bombs being found at another place at a later time.

Two journalists apparently filed the report in the newspaper. However, Simon Winchester, who was present amongst the crowd in Derry that Sunday afternoon, notes in his book *In Holy Terror*: "John Chartes, the *Times* reporter who headed his team that day, came from the army post he had remained in and told us he had seen one dead man with *nail bombs in his jerkin pockets* [emphasis added]. This single fact had convinced him that the day's military operations had been, in his words, a 'jolly good show'. I was to remember his phrase for some long while."[66] Here was a 'friendly' journalist – friendly, that is, to the army – who could be relied on to report in an uncritical fashion what he had seen, stating there was more than one bomb but they were in the *jerkin*

38

and not the trouser pockets. Could the other journalist, Brian Cashinella, have seen only one bomb? And if both saw the body, did they view the body of Gerald Donaghy at the same time and in the same geographical area? Did Cashinella see the body at the time of the photograph showing one bomb in the trouser pocket? Did Chartres then see more than one bomb in the jerkin pockets? Did the bomb disposal officer then appear and find the four bombs, one in each pocket? Lord Widgery's Report does not help on these points.

To compound the mystery, the forensic scientist Dr John Martin, who gave evidence to the Tribunal, did not regard as positive the hand swab test carried out for the purpose of determining whether Gerald Donaghy had discharged a firearm. The pathologist Professor Keith Simpson for some reason regarded the same test as positive[67]. So, according to one witness Gerald might have fired a gun, according to another he had not.

This test was important, not so much for its disputed result as for its purpose. A nail bomb is a home-made device about the size of a cricket ball, and has a gelignite explosive core. Embedded nails blow out like shrapnel when the bomb explodes after its fuse is lit[68]. No traces of nitroglycerine were found on Gerald's hands, indicating that he had not handled gelignite. Nor did he have in his possession any object which would have enabled him to light the fuses of the nail bombs.

These were matters which seemed not to have troubled Lord Widgery in his determining the truth about the possession of the four nail bombs. Indeed he found " . . . the matter of relatively unimportant detail of the events of the afternoon . . ."[69] Since the allegation of fabrication of evidence was forcefully and repeatedly made at the Tribunal, and if the allegation was true, then it followed that the witness who testified about finding the four nail bombs had either been deceived by the dishonest conduct of others, or he had planted, or been a party to the planting, those bombs on the dead body of a seventeen year old.

In such circumstances not everyone would agree with Lord Widgery that this was a matter of relatively unimportant detail. Lord Widgery certainly faces up to the two possibilities: either the bombs were in the pockets all the time and they had not been seen by those who examined the body, or they were planted on the body after the three medical examinations. Lord Widgery found the latter too horrific to contemplate and rejected it. He says: "I think that on a balance of probabilities the bombs were in Donaghy's pockets throughout. His jacket and trousers were not removed but were merely opened as he lay on his back in the car It seems likely that these relatively bulky objects would have been noticed when Donaghy's body was examined; but it is conceivable that they were not and the alternative explanation of a plant is speculation.

No evidence was offered as to where the bombs might have come from, who might have placed them or why Donaghy should have been singled out for this treatment."[70]

If Lord Widgery is correct in his conclusion that Gerald Donaghy and the three others who died with him in the courtyard of Glenfada Park were not acting aggressively, and shots were fired at them without justification, in circumstances that bordered on the reckless, then there was every reason for the army to plant nail bombs upon him. It may be correct, as a matter of law, that a soldier would not be entitled to shoot someone who was simply in possession of a nail bomb, as opposed to throwing it. In the court of public opinion, a soldier might be justified in shooting someone who had no less than four nail bombs in his pockets because, so the argument would go, the person would not have had the bombs with him unless he intended to use them. In matters concerning Northern Ireland, as in other colonies where Britain had purchased one part of the population and intimidated the other, it is the public perception of what has happened and not the reality that counts.

In his summary of conclusions, Lord Widgery says: "None of the deceased or wounded is proved to have been shot whilst handling a firearm or bomb. Some are wholly acquitted of complicity in such action;but there is a strong suspicion that some others had been firing weapons or handling bombs in the course of the afternoon and that yet others had been closely supporting them."[71] This conclusion is important because, in the application of the burden of proof in criminal cases, beyond reasonable doubt, or even the lower standard of proof applied in civil cases (viz. on the balance of probabilities), none of the dead or wounded were proved to have acted unlawfully and used firearms or bombs and therefore become legitimate targets for army fire.[72]

The basis of "the strong suspicion" is to be found in the evidence given to the Tribunal by a forensic scientist, Dr John Martin of the Northern Ireland Department of Industrial and Forensic Science, who was a "ballistics expert"[73], and by Prof Keith Simpson, who was a Home Office pathologist and Professor of Forensic Medicine at Guy's Hospital in London. In his professional career, Professor Simpson carried out 20, 000 post-mortem in the United Kingdom over a period of forty years. He was almost invariably a witness for the prosecution in cases of murder in the London area during that time. However, it is not possible to find any case where he gave evidence relating to ballistics. As noted previously, he disagreed with Dr Martin about whether the forensic tests were positive in the case of Gerald Donaghy.

In his biography *Forty Years of Murder*, Professor Simpson relates that "A Civil Rights Association march, hold in the Bogside district in defiance of an official ban, had been followed by a riot, which was broken up by paratroopers; they were given the order to fire and thirteen civilians lay dead as the mob dispersed."[74] Part of that statement is not accurate. No orders were given by anyone to the paratroopers to open fire. Lord Widgery says that "The soldiers were entitled to regard themselves as acting individually and thus entitled to fire under the terms of Rule 13 without waiting for orders."[75]

Simpson goes on to say: "Six of the dead men, however, had firearm powder discharge traces on their hands; they had been firing shots too, though no firearms were found on or near them as they lay dead." Although he had told Lord Widgery "a concentration of minute particles on the hand creates a 'strong suspicion' that the subject had been firing" [76], by 1978 when he published his biography, "strong suspicion" had substantially changed to become a concrete fact.

Prof Simpson refers to "firearm powder discharge traces" on the hands. That may be a much more emotive and inaccurate way of describing the test carried out by Dr Martin. It should be noted that the hands of the dead were swabbed by a member of the RUC and the swabs taken to Dr Martin at the Forensic Science Laboratory in Belfast, together with their clothing, for examination. No evidence was available to Dr Martin as to the chain of control and custody of the bodies from the time of the shooting until the swabs were taken.

As Dr Keith Borer told the makers of the television documentary *Secret History*, if the bodies has been swabbed and tested where they fell at the barricade, reliable results might have been obtained. In the event, on an overview of the scientific evidence, Dr Borer's professional opinion was that the tests on the bodies were flawed and Lord Widgery's conclusions must be viewed as being suspect.

Lord Widgery apparently misunderstood the very nature of the forensic test that was carried out. On no less than eight occasions in his report he refers to it as "the paraffin test". This test involves the taking of a wax mould of the hand and applying a chemical reagent to the mould to test for the presence of nitrates, which could indicate the use of gunpowder. According to Professor Dash the testimony of the forensic experts called by the Tribunal makes it clear that the paraffin tests were not used at all. The test that was used – the wet chemical test – involved swabbing the hands of the dead with cotton wool, and then subjecting the swabs to a chemical reagent to test for the presence of lead. The chemical, sodium rhodizonate, would show the presence of lead an a colour stain – purple or blue if 5% hydrochloric acid is added. The greater the amount of lead, the stronger the colour. Even in 1972 this was a relatively unsophisticated test, and scientists at the Home Office

Central Research establishment used a different one which had been developed in America. This test – neutron activation analysis – would show the presence of antimony, mercury and barium – all present in gun-shot discharges – as well an lead. Because of the time factor, which was lengthy, the wet chemical test was used in this case.

Lord Widgery accepts that a positive reaction to the presence of lead would not be conclusive that the subject had fired a gun, because of the other possible sources of lead contamination. He lists five in his report: "(a) being close to someone else who is firing; (b) being within 30 feet of the muzzle of the weapon fired in one's own direction; (c) physical transfer of lead particles on contact with the body or clothing of someone who had recently fired a weapon; (d) the passing at close range of a bullet which may spread lead particles from its damaged surface; (e) direct contact with lead in, say, the trade of a plumber or whilst loading a firearm."[78] Lord Widgery seems to have overlooked the fact that someone hit by a bullet, or fragments of a bullet, would show a positive response to a lead test. certainly on the clothing, if not on the body.

So far as the dead were concerned Lord Widgery finds that John Francis Duddy, aged 17, Patrick Joseph Doherty, aged 31, and Hugh Pius Gilmore also aged 17, were not carrying a weapon at any time. In the case of Bernard McGuigan, aged 41, Lord Widgery concludes that it "was not possible to say that he was using or carrying a weapon at the time he was shot" There was however ground " . . . for suspicion that he had been in close proximity to someone who had fired."[79]

John Pius Young, aged 17, had lead particles on the web, back and palm of his left hand. Michael McDaid, aged 20, had abnormal lead particles on his jacket and one large particle of lead on the back of his right hand. William Noel Nash, aged 19, had particles of lead on the web, back and palm of his left hand. All three were shot almost simultaneously at the Rossville Street barricade. Lord Widgery concludes that there is a very strong suspicion that one or more of these three was using a weapon.

But, says Lord Widgery, "No weapon was found but there was sufficient opportunity for this to be removed by others."[80] (The force of this comment is diminished by Lord Widgery's failure to consider that there was sufficient opportunity, in less dangerous circumstances, to remove the four nail bombs found in the pockets of Gerald Donaghy.) He further considers that John Pius Young had discharged a firearm, and that Michael McDaid was in close proximity to someone firing. William Noel Nash had been shot in the chest from the front, and Lord Widgery accepts the evidence of Soldier P that he had seen a man firing a pistol from the barricade: of four shots directed by the soldier at that man, one had hit the man in the chest. Soldier P thought that the pistol was removed by other civilians.[81] Whether this thought is based on clear evidence or mere speculation, simply because no pistol was found, is not discussed by Lord Widgery.

Michael Kelly, aged 17, was also shot at the Rossville Street barricade- The lead particles on the right cuff of his clothing was consistent with his having been close to someone using a firearm, but Lord Widgery concludes that he did not fire a gun or throw a bomb.[82] Kevin McElhinney, also aged 17, was shot whilst crawling along the pavement on the west side of No. 1 Block of Rossville Flats between the barricade and the entrance to the flats. Lead particles were found on the back of his left hand and on the back of his jacket. The bullet which shot him had been damaged on impact, so says Lord Widgery. Dr Martin thought the lead test inconclusive on this account. On this occasion at least Lord Widgery had properly identified the test that had been carried out; but he leans to the view that Kevin McElhinney might have been carrying a rifle at the time he was shot.[83]

This view cannot be justified in the light of the evidence of two eye-witnesses. Father T.M. O'Keefe told the Tribunal that he saw Kevin dragging himself to a doorway, when his body jerked and he was then pulled inside. A news photographer gave evidence that he saw Kevin crawling along and then fall into the doorway from a crouching position. He was standing inside the doorway and saw Kevin die within a few minutes of being shot. Both witnesses said that Kevin had no weapon in his hands.[84]

Lord Widgery accepts that Kevin was shot while crawling along the pavement and that he was shot from behind by a soldier, probably Sergeant K, whose rifle was fitted with a telescopic sight. That soldier fired only one shot that afternoon and he told the Tribunal he saw two men crawling from the barricade in the direction of the door of the flats and that the rear man was carrying a rifle. On any view of his evidence neither he nor anyone else was being attacked or threatened by a gunmen or bomber at the time he fired without warning. Lord Widgery passes over this point without comment, except to say by way of general discussion that Rule 13 of the Yellow Card leaves certain questions unanswered. For example, is fire to be opened defensively and restricted to that which is necessary to cause the attacker to desist and withdraw, or is he to be treated as an enemy in battle and engaged until he surrenders or is killed?[85]

Sergeant K was unable to say whether the single shot he fired hit the target. Thus Lord Widgery's assumes that, if Kevin McElhinney was the intended target, he was shot by that soldier, and that he was therefore

43

carrying a rifle. This overlooks the fact that even Sergeant K admits to seeing two men crawling along the pavement, and it may be therefore that he hit the unarmed man. Most important of all, however, Lord Widgery gives no reason why he rejects the evidence of both Father O'Keefe and the news photographer who said that Kevin was not carrying a weapon.

Of the four shot dead in the courtyard of Glenfada Park, Gerald McKinney and William McKinney were not using a weapon at any time. Despite the dispute between Dr Martin and Professor Simpson as to whether the results of tests on Gerald Donaghy were positive or not, both agree that the results of the tests on James Joseph Wray were consistent with his having used a firearm.

Before accepting the validity of such a conclusion in respect of any of the dead Lord Widgery should have considered carefully his own caveat that other sources of lead contamination have to be considered, before a finding of strong suspicion of firing can be reached on the basis of a positive wet chemical test disclosing the presence of lead particles. There is the strongest unchangeable evidence, from no less than the commanding officer of 1 Para, Lieutenant Colonel Wilford, that the bodies at the Rossville Street barrier were picked up and placed in a Saracen vehicle by a paratrooper.[86] The Saracen was then driven to Altnalgelvin hospital where, according to Ivan Cooper, the bodies ware lifted by the soldiers from the Saracen by the hands and legs and taken into the hospital. Shortly after they were taken to the mortuary, Mr Cooper says that the paratroopers were comparing "scores" or numbers of people they had shot.[87] The possibility of cross-contamination from the soldiers to the bodies was so high it must have been a virtual certainty. Yet, in spite of this evidence available to Lord Widgery, he still makes a finding adverse to some of the dead, John Pius Young, Michael McDaid, William Noel Nash, Kevin McElhinney and James Joseph Wray, on the basis of an unsophisticated test.

This finding has to be read in conjunction with Lord Widgery's express conclusion already noted, that at the time James Wray and the three others were shot the group of civilians was not acting aggressively and that the shots were fired without justification."[88] Dr McClean, who was present at the post-mortem, states that in the case of James Wray there were two entry wounds in the back. The trajectory line of the bullets were: wound 1, right to left,superficially across the body; there was an elliptical hole 7 mm x 5 mm on the right side of the back 4.5 cm below the scapula. The angle was upwards and towards the midline. The bullet exited, leaving a gaping hole on the top of the left shoulder. Wound 2, right to left, and from behind, forward travelling upwards towards the left shoulder; there was a circular wound on the right side of the back 7 mm in diameter situated 7 cm below and 2.5 cm to the right side of wound 1. The bullet exited, leaving a ragged circular hole on the left side of the body.

Dr McClean considers that this medical evidence is consistent with "several eye-witness accounts which stated that Jim Wray was shot in the back as he lay on the ground. Several eye-witnesses stated that they called to Jim Wray as he lay on the ground. He replied that he was alright but that he couldn't move his legs. This is consistent with the lower entry and exit wounds, caused by the bullet travelling across the lumbar region superficially. The bullet did not damage the spinal canal but could have created shock waves sufficient to have caused a temporary paralysis of both legs. The trajectory line of the second upper wound was consistent with his having been shot while lying on the ground with his head raised, apparently talking to others who were in hiding."[89]

There is not a single word about this eye-witness or medical evidence in Lord Widgery's report. Rather than try to elaborate on or explain in detail the circumstances in which James Joseph Wray was shot, Lord Widgery prefers to say nothing about this evidence at all.

Lord Widgery had been invited by the British Government to conduct the Tribunal of inquiry on 31 January 1972 into the circumstances in which thirteen people were shot dead. There was a preliminary hearing on 14 February, and the first substantive hearing of the Tribunal was held in Coleraine on 21 February. There were seventeen sessions between that date and 14 March during which 114 witnesses gave evidence and were cross-examined. After the evidence was heard, three further sessions were held in London at the Royal Courts of Justice on 16, 17 and 20 March 1972, at which Lord Widgery heard closing speeches of Counsel for the relatives of the deceased, for the army and the Tribunal.[90]

The scheduled date for publication of the Report of the Tribunal was Wednesday, 19 April 1972 in the afternoon. According to Simon Winchester, on the preceding evening, the Tuesday, "astute press officers of the Ministry of Defence telephoned the Defence Correspondents of the national newspapers . . . to leak, in highly selective terms, the Tribunal's conclusion to be published the next day. [91] Some of the newspapers duly obliged the next day. *The Daily Telegraph* stated: "Widgery clears paratroopers for Bloody Sunday". *The Daily Mirror* said: "Bloody Sunday Paras 'clear'. And the *Daily Express* said: "Widgery blames IRA and clears the army."[92]

None of these newspaper reports makes any reference to Lord

Widgery's findings that if the army had persisted in its low-key attitude and had not launched a large scale arrest operation the day might have passed off without incident; or that four men were not acting aggressively and were shot without justification; or "firing that bordered on the reckless"; or the twelve shots fired into the alleyway between the Rossville Flats, which were unjustifiably dangerous for anyone around. Nor is any mention made of soldier H's nineteen shots which were unaccounted for. These newspaper reports were based on the sanitised version of events according to the Defence Ministry press officers from a report which the press had not yet seen.

So there were really three versions: first there was the truth, then Lord Widgery's version which partly disclosed the truth, and then there was the Ministry of Defence version which concealed the truth. Significantly, on the day of publication of the Widgery Report the Defence Ministry held a press conference for accredited defence correspondents.

The Guardian journalist, Simon Winchester, wished to attend in company with that paper's correspondent, but his request to do so was refused. He was told that if he tried to get in to the press conference he would be stopped. He was, he says, furious, because none of the accredited defence correspondents, with one exception, was in Derry on the day of the shootings. (The one exception was Brigadier Thompson, who had admitted that he had missed the entire episode because he was parking his car.)[93] Winchester had himself been a eye-witness to some of the events in the Bogside. Indeed he had given evidence before Lord Widgery. His evidence – and there is no reason to doubt its truth – wholly destroys the army case. The army states that aimed shots were fired only at gunmen and nail bombers. But, as Simon Winchester narrates in his book: "A soldier below me suddenly turned my way. He pointed his rifle up and there were two sharp jerks of his arm. 'Christ, he's firing at us!' I yelled to a young boy, who was watching the scene, his mouth agape with horror, beside me. We dropped on to the road and stayed as still as we could for a minute . . . we had indeed been the targets of the paratroopers down below."[94]

Mr Winchester's presence at the press conference was undesirable and unacceptable only because of what questions he might ask and answers he might not accept at face value, for he had been in a very good position to learn the truth. He, personally, could supply first hand information that an innocent unarmed civilian, posing no threat or danger to the army, had been fired at by a member of the Parachute Regiment. He might not be surprised to find that the Northern Ireland Office has categorised the thirteen deaths that day in Derry as "terrorists"[95]. That categorisation may be as truthful and accurate as the newspaper summaries of the Widgery Report, which totally absolve the army from blame for those deaths.

Lord Widgery's Summary of Conclusions begins badly, for it states that "there would have been no deaths in Londonderry on 30 January if those who organised the illegal march had not thereby created a highly dangerous situation in which a clash between demonstrators and the security forces was almost inevitable." This is equivalent to holding the City of Westminster responsible for the deaths of those who jump into the River Thames from Westminster Bridge, simply because the Council built the Bridge. It is a false point as well, because on the following Sunday, 6 February 1972, there was a Civil Rights Rally held in the town of Newry, attended by 20,000 people. That passed off without any incidents of violence, although on the following day twenty-six summonses were issued, recipients included several Members of Parliament, for breaking the ban on marches[96].

The truth about the events leading to the shootings in Derry on Bloody Sunday has not been disclosed. The Independent Television journalist Desmond Hamill may have come nearest to discovering it when he was doing the research for his book *Pig in the Middle – the Army in Northern Ireland 1963-1985*, first published in 1985.[97] He notes that Major-General Ford, the Commander Land Forces in Northern Ireland, who was responsible to the General Officer Commanding for day-to-day military operation, was "on the ground with a company of 1 Para and in touch with brigade headquarters on a secure radio link." [98] In fact he was at barrier 14 with C Company. The Brigade Commander, Brigadier MacLellan, was in his headquarters across the Foyle in the City of Derry, in touch with events by radio contact with a helicopter hovering above the crowd in the Bogside. The Brigade Major was in an Operations Room in the same building. Hamill notes: "Just before 4 p.m. a Para Officer came through in the brigade net and asked for permission to send in the arrest unit. MacLellan turned down the request on the basis that the marchers and rioters had yet to separate . . . " Shortly after, he writes, "The General, out with the forward troops, felt that being on the ground gave him the right 'feel' for the operation, although he accepted that the Brigadier, with his helicopter, had a better overall picture. However, he himself now came through and spoke to the Brigade Major, *making it very clear that the time had come to 'get a move on and send in the Paras'*." [emphasis added].

This was said by a Major-General and the second most senior army officer in Northern Ireland talking to a Major. There must have been very substantial psychological pressure upon him and upon Brigadier

MacLellan to do what Ford demanded and send in the Paras.

At this point the stone-throwing at barrier 12 had abated. Hamill says that "The Brigade Major passed on the message, telling MacLellan 'The General has been on and says this is the time to go in. Again MacLellan said 'no' because the rioters and the marchers had not yet separated. A few minutes passed, and then came the word from the helicopter that the separation had finally taken place, and MacLellan gave the order to move."[99] Hamill then recites what was to become the official line: "He [MacLellan] had given the order himself, and the paratroopers had gone in with some encouraging words from General Ford."[100] Those encouraging words were heard by the London *Times* journalist Brian Cashinella who describes the scene as follows: "I was standing next to General Ford. He was waving his swagger stick and said 'Go on, the Paras, go on, go and get them.'"[101]

General Ford did not deny the substance of those words, indeed he admitted them almost in their entirety. During his examination by counsel for the army he told Lord Widgery that when C Company went through barrier 14 he spoke to the leading platoon and said to them "Go on, 1 Para, go and get them, and good luck."However, in cross-examination by counsel for the deceased and the wounded, General Ford denied that he gave any order for the scoop-up operation.[102]

The presence of the General Officer Commanding on the streets of Derry must have posed problems for officers junior in rank to him. Was he there because the Bogside had been a No-Go area for the previous six months, and "Free Derry" had become very politically unacceptable to the British Government in London and very embarrassing to the British Army in Northern Ireland, and they "were going to do something about it?"[103] In fact the Parachute Regiment were the first British soldiers to enter Free Derry in daylight for six months.

It is clear that General Ford was pushing for a decision to send 1 Para into the Bogside; it is equally clear that they were going in to carry out an arrest operation against stone-throwers at barrier 14. What could have been more logical for Brigadier MacLellan to order C Company – and only C Company – through that barrier, and limit the extent of the advance so as to avoid the peaceful marchers who were heading along Rossville Street towards Free Derry Corner? Such an order would have satisfied General Ford, who was standing behind barrier 14. That such an order was given is supported by the serial 159 in the Brigade log: "Orders given to 1 Para at 16:07 hours for one sub-unit of 1 Para to do scoop-up through barrier 14. Not to conduct running battle down Rossville Street."

In fact Support Company of 1 Para, as well as C Company, entered the Bogside. C Company penetrated the area by advancing down Chamberlain Street; Support Company went through barrier 12 and went down Rossville Street which runs parallel to Chamberlain Street. Brigadier MacLellan told the Tribunal that he had given the order entered in the brigade log as serial 159 and he interpreted it as authorising both Companies to advance. That evidence is in conflict with his own original Brigade Commander's plan and contradicts the plain meaning of the words of the order entered in the brigade log as serial 159.[104]

One sub-unit – one company – means one in any language , and that is what the log says. To add to the confusion, the commanding officer of 1 Para, Lieutenant Colonel Wilford "acknowledged that the only order appearing in the Brigade log authorising an arrest operation, specified Company C, and not Support Company. But he stated *he* [emphasis added] gave the orders to Support Company, since they were under his command, and he understood they were to participate in the arrest operation. This action on his part, however, would be in violation of the Brigade Commander's plan, which clearly specified that the order for the arrest operation could only be given by the Brigade Commander."[105] Wilford had no recollection of receiving any order instructing (or requesting, if the Brigade Major's evidence on this point is true) C Company to return to its original position at barrier 14. That such an order was given cannot be denied, for it is recorded in the brigade log at serial 164 – an entry which escapes mention in Lord Widgery's Report completely.

The Report of the Widgery Tribunal satisfied no one. The army continued consistently to maintain the line that aimed shots were fired at, and hit, identified targets. i.e. gunmen and nailbombers. The Independent Television programme *This Week* shows soldiers of 1 Para maintaining that position. They deny either firing without justification or that the firing bordered on the reckless. The Tribunal's finding and the soldiers statements on this point can hardly be accepted in the light of the soundtrack of the television film showing the army in action that Sunday afternoon, where a voice (possibly that of Lieutenant Colonel Wilford) is heard saying, "Do not fire back for the moment, unless you identify a positive target."[106]

Is that not the clearest evidence that the soldiers to whom this order was addressed were out of control and that there was a breakdown in army discipline? Amongst the soldiers involved might there have been Soldier H, with nineteen shots unaccounted for, and Soldier S firing twelve rounds, unjustifiably dangerously, into the alleyway of the Rossville Flats? Or was this the firing in the courtyard of Glenfada Park, where four men died in a group not acting aggressively, but who were innocent unarmed civilians running away?

Lord Widgery finds that, "Soldiers who identified *armed* [emphasis added] gunmen fired upon them in accordance with the standing orders in the Yellow Card."[108] This is confusing because it might have been difficult for the army to identify gunmen who were unarmed. Significantly Lord Widgery omits the evidence given to the Tribunal by an army captain, "who was in the midst of the paratroopers, up close to the Rossville Flats", who did not hear or see any civilian shooting. Indeed, he testified that he was concerned over the intensity of the army shooting and that he complained about it to the company commander.[109] Why should an army officer give such evidence, damaging as it was to the army's case, unless it was true?

Nor does Lord Widgery attempt to deal with the evidence of the army major, identified as soldier 236. According to *The Guardian* of 8 March 1972, he told the Tribunal that "He agreed that he had said in a report later that casualties included six nail-bomber's, seven gunmen and one acid bomber." His report was clearly based on what he had been told by someone else, for "he agreed that he had not seen any civilian firing, or with a gun; anyone with a petrol bomb or a nail bomb; anyone recovering a rifle from an injured person, or anyone recovering a nail bomb." None of this appears in Lord Widgery's Report, although he notes that Major 236 heard fifteen rounds of low velocity fire from the Rossville Flats.[110]

On 7 March 1972 Lord Widgery heard the evidence of a paratroop platoon commander, a lieutenant, who admitted that he had told a lie in a Thames Television interview – transmitted on 3 February 1972 – when he said he had seen a gunman. When asked by the interviewer if he had seen a rifleman, the answer "no" sounded lame, he said, so he decided to say what his soldiers had reported. In cross-examination he said: "The background was one of sniping at the army and I was asked to put the army's point of view. I was asked if I saw any riflemen and the answer to that was 'no', but it sounded very lame, so I decided to tell what had been reported to me by my soldiers."

Why this officer could not have simply told the truth that other soldiers had seen riflemen, so they said, but he had not, is not easy to understand. Nor is the answer to the next question. The lieutenant was asked at the tribunal by junior Counsel for the families of the dead and wounded: "Did you tell a deliberate lie to millions of people on television when you said you saw a gunman firing?" The answer was "No, sir." If this was not a purposeful, calculated and deliberate lie, it is difficult to imagine what is. The answer was given for the sole purpose of justifying the killings and the woundings by the paratroopers. Why this officer denied the deliberate lie before the Tribunal defies comprehension.

The lieutenant was also asked: "Now that we have the truth today, it is that you did not see a gunman firing on that Sunday at any time?"

He answered: "That is correct."

Counsel asked him: "If you felt that the army was being sniped at today, would you feel justified in lying about that today?"

"No, not on oath."[111]

This officer's capacity to tell the truth seems therefore to be governed by the fact that lying on oath is not acceptable to him, but telling an unsworn lie to defend the army from sniping clearly is. He lied not out of panic, or in accidental error, but because the army was being sniped at, in what circumstances and by whom he does not say.

One can understand that Lord Widgery might be reluctant to emphasise the evidence of this witness. Of course when the lieutenant lied on television he might not have expected that his conduct would be subject to scrutiny and cross-examination at a later date, as indeed it was. Lord Widgery makes no mention of the evidence of this witness, a self-confessed liar, anywhere in his report. Its absence weakens an already frail discourse on the events of Bloody Sunday.

On 1 August 1972, in answer to a Parliamentary Question about the shootings in Derry on that most dreadful day, the Attorney General said, "After consideration of the evidence, the Director of Public Prosecutions for Northern Ireland and I have decided that there is no evidence sufficient to warrant prosecutions of any member of the Security Forces who took part in those events."[112]

That is a statement with which not everyone agrees. Nor are its contents surprising, for it is doubtful if there was ever a competent, independent, investigation into the conduct of the army. Between September 1970 and September 1973 there was in operation an R.U.C. Force Order whereby, if an offence against the ordinary criminal law was alleged against military personnel in Northern Ireland, the interviewing of military witnesses and of the alleged offender himself was conducted exclusively by military investigation. Even the Lord Chief Justice of Northern Ireland did not know of the existence of this order until the appeal against conviction of the Hampshire Regiment corporal for the killing of Kevin Heatley in May 1974.[113]

It is not known whether the Attorney General knew of the contents and existence of the Force Order when he made his statement to the House of Commons. Certainly, he gave no indication either way. The limits on a police investigation into a breach of the criminal law was bound to lead to abuse, and it did, for it placed the British Army in

Northern Ireland above and outside the ordinary criminal process. One case at least discloses a fact which Lord Widgery was unable to face: that murder could be committed by soldiers, and there would be a conspiracy of silence to conceal the truth and protect the killers. On 24 October 1972, only six months after the publication of the report of the Widgery Tribunal, the bodies of two men – Andrew Murray, aged 24 and Michael Naan, aged 31 – were found on a farm in County Fermanagh. Both had been stabbed to death, probably with a doubled-edged dagger, with a blade up to one inch wide and not less than 5½ inches long.

Michael Naan's wounds, at least seventeen in number, were concentrated on the frontal chest area; the uppermost wound occurred just below the throat. Superficial wounds below the neck were shallow incisions indicating that a knife had been drawn slowly across the throat. There were no significant defence injuries on his arms or hands, indicating that either he had made little or no effort to resist his killer(s), or he had been prevented from doing so by having his arms held.

Andrew Murray received at least thirteen stab wounds. He had been stabbed in both the chest and the back. Many of the wounds had penetrated the chest cavity, damaging the lungs, heart and the major artery, the aorta. Because of the nature of the attacks, the RUC believed that they were looking for more than one killer. Whoever was responsible must have been heavily bloodstained.

Police inquires revealed that 13 Platoon of Delta Company, Argyll and Sutherland Highlanders had been billeted in a field adjacent to the farm owned by Michael Naan. They had left the field on 24 October, the very day the two bodies were discovered. The RUC were precluded by their Force Order from interviewing those soldiers on whom suspicion must have fallen from the very outset. Such inquiries, as may have been carried out by the army's Special Investigation Branch, got nowhere. It seems that they questioned the Company Commander, a major, but not the officer in charge of 13 platoon, a lieutenant, or any members of that platoon. These soldiers might have been witnesses to the incident, or at least noticed someone or something suspicious in the area at around the time the murders were committed. However, they were not even interviewed on this basis, let alone as suspects of murder.

It was not until six years later that the truth began to emerge, and then only because an unidentified man, a former soldier in the Argyll and Sutherland Highlanders, went to the police in Glasgow, because he believed he knew the identity of "The Yorkshire Ripper", a man who had carried out a number of killings in the Leeds area. All his victims had been women, but the former soldier thought that the use of a dagger in those killings linked him to the unsolved murders of the two men in County Fermanagh in 1972. This man came forward not out of any sense of regret or remorse for two savage killings of defenceless innocent men in Ireland, but because of what he feared a former fellow soldier might do in England.

As a result of this information, in January 1981, four men of 13 Platoon appeared before Belfast Crown Court. Sergeant Stanley Alexander Hathaway and Sergeant John McFayden Byrne pleaded guilty to the murder of Michael Naan and Andrew Murray and were sentenced to life imprisonment.

Former Lance-Corporal Iain Fletcher Chestnut pleaded not guilty to the murder of Andrew Murray, but guilty to manslaughter. On what basis this plea was offered and accepted is not known, but he was sentenced to four years imprisonment. Because he had spent two years on remand, with all the privileges of an unconvicted person awaiting trial, that meant his almost immediate release. Chestnut had been either dismissed or dishonourably discharged from the army in May 1973. There are two versions of reasons for his discharge: his own, that he had been "involved in an escapade involving an air rifle", and that of the journalist, Martin Dillon who states in the second of his trilogy of books on Northern Ireland[114], that Chestnut had been dishonourably discharged and "His crime was putting nuts and bolts into a rubber-bullet gun which converted it into a lethal weapon rather than a gun designed for riot purposes." [115]

Those who consider that the British Army is in Northern Ireland as a peace-keeping force between the Ulster Loyalists and the Irish Nationalists should ponder upon the Cheshnut case and his rather unique contribution towards keeping the peace.

The fourth accused was the officer commanding 13 platoon, Andrew Malcolm Burlton Snowball, who by 1978 had been promoted from lieutenant to captain. At the first interview with the police, Captain Snowball lied. On 12 June 1979 he decided to tell the truth. He admitted in a statement that either Sergeant Hathaway or Byrne has spoken to him and he asked them what had happened when they were out on patrol. They said " . . . they had killed two men at Naan's farm . . . I mulled the whole thing over in my mind and *decided for the good of the army and the regiment it must never go any further."* [emphasis added].[116]

Such an attitude – that it is better to conceal the truth than damage the reputation of the army and the Regiment – has a familiar ring to it. It echoes the words and the attitude of Lieutenant N of Support Company of 1 Para. Such an approach may not have been confined to him; it may have been shared by many other serving soldiers in Northern Ireland.

For his part in the cover-up of those two most terrible murders, Captain Snowball received a one year suspended sentence of imprisonment. Other soldiers in 13 Platoon must have known about the killings but they, like him, said nothing. The sentence he received meant that he would not be automatically discharged from the army under Queen's Regulations. He did however resign his commission. His case surely called for a deterrent sentence of imprisonment, so that others in his position would not stay silent as he had, but have the courage to come forward and tell the truth. The court may however have taken into account the fact that at the time of the incident he was only 20 years old, and the actual killings had been carried out by more experienced and mature men than he.

The truth of what goes on in Northern Ireland is often obscured and concealed, especially with the often unquestioning British attitude to matters involving national security. There are many unsolved murders where army involvement is suspected but proof is lacking. What actually happened in Derry on Bloody Sunday has not yet been disclosed. That fact may well have contributed to the continuation of violence in Northern Ireland for the past twenty years, for there is strong evidence, contrary to the Attorney General's statement, to support the view that some soldiers acted without orders, or in defiance of orders, and unlawfully killed innocent people on that day. If Soldier H fired nineteen shots which were unaccounted for, and he lied to justify his conduct, at whom did he in fact fire his rifle? If the three other soldiers with him in the Glenfada Park courtyard fired without justification and in a manner which bordered on the reckless, and shot young men who were unarmed and posed no threat, did they not have a case to answer before a criminal court?

Lord Widgery, however, provides a ready explanation for the conduct of the paratroopers and considers that they generally acted in good faith. He wanted to believe the army evidence and did so; any evidence he found inexplicable, such as that of the army captain, or the lying lieutenant on television, he ignores. Telling the truth, however painful and unacceptable, about events in Derry on that Sunday afternoon might have helped in the defeat of terrorism. But an exercise in whitewash in covering up the brutal and illegal behaviour of the army has only helped to prolong and intensify it, for in the days following 30 January 1972 men who did not support violence flocked to join the IRA. They thought, rightly or wrongly that force had to been met with force. Most of all, Lord Widgery damaged the reputation for firmness, courage and impartiality of Britain's judiciary, of which he was the most senior permanent judge. Whatever the truth may be about the terrible tragedy of Bloody Sunday, from whatever viewpoint, was it really "a jolly good show" after all?

Chapter 2

THE CASES OF THE MAGUIRE SEVEN AND THE GUILDFORD FOUR

The Maguire Seven were convicted of knowingly having in their possession or under their control an explosive substance – nitroglycerine – between 1 and 4 December 1974. The circumstances were said to give rise to a reasonable suspicion that they did not have it in their possession or under their control for a lawful object. They were: Anne Maguire, aged 40, and her husband Patrick Maguire, aged 43, both sentenced to fourteen years imprisonment; their sons Vincent, aged 17, sentenced to five years imprisonment, and Patrick, aged 14, ordered to be detained for four years; Guiseppe Conlon, aged 52, Patrick O'Neill, aged 35, and Sean Smyth, aged 38, all sentenced to twelve years imprisonment. (O'Neill's sentence was reduced to eight years on appeal.)

On 26 June 1991 the Criminal Division of the Court of Appeal (Lord Justice Stuart-Smith, Lord Justice Mann and Lord Justice McCowen) quashed the convictions of Mrs Anne Maguire and six others, known as the Maguire Seven, for unlawfully possessing nitroglycerine, "on the ground that the possibility of innocent contamination could not be excluded and on that ground alone, the appellants' convictions were unsafe and unsatisfactory and the appeals were allowed"[1] The Director of Public Prosecutions had already indicated that the appeal would not be opposed on that ground.[2] Five other grounds of appeal were rejected by the Court.

The decision of the Appeal Court has been described as "grudging" and "a hollow victory".[3] Mr Chris Mullen, the MP for Sunderland South, accused the judges of "an awesome display of stupidity."[4] Outside the court, Mrs Anne Maguire said, "I am glad we got the decision, but I had hoped that would be the end of it. We will have to go on and fight at the (Sir John) May inquiry, because there were a lot of things said in there that weren't right."[5]

Two academic lawyers, David Schiff and Richard Nobles in their interpretation of the judgement, pose two questions about the case: "First, could anything less than an authoritative statement of your innocence, which was at least as strong as that represented by your conviction, enable you to rebuild a normal life? Second, would you be satisfied with a judgement which said, in effect: 'At least one of you handled explosives, but we do not know who, so we have to let all of you go'."[6] These views have to be considered alongside the statement of Neil Butterfield Q.C., to the Court on 8 May 1991 when he said, "It would be quite wrong for me to infer guilt while conceding that the convictions were unsafe and unsatisfactory."[7]

This statement was described by Patrick O'Connor, counsel for Guiseppe Conlon, as being "diametrically opposed" to what the DPP had set out in his skeleton argument to the Court of Appeal.[8] In addition, the Home Secretary has told the House of Commons: "It is a matter of concern that there should have been such a serious miscarriage of justice, which has resulted in wrongful imprisonment."[9]

So what now is the position? Are the Maguire Seven innocent, or is at least one of them guilty? Or are they all guilty as charged, and their convictions simply set aside on technical grounds?

Their case really began with the arrest of four people, the Guildford Four. The Guildford Four were Gerard Conlon, aged 21, convicted of five counts of murder and conspiracy to cause explosions, sentenced to life imprisonment; Carole Richardson, aged 18, convicted of five counts of murder and conspiracy to cause explosions; Patrick Armstrong, aged 25, convicted of five counts of murder and conspiracy to cause explosions, sentenced to life imprisonment; Paul Hill, aged 21, convicted of five counts of murder and conspiracy to cause explosions, sentenced to life imprisonment. The charges related to the bombing of two public houses in Guildford, Surrey, on Saturday, 5 October 1974. Armstrong and Hill were also convicted of bombing a public house at Woolwich, killing two people, on 7 November 1974.

This was the sequence of events, extracted from the Interim Report of Sir John May.[10] Paul Hill was arrested in Southampton on Thursday, 28 November 1974 and taken to Guildford Police Station. Gerard Conlon (Mrs Anne Maguire's nephew) was arrested in Belfast on Saturday, 30 November 1974 and on the following day was taken to Godalming, Surrey. That same day, 1 December 1974, Gerard Conlon's father Guiseppe was told by a firm of solicitors that his son had been arrested in connection with the Guildford bombings.

On Monday, 2 December 1974, those solicitors sent a telegram addressed to Patrick Maguire, Anne's husband, at the family home in North West London, about Gerard's arrest. It was received by Mr Maguire at around 6 p.m. that day. He didn't tell his wife Anne about the telegram. What he did do was to telephone the London solicitors, whose telephone number had been give in the telegram, and tell them he didn't want to have anything to do with the matter.[11] Guiseppe Conlon, who was chronically ill with tuberculosis, in the meanwhile decided to travel from Belfast to London, arriving at Heysham in

Lancashire at about 6 a.m. on Tuesday 3 December 1974 and thence by train to London. His exact time of arrival is not stated, but it is known that perhaps about 1:30 p.m. Mr Conlon and Mr Maguire went to a public house for drinks, and returned home between 3 and 3:30 p.m. Anne Maguire was then told of her nephew's arrest in connection with the Guildford bombings.

That same day, Tuesday, Paul Hill and Gerard Conlon made statements implicating Mrs Anne Maguire in the Guildford bombings. Also on that day Carole Richardson and Patrick Armstrong were arrested in Kilburn, North London. In Sir John May's words, "As a result of what Hill and Conlon had said – whatever exactly it was – Metropolitan Police officers were deployed that evening to watch the Maguires' house.[12] He puts the time that police observation began at around 7 p.m.[13] That time is of fundamental importance to the case of Patrick O'Neill.

Mr O'Neill had been a friend of the Maguires for many years and at one time had lodged with them.[14] He was the father of three little girls: Jacqueline, aged 8, Sharon, aged 6, and Jean, aged 4. Patrick O'Neill had telephoned Anne Maguire to ask her to look after the three children as his wife was in hospital. The children had been staying with their aunt until Mrs O'Neill's planned release from hospital on the Tuesday; that arrangement had been changed, for she was not coming out of hospital on that day. The aunt could no longer care for them as her own father was ill. Mrs Maguire agreed to look after the three girls for a few days.

According to Mr Robert Kee[15], the time of that phone call between Mr O'Neill and Mrs Maguire was around 6 p.m. on Tuesday, 3 December 1974. Sir John May thinks it was shortly after 6 p.m. that day, or it may have been about the same time the previous day, or even possibly Tuesday morning.[16] In any event, the phone call was clearly made and Mr O'Neill arrived, with the children, perhaps just before 6:40 or 6:45, although their arrival could have been nearer 7 p.m.[17]

If the Crown case against the Maguire Seven was true, Mr O'Neill was bringing those young children to a bomb factory. He was arrested at about 9 p.m. that evening, in the Royal Lancer public house, together with Patrick Maguire, Guiseppe Conlon and Sean Smyth who had been lodging at the Maguire house. Mrs Maguire and her three sons were also taken from the house into custody.

Leading Counsel for the Crown at the Maguire Seven trial in January 1976 was Sir Michael Havers Q.C. – as he then was. He was the Conservative and Unionist Member of Parliament for Wimbledon. He had been the Solicitor General in Mr Edward Heath's Government from 1972 to 1974. He had also prosecuted the Guildford Four. According to *The Times*, in his opening speech to the jury, on 14 January 1976, he said: "Alarm bells had started ringing", and it was "all hands to the pumps" after a telegram had been received from Northern Ireland stating that a relative had been arrested there in connection with the Guildford public house bombings two months earlier.[18] "There had been 'a gathering of the clans' for that purpose."[19] Evidence would be given during the trial, said Sir Michael Havers, "that all had not only handled the explosives but had 'kneaded and manipulated' it to pack it into small bags to get rid of the evidence.[20]

Therefore, the telegram from Mr Guiseppe Conlon had arrived at the Maguire house at about 6 p.m. on Monday, 2 December 1974. He himself had arrived around the middle of Tuesday, 3 December. His hands were swabbed for forensic testing. The tests showed positive for all swabs except for his dry, left hand. Did the panic start when the telegram arrived on the Monday evening. But why did it not induce any action until after Mr Conlon's unexpected arrival on the Tuesday? Or had there been some panic action by the Maguires immediately on the Monday, and some bulk of nitroglycerine was left over so that Guiseppe Conlon could be involved in its handling and disposal at a later stage?

The one count in the indictment against the Maguire Seven alleged the possession of nitroglycerine "between the 1st and 4th days of December 1974". In the summing up[21] the trial judge – Sir John Donaldson, who had also tried the Guildford Four – said: "The Crown say that the Guildford arrests would create panic amongst these people, that they were in possession of explosives, and they say there is some evidence of panic, or at least grave concern, in relation to the arrest of Gerry Conlon . . . The Crown do not say that all those people necessarily handled the nitroglycerine simultaneously, they do not express any view about that at all; they simply say they handled it somehow or other; they do not even say where it was handled. You may think that the probabilities are that if it was handled at all it was handled at or near 43 Third Avenue (the Maguire home). You may also think it is probable that it was handled *during the afternoon* [emphasis added] of 3rd December. But the Crown do not have to prove that and they do not allege any particular time of handling it or, as I say, that they all handled it together."

This is difficult to follow. Was it the fact of arrest of Gerard Conlon, or the notification of that fact by telegram which induced the panic? Assuming that the Maguire Seven were bombers and one of their family was arrested in Belfast on 30 November 1974, would they not be told? They did nothing for the first day, whether told or not. Did they do anything on the second day or even the third? Some nitroglycerine has to be left for Guiseppe to handle on 3 December – and on the Donaldson scenario the probability was that the handling took place on the Tuesday in the afternoon following his arrival.

If that is right what about the case of Patrick O'Neill? He had arrived with his three daughters at some time between 6:40 and 7 p.m. The Donaldson scenario might exclude him on those timings, but the difficulty was that when his hands were swabbed, although the swabs were negative, "The nails on both hands and paper scrapings were positive."[22]

It should be stressed that "The scientists called for the prosecution asserted at the trial that the traces of nitroglycerine found under the fingernails of certain of the suspects established that they had been manipulating or kneading explosives."[23] This evidence, highlighted by the extravagant and theatrical language of prosecuting counsel – "all hands to the pumps", and "the gathering of the clans" – ruled out any possibility of innocent contamination. Sir John Donaldson's suggestion to the jury that "The Crown do not say that all those people necessarily handled the nitroglycerine simultaneously . . . *They do not even say where it was handled* [emphasis added]." is directly contradicted by *The Times* report of the opening day of the trial: "Swabs showed that they had been handling nitroglycerine although no explosives were found when police raided the premises. The explosives were packed up either at the house in Third Avenue or in one of the derelict houses situated behind, Sir Michael added."[24]

For some reason which defies comprehension there was a bulk of nitroglycerine available to Mr Patrick O'Neill at the 59th minute of the 23rd hour, on that fateful Tuesday evening, just before the police took up observation at the Maguire house; he kneaded and manipulated it into small bags to get rid of the evidence, just like the other six accused, and did so in such way no small bags were ever found. A search of the house with dogs and a mechanical device known as "a sniffer" failed to detect any trace of explosives in the house.

One fact seems not to have troubled the jury at the trial: following the tests at Harrow Road police station, Mr O'Neill was then released on bail to await the results of the forensic tests. The police had power to hold him for seven days without charge under the terms of the Prevention of Terrorism (Temporary Provisions) Act 1974. Since the timings were so vague, did the police release him because they saw him arrive at the house with the three children? Mr O'Neill, still available to the police for questioning, and making no attempt to abscond, was told four days afterwards that the forensic results were positive; he was arrested and detained. On conviction he was sentenced to twelve years imprisonment. On appeal that was reduced to eight years.[25]

It may be significant, in the light of the Appeal Court finding that it was possible that those whose hands were contaminated by nitroglycerine were innocently contaminated by contact with the towel in the bathroom at the Maguire house."[26]At Guildford Police station Mr O'Neill said that he had used the toilet at the Maguire house, "but I washed my hands after and dried them on a towel there. That's the only thing I did. Whether I could have got it off the towel or not I don't know."[27] If that was the source of the contamination then Mr O'Neill was an entirely innocent man, wrongly convicted, wrongly sentenced, and on his release he was made the subject of an wrongful exclusion order under the Prevention of Terrorism Act[28], excluding him from the mainland part of the United Kingdom where he had made a home for himself and his young family. Did the police even look for a contaminated towel?

On 23 May 1990 a laboratory liaison officer, Detective Sergeant Vickery, told the May inquiry in reply to a question from Neil Butterfield Q.C., as to whether dogs would have found "a heavily contaminated towel" in the house. The officer replied, "I'm sure they would have found it."[29] Whether that evidence was given to the Appeal Court is not known to me.

When Mrs Anne Maguire's hands were swabbed they were clean. There was no forensic evidence against her at that stage. However, based on what her nephew Gerard Conlon and Paul Hill said to the police about her, she was charged with the Guildford pub bombings and offences of murder. Three other people were likewise charged with her and the Guildford Four. Mrs Maguire was able conclusively to prove her movements on 5 October 1974, and the murder charges against her were withdrawn by the prosecution at the Magistrates Court.

On the night of 3 December 1974, Mrs Maguire had been arrested and her house searched. Thirty-nine plastic gloves "were apparently left in the drawer on the table in the living room overnight and remained there until 5 p.m. the following day, Wednesday 4 December, when they were collected by Detective Sergeant Lawrence Vickery in a single plastic bag."[30] It was one of those gloves which was to found the prosecution case against Mrs Maguire and result in her conviction. On testing, a positive result for nitroglycerine was obtained,"though it could perhaps have been from only one glove. Mr Elliott, one of the Crown's principal scientific witnesses, further admitted that the contamination might have been on the outside of a used glove; or the inside or a used glove; or the outside of an unused glove."[31]

The point seems not to have been raised at the trial or on appeal, or even before Sir John May, but what was the legal authority which the officer was exercising when he returned to the Maguire house where the arrests had made, to search for and to seize evidence? If there was no lawful power to do so, then Mrs Maguire may have been convicted on the basis of illegally obtained evidence. In McLorie -v- Oxford[32], the Divisional Court of the Queen's Bench Division ruled that, "Once a person has been arrested on private premises for a serious offence and the arrest was completed, a police officer had no right at common law subsequently to enter the premises without a warrant in order to search for or seize an instrument of the crime known to be on the premises."[33] Ironically, the judge who read the judgement of the Court was Sir John Donaldson.

The travels of the gloves were traced at the trial and at the May inquiry. They were taken "with further exhibits [a pair of rubber gloves and two boxes of ointment] to New Scotland Yard where he [Sgt. Vickery] put them all in a locked cupboard in the Bomb Squad Exhibits Room. They remained there for five days."[34] On Monday, 9 December, he collected the plastic gloves and the other two exhibits, gave them to another officer who eventually took them to the RARDE at Woolwich where the positive test on one of the gloves was carried out.[35] A statement of 13 December 1974 to this effect was made by Mr Elliott – so that may have been the day of the test. If it was, then traces of nitroglycerine seem to have lingered on one glove for about ten days.

When he gave evidence to the May inquiry, Detective Sergeant Vickery was unable to recall if he had been wearing gloves when he removed the plastic gloves from the Maguires' house. He also told the inquiry that he was unable to remember if he had washed his hands between the swabbing of each suspects, as laid down in the rules, to avoid possible contamination of the tests.[36] He said, " . . . at the time, bomb squad officers were not supplied with protective clothing or specific instructions on the possibility of cross-contamination, though since then new procedures had been brought in."

Detective Sergeant Vickery, it emerged, had attended the scene of a bomb explosion at the Talbot Arms public house in Chelsea, West London, on 30 November 1974, just forty-eight hours before he entered the Maguire house."[37] In Chelsea, " . . . he had taken charge of an unexploded device."[38] If traces of nitroglycerine can linger for about ten days on a plastic glove, could not have this officer have been the innocent source of the contamination of at least some of the Maguire Seven samples?

Of equal importance, some of the notes made at RARDE by an

eighteen year old trainee relating to Mrs Maguire's gloves, " . . . were marked Tite Street at the top, which was then crossed out."[39] Tite Street, Chelsea is the site of the Talbot Arms, the scene of the IRA bombing on 30 November 1974. Was it just an unhappy coincidence that the property named in the notebook should appear on the same page as Mrs Maguire's name and test results?

The conduct of the scientists who gave prosecution evidence in the case gives cause for concern, but it does not stand alone. Sir John May recounts the fact that "Evidence was given at the Maguire trial that second tests [on the hand swabs and gloves] were not necessary or practicable."[40]

At the outset of the inquiry, on 24 May 1991, *The Guardian* reported: "An 18-year old trainee with two months experience carried out tests on hand-swabs taken from the Maguire defendants, which uncovered nitroglycerine traces and led to their convictions on IRA bomb-making charges, the May inquiry heard yesterday. The forensic evidence, the basis of the Crown's case against the Maguires at the 1976 Old Bailey trial, was destroyed in the test, leaving no opportunity for secondary confirmation of the results."

In fact that was not correct, because " . . . the inquiry's examination of the RARDE notebooks revealed *for the first time* [emphasis added] that there had been a second test on the samples taken from the Maguires." [41] Those second tests were negative.[42]

Of the two scientists who had given evidence for the prosecution at the trial, Mr Higgs and Dr Hayes, Sir John May says, perhaps more in sorrow than in anger: "Both Mr Higgs and Dr Hayes denied knowledge of these second tests until they examined the papers at RARDE shortly before my public hearings began. Even then, when they first gave evidence before me, they did not tell me of the second tests." [43]

Worse still, in relation to the first named scientist, Sir John May notes at paragraph 11. 19 that, "In 1983 Mr Higgs wrote a note for a meeting at the Home Office that the technology as it existed in 1973/74 did not permit an alternative TLC procedure to be used. Furthermore, at his first appearance before my inquiry Mr Higgs maintained this position." There is a further ground on which Mr Higgs can be criticised. At the trial the prosecution had maintained that traces of nitroglycerine under the fingernails established that the suspect had been manipulating or kneading explosives. That assertion was based, of course, on the evidence of the scientists called by the prosecution, of whom Mr Higgs was one.

In a study carried out in 1977, whilst the Maguire Seven, including Vincent, aged 17 and Patrick, aged 14,were at the outset of their sentences, it was shown that assertion was no longer sound and accurate; nitroglycerine can migrate under the nails without the explosives being kneaded.

When the study was published in the Journal of Forensic Sciences in 1982, one of the authors was Mr Higgs.[44] He fared little better when he gave evidence before the Court of Appeal. He admitted to that court that "he knew about a set of negative tests for explosives carried out on the Maguire Seven, but that he must have 'forgotten' about them when he gave prosecution evidence." He also told the appeal judges that he did not know about the experiment during the trial which was aimed at discovering how nitroglycerine traces can be transferred from one hand to another. If he had, he said, he would certainly have told the prosecuting counsel, Sir Michael Havers, about it. However. he admitted later that he must have authorised the test when presented with RARDE documents showing his initials. Patrick O'Connor pointed out to Mr Higgs, "That is diametrically opposed to your denial this morning to their lordships."[45]

What would a jury have made of this? The Court of Appeal, perhaps looking more at evidence which might have proved the guilt of someone in the Maguire house than that which discredited the scientists, considered that "No miscarriage of justice occurred by the irregularity concerning the non-disclosure of certain tests.[46]

At the trial the defence called as an expert witness Mr John Yallop. He was a former Director of RARDE. He had helped to develop the Thin Layer Chromatography (TLC) test. His professional opinion was that he no longer thought a single TLC test was a satisfactory basis on which to form a conclusion that nitroglycerine had been present. A confirmatory test was necessary.[47]

Mr Yallop clearly had deep feelings of troublesome unease about the case. No less than six people with nitroglycerine on their hands were in a house in which no trace of explosive had been found. Had they cleaned the house but not their hands? Moreover, the police dogs and the sniffer device had found no trace in the drawer where Mrs Maguire's contaminated glove had been stored. Finally, he found it hard to believe that, knowing the dangers of handling nitroglycerine, Anne Maguire should apparently have been alone in protecting herself with gloves. nitroglycerine is rapidly absorbed through the skin into the bloodstream and gives the handler a blinding headache known to scientists as "an NG headache". Would Anne Maguire have worn gloves – especially since there were so many available for use – while allowing her children to use their bare hands?[48] The reaction of the trial judge was to comment that this was hardly expert evidence.[49]

The reaction of prosecuting counsel, Sir Michael Havers, was markedly different. He attacked Mr Yallop's credibility as a witness. In the words of the former M.P. Christopher Price[50], Havers " . . . decided to destroy Mr Yallop. He laid into him, accusing him of dishonesty, lack of frankness, and selecting his evidence to suit his case. It was a cross-examination of which he was particularly proud, saying so to acquaintances afterwards, including myself."[51]

Why should Mr Yallop, who had many years distinguished public service to his credit, have given false evidence in the defence of those who might be terrorists defies explanation. He had ranged against him the expert evidence of Mr Higgs, who told the jury, "I seek to establish that the TLC test is infallible and I believe it to be."[52] Of course, if Mr Yallop was right, or might have been right, in his assertion that the TLC test was a preliminary screening and not conclusive test for the presence of nitroglycerine, the Maguire Seven should have been acquitted by the jury. As Sir John May notes[53], "There is no doubt that cross-examination of Mr Yallop by Sir Michael Havers Q.C. was very effective. In the course of it, Sir Michael clearly put to him that he had not been honest; that he had not complied with his duty to be frank with the court; that he had selected and given evidence about the results of experiments which best supported his thesis and discarded the rest. Reading the transcript of Mr Yallop's evidence at the trial, it is quite clear that an effective challenge was mounted not only against his scientific expertise but against his credibility generally."

In other words, Mr Yallop was the kind of person who should not be believed when giving evidence on oath. No reason why Mr Yallop should perjure himself by giving false evidence for the defence, and thereby run the risk of a substantial prison sentence if his evidence was shown to be false has ever been advanced by anyone.

The case of the Maguire Seven is obviously closely connected with that of the Guildford Four. Apart from the family connections, there are other clear links between the two cases: first, the prosecution team in both consisted of the same four barristers, and second, the trial judge was the same, Sir John Donaldson.

Leading counsel for the prosecution was Sir Michael Havers Q.C. He was born in March 1923 and educated at Westminster School and Corpus Christi College, Cambridge. His father, Sir Cecil Havers, had been a High Court Judge. Sir Michael was called to the Bar of England and Wales by the Inner Temple, one of the four Inns of Court, in November 1948. He became a Queen's Counsel in 1964. He was a Conservative Member of Parliament for Wimbledon from 1970 until 1987. During his time in the House of Commons he was appointed

Solicitor General, in 1972 in the Conservative Government headed by Mr Edward Heath. When the Government was defeated in the General Election in March 1974, he vacated that post and returned to the back benches in Parliament. He was on any view a rising star both in the law and in politics, and he would be a formidable opponent to cross in or out of court.

It was whilst he was shadow Attorney General and Legal Adviser to the Shadow Cabinet that he led the prosecuting team in both the Guildford Four and the Maguire family trials. When the Conservatives, under Mrs Margaret Thatcher, were returned to power in May 1979, Sir Michael Havers was appointed Attorney General in the new administration. He held that post until 1987.

The Attorney General is the government's chief legal adviser, and speaks in Parliament from the Front Bench on legal administration and government legislation. Havers was not a complete success as Attorney General and was criticised for his role in several high profile cases, such as the Spycatcher case and the prosecution of a junior civil servant who passed secret information to the *Guardian* newspaper. His physical health was not good; nevertheless on 13 June 1987 he was appointed Lord Chancellor. He held that office, the highest judicial post in the United Kingdom, for six months, until 26 October 1987, the shortest term of appointment of any Lord Chancellor certainly in the last 107 years.

The second prosecuting member of the team was Eliot Michael Hill, who was born in 1935 and educated at Bancroft's school in Essex and Brasenose College, Oxford. He was called to the Bar by Gray's Inn in 1958. Between 1963 and 1974 he was prosecuting counsel to the Crown at Inner London Sessions. Between 1974 and 1979, when he was appointed Queen's Counsel, he was a member of the prosecuting team at the Central Criminal Court in London, the Old Bailey. He was chairmen of the Criminal Bar Assocation for four years from 1982 to 1986. He appeared for the defence of a tabloid newspaper which had been sued for libel by the author Jeffrey Archer. He was instructed, presumably, on the basis that a forceful cross-examination might be helpful to the defence case, and with his background in the criminal trial process he might at least undermine if not destroy Mr Archer's credibility.If that was indeed the purpose, he failed, for when faced with witnesses, especially Jeffrey Archer's wife, Mary, and others who were of an different level of intellectual attainment and capacity than those to whom he was normally accustomed, certainly on one view, Mr Hill floundered. The amount of damages which the jury awarded against Mr Hill's clients was the not insubstantial sum of half a million pounds. The plaintiff was also awarded his costs against the defendant newspaper.

The third member of the team was Paul Oliver Purnell, who was born in 1936 and educated at the Oratory School in London and Jesus College, Oxford. He was a former member of the British Army, having served[54] in the 4th/7th Royal Dragoon Guards from 1958 until 1962. He was called to the Bar by the Inner Temple in 1962 and was appointed Queen's Counsel in 1982. He was also prosecuting counsel at the Old Bailey between 1976 and 1982.

There was a fourth member of the prosecuting team: Philip Havers, who had been called to the Bar by the Inner Temple in July 1974. When the trial of the Guildford Four opened in September 1975 therefore, he had been a practising barrister for a year and two months. Twelve months of that time had to be spent as a pupil, or trainee, with another, more experienced barrister. It was the practice then that if a case was conducted by the Director of Public Prosecutions outside of the London area where special rules applied, it was the responsibility of the Attorney General to nominate counsel to conduct the case on the Director's behalf from a list of names of those barristers with experience of criminal law, and of more than ten years seniority since being called to the Bar. Why such an inexperienced beginner as Philip Havers was nominated as prosecuting counsel in two cases of such importance can perhaps only be explained by the fact that his father, Sir Michael Havers, was heading the prosecution team.

However, the other three experienced criminal practitioners made quite a formidable team when ranged against all the defendants in both the Guildford and Maguire cases.

Their backgrounds could not have been further removed from that of any of the accused; they might have lived in different parts of the world for all that they had in common. Of the Guildford Four, Paul Hill left school at the age of fourteen without a single academic or trade qualification. Gerard Conlon, who left school at fifteen, was in the same position. Patrick Armstrong was three years older than Paul Hill and Gerard Conlon, and like them was a native of Belfast. He too left school at the age of fifteen with no formal qualifications of any kind; he worked in various places at jobs with low pay and no prospects. He was the only one of the Four not to have a criminal record for petty crime but, like Gerard Conlon, was involved in drug-taking and at the time of his arrest was living in a squat.

Carole Richardson had no qualifications of any kind. She was born in London; her father had deserted her mother before her birth so she never knew him. At the age of 13 she drank alcohol and smoked cannabis; her only graduation was from soft drugs to LSD, cocaine and morphine. She left school, where she had a history of truancy, on her fifteenth birthday. She had been made the subject of a supervision order by the Magistrates at Willesden Juvenile Court for minor offences of dishonesty. At the time of her arrest for the Guildford bombings, aged 17, she was living in a squat, with Patrick Armstrong and others in North London. She did not give evidence in her own defence at the trial when she was charged with murder. The right to silence, the privilege against self-incrimination, is an important constitutional right jealously guarded by the law.

In his book *Trial and Error*, Robert Kee writes that she was "in such a psychological condition so precarious that her counsel would not take the risk of letting her go into the witness box where she could be cross-examined on oath." In a review of Mr Kee's book[55], Lord Rawlinson of Elwell, a former Conservative & Unionist politician and Queen's Counsel who had been Attorney General between 1970 and 1974 (when Havers was Solicitor General for part of that time) comments on that failure to give sworn evidence: "The risk of what? That the truth will come out?" Is that not a clear indication from a former Law Officer of the Crown that, contrary to well established legal principles that no inference of guilt is to be drawn from a failure to give evidence, that Carole Richardson stayed out of the witness box to conceal the truth, and that truth was that she was guilty as charged?

A criminal trial on indictment in England begins with the identification and arraignment of the accused; they are asked to plead formally, guilty or not guilty, to the indictment, the written document which sets out the charges against them. After the arraignment, the jury is sworn to try the case according to the evidence. They are told by the judge and often by prosecuting counsel to forget everything they may have read or heard about the case they are to try, and to pay regard only to what is established by the evidence of the witnesses in the course of the trial.

The next step in the criminal process is the opening speech of counsel for the prosecution to the jury. It is then that the prosecution outlines and explains the evidence which it proposes to adduce to establish the guilt of each of the accused. Reference is almost always made to the obligation on the Crown which brings the case to prove it, and that the defence generally need prove nothing. The burden of proving the case against an accused at a criminal trial lies from first to last upon the prosecution; the standard of proof, a high one, is that the jury must be satisfied of the guilt of the accused beyond reasonable doubt.

In outlining the case, the prosecuting counsel has of necessity to rely upon the written statements made by witnesses to the police in the course of the investigation into the crime. It is anticipated by the prosecution that the witness will say in evidence on oath from the witness box exactly what he/she said to the police in the statement. Of course, what counsel says is not evidence; it is of great importance that he opens only that evidence which it is expected will be given to the jury.

At the time of the trial, the duty of Counsel for the Prosecution was set out in the principal opinions or rulings given by the General Council of the Bar, in their Annual Statements on matters relating to professional conduct and etiquette. In the 6th Edition of Conduct and Etiquette at the Bar, compiled by W.W. Bolton, Secretary of the General Council of the Bar, the rulings state: "Crown counsel is a representative of the state, a 'Minister of Justice'; his function is to assist the jury in arriving at the truth. He must not urge any argument that does not carry weight in his own mind, or try to shut out any legal evidence that would be important to the interests of the accused person. It is not his duty to obtain a conviction by all means; but simply to lay before the jury the whole of the facts which compose his case, and to make them perfectly intelligible and to see that the jury are instructed with regard to the law and are able to apply the law to the facts. It cannot be too often made plain that the business of counsel for the Crown is fairly and impartially to exhibit all the facts to the jury . . . In opening a case, counsel must not open any fact as a fact in the case which he is not in a position to prove."

This last sentence is of immense importance in the case of Gerard Conlon (Mrs Maguire's nephew), Paul Hill, Patrick Armstrong and Carole Richardson – the Guildford Four.

When Sir Michael Havers opened the case for the prosecution against the Guildford Four a most important question arises: did he open as a fact a fact which he was not in a position to prove? If a senior and experienced television journalist is correct in his reporting of the opening speech, then that is exactly what Sir Michael Havers did.

On the opening day of the trial, Tuesday, 16 September 1975 Mr Norman Rees was shown, face on to camera, on Independent Television News relating these words: "Two soldiers had seen the couple kissing and cuddling in the corner of the bar on the night of the explosion. At the time (he said) they were in the process of planting a time-bomb under their seat. Sir Michael said the couple would be identified by the soldiers as Patrick Armstrong aged twenty-four and Carole Richardson aged seventeen."

These words are a crucial point in this case, for the truth was that Patrick Armstrong had never been identified by anyone; nor was he ever placed on an identification parade at any stage. Carole Richardson had stood on no less than eight such parades, all held on Friday, 13 December 1974 at Guildford Police station.[56] No one identified her at those parades. At that date the dangers of wrongful conviction arising out of mistaken visual identification evidence were under consideration, especially since the setting up of the Committee under the chairmanship of Lord Devlin on 1 May 1974 to examine all aspects of the law and procedure relating to evidence of identification in criminal cases.

Amongst the eight witnesses who attended the parades on which Miss Richardson stood were indeed two soldiers, Paul Lynskey and John Cook, both paratroopers. Both had given detailed descriptions to the police of "the courting couple" and neither soldier had been injured in the bombing on 5 October 1974. Therefore,there was no question of their powers of observation, recollection or description being impaired in any way. As Robert Kee relates: "John Cook passed down the line: 'I can't remember'." Paul Lynskey was more categorical: "I can't see her there."[57]

No witness at the trial, soldier or civilian, ever identified Armstrong and Miss Richardson as the courting couple. In a letter to me dated 26 February 1987, the television reporter Mr Norman Rees states: "My reference to the fact that Armstrong and Richardson would be identified during the course of the trial by two soldiers who were in the pub at the time would have come from my shorthand note. Unfortunately I have not kept my notebooks from this period. My recollection however is that the Havers statement was not challenged at the time and certainly my report was never the subject of any complaint from any source on the ground of accuracy."That filmed report from the ITN broadcast is still available.

There is an additional matter to be considered on this point. Reference has already been made to the extravagant and theatrical language used by Sir Michael Havers in the case of the Maguire Seven. According to the television documentary programme produced by the *Today, Tonight* team and broadcast by the Irish national television service, Radio Telefis Eireann, Havers used an unforgettable phrase, directed this time at the hapless Pat O'Neill, who had taken his three daughters to Mrs Maguire's house. O'Neill was, as Havers put it in cross-examination "another homing pigeon going down to Paddy Maguire's." This suggestion, expressed in evocative and emotive language was no doubt in support of another suggestion made, according to *Today, Tonight,* by Havers in his opening speech that, "The Maguires had *called a hastily convened council of war*" [emphasis added]. There was simply no evidence of this fact presented as a fact in the prosecution opening speech. Moreover, that statement was manifestly untrue.

Sir John May narrates the chronology of events of 3 December[58]: "In the Maguire household Tuesday 3rd December began as a normal working day. Sean Smyth (who is Anne Maguire's brother and was at the time lodging at the house) left for work at about 6.45 am; Annie Maguire left for her cleaning job at a firm of accountants about half an hour later. At about 8 a.m. Paddy Maguire, having tried without success to contact his brother Hugh to discuss the telegram, rang the number of Hugh's close friend Sean Tully and spoke to Mrs Tully about Hugh's whereabouts. At around 8.45 a.m. Annie Maguire returned home. By this time two of her three sons, John and Patrick had gone to school; Vincent, her eldest son, had gone to work. At around 9 a.m. Annie Maguire took her daughter Ann Marie (aged 8 years) to school, getting home again about a quarter of an hour later, when she made some tea for her husband. After about 9.40 a.m. she left the house again for two more cleaning jobs, the first at a betting shop, the second, having stopped off at a bakers on the way, at a greengrocers. Afterwards she went to a jumble sale, did some more shopping and eventually returned to 43 Third Avenue at between 1. 30 and 2 p.m..

"Meanwhile, much to Paddy Maguire's surprise, Guiseppe Conlon had arrived at the house and, after 20 minutes or so, they went to a public house. This was perhaps getting on for 1.30 p.m. Not long after, John Maguire arrived home with his friend Hugh McHugh – 'Ginger' – followed by Vincent Maguire who probably had to let them into the house . . . At about 2 p.m. Annie Maguire had lunch with the boys. Between 3 and 3.30 p.m. Paddy Maguire and Guiseppe Conlon returned from the pub . . . At about 4 p.m. John Maguire's girlfriend Maxine Ryan visited the house, staying for about half an hour. Soon after 4 p.m. Ann Marie came home with a school friend. Between 4.15 and 4.30 p.m. a neighbour, a Mrs Roach, came to collect a package from Annie Maguire, staying about 5 minutes."

Mr Robert Kee's account of this incident is slightly different both in time and content and perhaps a rather more homely setting. He states Ann Marie came back from school with a friend of hers, Marie Baker. Anne made them tea and sandwiches in the kitchen. At about 5:30 Mrs Roach, whom Anne had met in the street that morning, came in to ask if she had any Bisto. She had none but let her have an Oxo cube and Mrs Roach left again, saying how good the stew smelt.[59]

Sir John May continues: "At about 4.30 p.m. John and Ginger left the house." Up to this point in time, four people – Hugh McHugh, Maxime Ryan, Ann Marie's school friend Marie Baker and Mrs Roach – all unconnected with the Maguire family, had open and uninterrupted

71

access to the supposed bomb factory at the Maguire home.

The narrative goes on: "John Maguire returned home between 5.15 p.m. and 5.30 p.m., Patrick (aged 13) not long after. Soon after this, though probably no later than 5.40 p.m., Vincent left for his evening class. Vincent was an assistant gas fitter with the North Thames Gas Board; he was studying in the evenings at Paddington Technical College. His father left soon after to inquire after Hugh at Harrow Road Police Station."

In the sequence of events this is important for Vincent Maguire's case, because he was at classes at the Technical College between 6 p.m. and 8 p.m., and when he returned home about 9 p.m., " . . . he saw two police vans and a car parked at the house. A man was standing outside. Vincent walked up to the front door and could see through it a group of men in the hallway. He also caught sight of a dog. The man outside told him to move on. 'What do you mean?' said Vincent, 'I live here.' The man called in to the others, 'Here's another of them.' He hauled Vincent into the house."[60]

Vincent was taken to Paddington Green Police Station and his hands were swabbed, as were those of his mother and two brothers, by Detective Sergeant Kenneth Day. The Laboratory Form 1 which accompanied the swabs on their journey to Royal Armament Research and Development establishment for forensic examination were marked "Offence – Murder" and the entry on the form under "Circumstances of Offences" was "Suspects for Guildford and other bombing offences."[61] In Vincent's case, the scrapings from under "his right hand nails and the paper were positive".[62] The results were not known until the afternoon of Thursday, 5 December.

In the meanwhile, Vincent and his two brothers John and Patrick were allowed to go home in the early hours of the Wednesday morning. Since Vincent was suspected of murder, that must have seemed a somewhat odd approach to the investigation of that crime. Moreover, despite the forensic test being positive, Vincent was not charged with an offence until three months later, on 24 February 1975. On the same day his mother, Anne Maguire, had the charge of murder – laid against her solely on the basis of inadmissible hearsay evidence of others– withdrawn on the instructions of the Director of Public Prosecutions in the magistrates court.

Vincent's case does pose the question: what part, if any, did he play in the Havers scenario of the "hastily convened council of war"? He had gone to work in the morning long before Guiseppe Conlon arrived unexpectedly at the family home. When he returned to the house, Guiseppe was at the public house with Vincent's father. But, according to the prosecution, Vincent Maguire had not merely handled nitroglycerine: Sir Michael Havers told the jury that finding the substance under the fingernails indicated that the accused had been not just touching it but manipulating and kneading it. Could Vincent, Conlon and Vincent's father have handled the substance between the pair's return from the pub at 5:30 p.m. and before Vincent's departure for college at 5:40 p.m.?

Besides, did Vincent handle it in such a way that only the area under the fingernails of his right hand were contaminated? Did he decide to forgo his place at the table for the council of war in order to attend his gas fitters class at Paddington Technical College? By the time of his departure from his home, neither his uncle Sean Smyth nor the family friend Patrick O'Neill (the "homing pigeon", according to Havers) and the three little girls had arrived at the house. This leads to yet another question: who called the council of war, where, when and at what time was it to be held? If Vincent manipulated and kneaded explosives, but missed the council of war, why on his return did he identify himself at the house where the handling took place, instead of running for cover?

Paddy Maguire left the house shortly after Vincent; his destination was Harrow Road Police Station and his purpose was to make inquiries about his brother Hugh Maguire. If Vincent had been in contact with nitroglycerine that must have happened at a time prior to Paddy Maguire's departure for the police station. Had the father, like his son, manipulated and kneaded the explosives at or about the same time, and having done so just nipped down to the nearest police station to inquire about a near relative? Or did Paddy Maguire do a bit of manipulating and kneading after the visit to Harrow Road; did he know what Vincent had been up to and perhaps decide to keep his hands clean until his return to the house?

Paddy Maguire visited the Harrow Road Police Station between some time shortly after 5:40 p.m. and before 7 p.m. There he saw a young policewoman to whom he explained his anxiety about his brother. He was told that another person had been making inquiries about Hugh Maguire. When Paddy suggested that a policeman might come with him and if necessary break down the door of Hugh's flat, in case he was ill or injured or worse, he was told: "There is no need for that."[63] He then returned home.

In fact Hugh Maguire and his wife had been arrested at their home in Westbourne Terrace Road, Paddington between 4 a.m. and 5 a.m. on Saturday, November 30. No information about those arrests four days earlier, in a place not far from the Maguire home was communicated to any of the family by anyone. Hugh Maguire was taken first to Harrow

Road Police Station, then to Cannon Row, and then to Guildford. In making inquiries about his brother, who of course had the same family name as himself, Paddy Maguire was drawing attention to himself at the very same police station where Hugh had been detained, at a time when Hugh was in police custody. Therefore, all the more important to decide whether Paddy Maguire had kneaded and manipulated the nitroglycerine before that visit to the police station, or whether the bulk or at least some of it was awaiting his return to 43, Third Avenue. As for the "hastily convened council of war", had that been held prior to the police station visit, or was it held in Paddy Maguire's absence? Or was it awaiting his return, if he did return, for it was possible that some police officer might link the two Maguire names and arrest Paddy at Harrow Road?

Paddy's son Patrick was a thirteen year old schoolboy. He had left home for school before 9 a.m. and, according to Sir John May's report, returned home not long after 5:30 p.m.[64] Whether Vincent had left for his evening classes at that time is unclear, but if the two brothers met that early evening of 3 December, it could not have been for any great length of time. Patrick sat down to supper with some other members of the family at about 6 p.m.. He left to go to the local youth club shortly before 6:30. p.m.[65] He had, on those timings, about sixty minutes in which to come into contact with nitroglycerine. His hands were swabbed and fingernails scraped at Paddington Green Police Station. The scrapings from under his right hand fingernails were positive. He too, if this evidence was worth anything, had manipulated and kneaded nitroglycerine, but just like his brother Vincent he had used only one hand to do so. In both their cases therefore, it was one hand to the pump, not "all hands" as Havers was alleging.

It is yet another odd feature of this case that the forensic tests on the hands of the remaining brother, John, aged 15, were negative. Although he had been arrested at the house he was never charged. Yet it is a fact that he had spent more time at the house, almost the entire afternoon, than Patrick, and although he left home about 4:30 he was back again at some time between 5:15 and 5:30 p.m.[66] Patrick had arrived home from school at around 5:30 p.m. and left again before 6:30 p.m. John did not leave the house again until about 7:20 p.m. If the kneading and manipulating of nitroglycerine was done on that Tuesday afternoon or early evening, for some reason which cannot be explained thirteen year old Patrick put one hand to the pump but John put neither. If he was offered a place and declined, or there was no offer at all to be present at the "hastily convened council of war" is not known. What is known is that at about 7 p.m. John's girlfriend, Maxine Ryan, called for him. She got into the house with no apparent difficulty. She went on to a local youth club having arranged that John would join her there later.[67]

Sean Smyth, their lodger, had left the house early on the Tuesday morning. He was a tractor driver for a building company working at a site at Wembley Stadium.[68] He arrived back at the house at about 6:30 p.m., shortly before Paddy Maguire's return from the Harrow Road Police Station. That time of arrival could be confirmed by independent evidence from one of Sean's work mates.[69] Smyth had lived at the house since July 1974 when he came to England from Belfast in order to find work. He was sending money weekly to his wife and four children in Belfast.[70] What he did on that Tuesday was all part of a regular routine. There could be no question, therefore, that he had been summoned to the house to attend a council of war. Sir John May notes that Smyth " . . . had a wash and changed out of his work clothes. Anne Maguire told him of Gerard Conlon's arrest. The others had finished their meal by the time Sean Smyth sat down to his."[71]

The time and circumstances of the arrival of Patrick O'Neill and his three daughters have already been examined. Sir John May states that "Police observations of the house began at around 7 p.m.[72] Against this, one can compare and contrast what a journalist of the London *Times*, Clive Borrell, wrote in that newspaper on 5 March 1976, after the conviction of the family. He wrote a background article to the case headed "Mother taught IRA recruits to make bombs." Some of the material for the article was clearly supplied to Mr Borrell by police officers: "Members of Scotland Yard's anti-terrorist squad and Surrey Constabulary are convinced that Mrs Maguire was a vitally important cog in the Provisional IRA network operating in London." The article concludes with this: "A telegram from a Belfast firm of solicitors to the Maguires gave a warning that Mr Conlon senior was arriving that day after his son had been arrested in Ulster in connection with the public house bombings."

That statement was quite untrue. There was no warning of any impending arrival of anyone. In fact the telegram read: "Re your nephew Gerard Conlon arrested and held in Guildford London. Father has instructed as solicitors Nurse and Jones 7 Lower North Street Belfast. Please telephone 45471 or 2 or after 6 phone 652565 or 23175. Bernard Simon Solicitor 40 Bedford Street London telephone 018367023 will be in contact tonight or tomorrow. Please reply. Nurse and Jones."[73]

What follows that untrue statement in the *Times* article may or may not be accurate, but if it is correct then it is highly significant. It states: "Mr Conlon's movements were followed by the police the moment he got off the ferry at Heysham. He was followed to Willesden, where seven hours later he was arrested with the members of the Maguire family." Did the police observation begin at about 7 p.m. that Tuesday evening or was it much earlier in the day? Is that statement pure invention on the part of the journalist or did it really happen?

What is not commented upon in the article is the rather unusual means of communication between these supposed terrorists, a telegram, open to public scrutiny, which when received, "alarm bells had started ringing" and it was "all hands to the pump". It was not even sent in any coded fashion, and it was not sent directly from one person to Annie Maguire, supposedly a "vital cog in the Provisional IRA operating in London". Instead, it was addressed to her husband and sent by a Belfast firm of solicitors, openly so it could be read by anyone. The firm had not only sent the telegram but had also communicated with a London solicitor, Mr Bernard Simon, to instruct him in the case, and had in addition provided him with either the address or the telephone number of the Maguires, so that Mr Simon could be in contact either that night or the next day.

The telegram had arrived at around 6 p.m. on Monday, 2 December, and rather than communicate its contents to his wife, the "vitally important cog", Paddy Maguire told her nothing. Instead, he had telephoned the London solicitor whose name and number were given in the telegram and told him he didn't want anything to do with the matter. Mrs Maguire knew nothing of Gerard Conlon's arrest in Belfast on that previous Saturday morning until after the arrival of his father Guiseppe on the Tuesday.

The forensic evidence was at the heart of the prosecution case against the Maguire Seven. There was no confession evidence, no direct or circumstantial or eye-witness evidence. Everything depended on the jury accepting the scientists' assertion that the TLC test was proof positive of contact with nitroglycerine. However, there was the danger of prejudice against Anne Maguire resulting from the extensive publicity given to the trial of the Guildford Four which took place between 16 September and 22 October 1975. In a statement read at that trial Gerard Conlon had said "he had visited his auntie Annie [Mrs Maguire] with other young Provisional IRA terrorists at a house in north London, where she gave them a lesson in making time bombs. 'Watch carefully; you may have to do this yourselves one day' she had told the assembled 'class'."[74]

Who can say whether any jury member, sworn to try Mrs Maguire according to the evidence at her trial which began on 14 January 1976, could disregard Gerard Conlon's statement read to the court at his trial only about four months earlier?

76

The defence solicitors in the case of the Maguire Seven appreciated the importance of the scientific evidence; if it could be explained or discredited or disregarded there was no case against any of the Seven. Sir John May notes[75] that Messrs Birnbergs, solicitors, wrote to the Director of Public Prosecutions asking for a copy of a further statement by the scientist Mr Walter Elliott served at the committal proceedings (where the prosecution must normally disclose the evidence of witnesses they propose to call at the trial). The solicitors asked if they could have sight of "any more detailed notes or reports that there are by Mr Elliott or his assistants who did the tests, to explain more precisely the procedure used and results obtained."

That was a perfectly reasonable request, addressed to the prosecuting authorities, whose duty is not to obtain a conviction by all means, and to counsel whose function it is to assist the jury in arriving at the truth. There seems to have been no reply to that request, because it was renewed six months later on 9 October 1975. This did prompt a response, though not a helpful one. On 22 October 1975 a reply was sent on behalf of the Director of Public Prosecutions. It said: "On the advice of Counsel I regret I am unable to supply you with copies of any notes made by Mr Elliott. The procedure used was the normal thin layer chromatography process."

On 18 December 1975 the defence tried again, this time at the hearing of a pre-trial review when the issues between the parties can be identified and indications given on what evidence may be agreed, so that court time and costs are saved.

According to the defence solicitors, Messrs Birnbergs, they noted in writing that the prosecution refused the request from the defence for the notes on the grounds of irrelevance. Whether the notes were relevant to the defence was surely a matter for the defence to decide, and if they wished to inspect them and waste time on irrelevant material is not really something which should concern the prosecution.

Mr Paul Oliver Purnell of counsel attended the pre-trial review on behalf of the prosecution. In an Advice on Evidence Consequent upon Summons for Directions dated 22 December 1975 Mr Purnell noted: "Defence seek in advance of trial bench notes of Elliott. Prosecution hedge."[76] What that actually means may not be the subject of universal agreement. To me it means, "Don't say yes and don't say no, but stall and play for time."

Mr Purnell was given notice in the course of the public hearings of the May inquiry that he might be criticised for the prosecution's attitude to the disclosure of this information. Accordingly, he appeared and gave oral evidence to Sir John May. "He explained to the inquiry that this was no more than a report that at the pre-trial review that he had hedged on this point."[77]

He further explained in evidence that his reluctance to agree to disclosure stemmed from anxieties about security. He believed that other similar trials could be anticipated and he wanted to ensure that RARDE did not disclose accidentally any other notes, and that the notes they did disclose were indeed relevant. He was also anxious, he said, that the prosecution should know in advance of any unusual features about the notes before the disclosure was made.

Sir John May thought that this attitude to the disclosure of the scientists' notebooks was both regrettable and significant. He believes that had the prosecution been more open minded to disclosure of the scientists' notebooks it is very possible that events would have taken a different turn.[78] Does this mean that if the full and frank disclosure of the scientific information had been made at the time it was first asked for, in April 1975, eight months before the trial began, this would have enabled the defence to prepare their case more fully? If that had happened would the Maguire Seven have been acquitted, and Paddy and Anne Maguire not be sentenced to fourteen years imprisonment, their son Vincent to five years imprisonment, Patrick to four years in custody, Sean Smyth, Patrick O'Neill and Guiseppe Conlon to twelve years imprisonment for a crime they did not commit?

Because of Purnell's anxieties, he told Sir John May that "he asked for steps to be taken to meet those concerns" regarding security, other similar trials, no accidental disclosure, only relevant disclosure, and the need for the prosecution team to know in advance, any unusual features about the notes.[79] What those steps were, and if they were taken, is not mentioned in the Interim Report. The security point was spurious. Was it suggested that the defence solicitors were not to be trusted? They no doubt wished to consult Mr John Yallop, who had worked for thirty-five years at the very establishment, RARDE, which had carried out the tests. On this issue Sir John May says: "We know from the case files made available towards the end of our hearings that Dr Carver did not believe that any objection could be taken to Mr Yallop's having access to the notes."

The other objections were equally spurious. Why should the professional witnesses in the Government Service not be trusted to disclosure only the notes which related the tests on the Maguire Seven? How could they accidentally, or otherwise, let the defence have sight of other unrelated tests? Just what unusual features about the notes did Purnell have in mind when he raised this objection? In the event the prosecution team agreed on 13 January 1976, the day before the trial of the Maguire Seven began, that photocopies of Mr Elliott's notes should be supplied to the defence at once and that laboratory notes would be available at the trial.[80] It way have been a case of "better late than never", but can there be any doubt that the defence of the Seven was placed at a great disadvantage by the "hedging" tactics of one of the counsel on the prosecution team?

The significance of this conduct became even more marked when Sir John May's inquiry resumed its sittings in September 1991. A prosecution under section 4 of the Explosives Substances Act, 1883, making or possessing explosives under suspicious circumstances – the charge laid against the Maguire Seven– requires the consent of the Attorney General for its continuance. The absence of such consent invalidates the proceedings.[81]

The Attorney General of the day was Mr Samuel Silkin Q.C. He died in 1988. He was not regarded by lawyers as having one of the best legal minds to hold that office, but of his personal and professional integrity and intellectual honesty there was no doubt. It was the practice that the Director of Public Prosecutions, whose responsibility it was to obtain that consent, would send the papers in the case to the Attorney General, for him to sign personally the form consenting to the prosecution being pursued.

Mr Silkin had doubts about the prosecution's forensic evidence. He expressed reservations about it on 17 February 1975. In a note to his legal secretary, Thomas Hetherington, who later became Director of Public Prosecutions, he said that there was some evidence to support charges of unlawful possession of explosives, "but only just." There was no basis for charges of conspiracy to cause explosions. Those charges did not receive his consent and were dropped. The note also referred to serious doubts by Mr Roger Maitland, a legal assistant in the law officer's department, about the forensic test that had been used.[82]

On 9 September 1991 David Clark Q.C., counsel to the May inquiry, said that "Crown counsel and the DPP representatives visited the Royal Armaments Research and Development establishment at Woolwich, southeast London, to see how the thin layer chromatography test for the presence of nitroglycerine was carried out on samples from swabs, the week before Mr Silkin's consent was sought for the prosecution . . . Sir Michael Havers and Michael Hill (Crown counsel) advanced the Woolwich theories that traces of nitroglycerine found under nails could come only from kneading the substance like dough *or suggested a finger had been used to force in a detonator. The two men also suggested no traces of explosives had been found in the house because plastic sheeting had been used*" [emphasis added].[83]

These suggestions about the detonators and the use of plastic sheeting seem not to have surfaced at the trial. It is a fact that no detonator and no plastic sheeting were ever found in or near the Maguire house at Third Avenue. Nor indeed were the small bags into which the nitroglycerine was, according to Havers, packed prior to disposal.

Clearly, the Attorney General had doubts about the forensic evidence. The *Independent on Sunday* of 1 September 1991 reported him as thinking that the case against the Maguire family was flimsy. As a result of his doubts, there was a meeting between himself and lawyers for the prosecution who had visited the laboratory where the tests were carried out.

Sir Thomas Hetherington Q.C.[84], in a written statement to accompany his oral evidence to the May inquiry, said Mr Silkin was "emphatically assured" by the lawyers that the particular scientific test used to detect explosives in the case provided conclusive proof of the presence of nitroglycerine. Mr Silkin had also received the "unanimous assurances" of the DPP's representatives, who had also visited the laboratories, and of prosecution counsel that the evidence was satisfactory.[85]

Mr Roger Maitland, who had been a legal assistant in the Law Officers Department in 1975, told Sir John May on September 10, 1991 that he had doubts over the way the scientists wrote up their statements generally in cases involving explosives charges. He said of the statements; "I had not liked them for some time. I thought they [the scientists] were being secretive. It was difficult to penetrate this veil." The nature of the statements from the Royal Armament Research and Development establishments scientists led him to feel "unease".

In a written statement to accompany his oral evidence, Mr Maitland said: "For some time, I had been worried about the evidence statements of the Woolwich scientists, *which seemed strangely reticent, sometimes asserting the presence of nitroglycerine without even naming the analytical technique which had been used*" [emphasis added].

Mr Maitland said he was "doubtful" about the technique used by the scientists to test for nitroglycerine "and the capacity of the Woolwich establishment to carry it out accurately every time."[86]

There was a compelling reason why Mr Maitland's view should have prevailed: he had received scientific training whereas those lawyers who maintained the TLC test was conclusive proof of the presence of nitroglycerine, as far as is known, had not.

What is distasteful about the conflict between Maitland's approach and that of the prosecuting team – Havers, Hill and Purnell – is that, when the defence solicitors asked for a sight of Mr Elliott's notes in April 1975, those barristers must have known how important and significant they were to the case – from both sides. To send a letter, as the department of the Director of Public Prosecutions did on 22 October 1975, "On the advice of Counsel I regret I am unable to supply you with copies of any notes made by Mr Elliott. The procedure used was the normal thin layer chromatography process", and then at the pre-trial review to refuse the notes on the grounds of irrelevance is the very essence of those factors leading to the wrongful conviction of the innocent.

Small wonder that on 12 September 1991 the Government scientists who had taken most of the criticism for the wrongful conviction of the Maguire family fought back. They blamed lawyers for the miscarriage of justice. Dr Maurice Marshall, the current head of the explosives division of RARDE, said that the scientists only "expressed an opinion." He said: "The Attorney General's decision to prosecute . . . was based upon *the positive assertions by prosecuting counsel* [emphasis added]. I have found no record that RARDE scientists made similar positive assertions to prosecuting counsel in the Maguire case."[87] If that is right, then the prosecution misrepresented to the senior law officer of the Crown, the Attorney General, just how strong the prosecution case against the Maguire Seven actually was.

However, the scientists cannot be absolved from blame in this case. Sir John May's inquiry was told in June 1990 that laboratory notes, which had only recently been handed to the inquiry by the Ministry of Defence, raised doubts about key areas of the forensic evidence which was relied upon to convict the Maguires. Those notebooks appear to contradict accounts of tests and procedures given to the trial by Douglas Higgs, Dr Thomas Hayes and Walter Elliott, scientists at the Royal Armament Research and Development establishment at the time of the testing in December 1974. The notebooks indicated that the scientists were apparently prepared to declare as positive tests for traces of explosives, although the results fell outside their own stated margins of error. Mr Maitland's reservations about that establishment's practices and conclusions were seemingly well founded.

Junior Counsel to the inquiry said that the notebooks raised four other areas of concern in addition to the margins of error. First, second tests were carried out on some of the hand swabs, showing negative results for other explosives. The jury had been told at the trial – and the inquiry had been told – that there was insufficient swab sample to do a second test to check the results. It was not until the contents of the notebooks were disclosed that it was clear that the jury had been misled, as well as the inquiry. Sir John May notes[88]: "My investigation of the RARDE notebooks revealed a number of disturbing features". But he was now told the true position; the jury of course were not.

Second, during the trial a number of experiments were carried out at RARDE, but the results were not disclosed to the jury trying the Maguire Seven. Two of the experiments were of great significance. On Wednesday, 21 January 1976, Mr Elliott gave evidence to the effect that when heart tablets containing nitroglycerine were crushed on the hand a positive result for nitroglycerine was obtained. But if the hands were left for a period of time, no nitroglycerine was detected. He maintained[89] that traces could only be detected if the hands were tested immediately after contact with the tablets. If left for a period of time, nothing would be detected.

Three weeks after this evidence was given to the jury there is a note in the notebook of a Scientific Office at RARDE, a Mrs Brooker which indicated that a test was carried out of 12 February 1976 involving crushing one tablet in the left hand and three tablets in the right hand. Each hand was swabbed three and a half hours later and produced a positive result for nitroglycerine. This result clearly conflicted with the evidence given earlier in the trial by Mr Elliott. Mrs Brooker gave evidence to the jury on 19 February 1976, seven days after the conduct of those tests, but she did not tell the court of the conflict of evidence.

However, what she did tell the court was evidence which advanced the prosecution and did not assist the defence of Vincent Maguire. He had told the court that he had been fingerprinted before his hands were swabbed. The jury in a note to the trial judge asked whether there would be any adverse effect on the swabs if fingerprints were taken before swabs. The Prosecution, according to Sir John May[90] – but without his identifying whether it was prosecuting counsel or the representative of the DPP – clearly asked RARDE to do an experiment to enable the jury's question to be answered. In her evidence Mrs Brooker told the court that she had, on 13 February 1976, carried out TLC tests with fingerprint ink and nitroglycerine to establish whether the ink could interfere with the performance of the nitroglycerine in the TLC test. She told the court that it would have little affect on the test.

There was a third experiment; its results were not disclosed to the jury. One of the RARDE scientists, Mr Higgs, gave evidence on 27 January 1976 that he could not see how nitroglycerine could be transferred under the fingernails after merely clenching the hand. Clearly at that stage of the trial, counsel for Mrs Maguire was putting in cross-examination to the witness, so that he could deal with it – a matter of evidence giving a contrary explanation to that advanced by the witness. It was of course the prosecution's case, based on Mr Higgs' evidence which he had given earlier, that nitroglycerine under the fingernails indicated manipulating and kneading.

On 8 February 1976 Mrs Maguire gave evidence on oath from the witness box in her own defence. She said she had received medical treatment for a skin problem, and her hands had been very itchy and she kept scratching. The next day Mr Yallop gave evidence on the possibility of migration of nitroglycerine under the fingernails after no more than touching a contaminated object. It will be remembered that no trace of nitroglycerine was found of Mrs Maguire's hands or under her fingernails; only the one glove was contaminated. But in the case of Vincent and Patrick Maguire, traces were found under the righthand fingernails of both, if the scientific evidence was right. In the case of Patrick O'Neill, traces were found under the fingerprints of both hands, but again only if the scientific evidence was right.

When the RARDE notebook was shown to the May inquiry it became known that on 11 February 1976 hand trials had been carried out by Mrs Brooker to investigate the presence of nitroglycerine on the hands and under the nails after the fingertips and nails of one hand had been scratched on the other. The procedure was carried out on a person with long nails (Dr Carver) and a person with short nails. The results indicated a faint trace of nitroglycerine under Dr Carver's nails but nothing under the short fingernails.

The connection is easy to see. The prosecution said that Patrick O'Neill and Vincent and Patrick Maguire had no accidental contact with nitroglycerine, because its presence under the fingernails indicated that they had been kneading and manipulating it like a piece of dough as if making a loaf of bread. Mr Yallop thought that when the hand came into contact with either nitroglycerine or an object already contaminated by that substance, then when clenching the hand that touched the object, nitroglycerine would migrate from the hand under the fingernails. Sir Michael Havers and Mr Elliott Michael Hill's theory – that traces under the fingernails indicated forcing in a detonator – to the Attorney General seems to have been somehow forgotten and not raised at the trial. However, Mrs Brooker did not tell the trial judge and the jury about the experiment carried out with Dr Carver's and another person's fingernails.

This was the position. On 21 January Mr Elliott gave evidence about the effect of crushed tablets on the hand. On 8 February Anne Maguire gave evidence about the itching hands. On 9 February Mr Yallop gives his evidence about migration from the hand to under the fingernails. On 11 February Mrs Brooker carried out the fingernail tests. On 12

February the heart tablet tests were carried out and noted in Mrs Brooker's notebook.

On 13 February, Mrs Brooker carried out the test involving fingerprint ink and nitroglycerine. On 19 February 1976 she gave evidence to the court. She was called by the prosecution in rebuttal of evidence already given by the defence. She had carried out tests on three successive days in the previous week. She told the court only of the test carried out on the third day. Of the first two tests, both of which substantially assisted the defence case, there was no mention. One is bound to ask: why not? The answer can only be found in determining who directed her to carry out the tests.

The Independent[91] reported that Mr Elliot Michael Hill told Sir John May that had the prosecution lawyers known of the tests, they would have informed the defence teams.

In the event, evidence about the experiments should have been presented to the court. Sir John May accepted that evidence as true. He states[92]: "It seems to me clear that the results were not communicated by RARDE to the prosecution despite the fact that the experiments were carried out on three consecutive days a week before the person who conducted them gave evidence. While I accept that it was not Mrs Brooker's responsibility to convey the results of her tests, it is to say the least strange that no one at RARDE saw fit to tell at least the office of the Director of Public Prosecutions of the two further tests Mrs Brooker had done. She can only have been asked to do them by a senior scientist at RARDE and one who knew what questions were being raised at the trial. As Mr Elliott has died since the trial and thus I heard no evidence from him, I am not able to identify who this senior scientist was. Whoever he may have been, however, it should have been apparent to him that prosecuting counsel ought to have been told of all three further tests."

It was during the hearing of the Maguire Seven Appeal against conviction in the Court of Appeal on 17 May 1991, that Mr Higgs admitted, when presented with the RARDE documents, that he must have authorised the test showing the transfer of traces of nitroglycerine from the contaminated hand to under the fingernails.

There are two other vital points. First, who exactly, on the prosecution side, asked for the test on the fingerprint ink and when and whom did they ask? Was the request made orally or in writing? For a scientist to ask for the other two tests to be done, would he not have to know that the prosecution could call this evidence in rebuttal? Moreover Mr Higgs had told Sir John May[93] that he did not know that the fingernail scraping test on the hand had been carried out, so he did not ask for it to be done. Yet he was the witness who was directly affected by the test and its result. There was always an inherent danger for a witness, even after he has given evidence, in contacting others who might be called as witnesses themselves.

The second point is: before giving evidence, Mrs Brooker would have been required to make a witness statement setting out the evidence which she proposed to give from the witness box. That statement would then be attached to a Notice of Additional Evidence, and both would be served on behalf of the Director of Public Prosecutions upon each of the defence solicitors acting for each of their respective clients. When Mrs Brooker came to write the witness statement did she do so unassisted, as often happens in the case of an expert witness, or was a statement prepared in conjunction with someone else, either a police officer or a representative from the DPP's office? If she wrote it unassisted, then why should there not be, in the statement, as opposed to the evidence which she ultimately gave in court, direct reference to all three tests that had been carried out on three successive days? Obviously she had not carried them out on her own initiative; she had been directed to do so.

In one of the tests, Dr Carver and another person had actively taken part. Why should she omit all reference in her witness statement to what happened on 11 and 12 February and deal only with 13 February and the fingerprint ink? There are at least three possibilities. First, acting entirely on her own, she appreciated that the first two tests damaged the prosecution case and therefore, although an examination of her notebook would have revealed it, she decided to conceal the results. To have done that would have involved a conscious decision to commit a criminal offence. There is not the slightest evidence to indicate that she would, or that she did, do that. Second, she accidentally omitted the first two tests both from her witness statement and consequently from her evidence. In that event she might have expected to be questioned about the tests by the person who asked that they be conducted. Third, she did mention all three tests in the witness statement, but someone on the prosecution side caused that to be omitted from the actual document which was handed to prosecuting counsel, and handed on by them to the defence.

It must be asked whether that person was Mr Douglas Higgs. After all, he had admitted to the Court of Appeal that he must have asked for the test to be done, although he had told Sir John May's inquiry he had not done so. Once the test was carried out and it was known that it contradicted his evidence to the trial court, he had a vested interest in concealing its result. In doing so he might have preserved his scientific reputation for a short time, and retained his accuracy and credibility as a witness, but at what cost to the Maguire Seven?

The whole issue of the heart tablets crushed in the hand must have seemed one of complete irrelevance to the jury, since no one suggested that any of the Maguire Seven had such tablets in his or her possession in the house at Third Avenue or elsewhere. However, it was important evidence in the case for this reason. One of the RARDE scientists, Douglas Higgs, suggested that a number of hand test kits should be sent to scenes of crimes officers throughout the Home Counties, asking them to take swabs from members of the public as and when the opportunity arose. In the result, Mr Higgs received back well over 900 hand test kits and of these it was possible to subject 916 to the same tests as had been used in the TLC tests at Woolwich. The purpose of this exercise was to strengthen the prosecution assertion that there was no other substance which would closely resemble nitroglycerine on the TLC test.

Mr Robert Kee explains[94] the TLC test in a clear and concise way, which may not be an apt description of how it was canvassed before the jury at the trial by the scientists and lawyers: the substance to be tested is first dissolved in a powerful solvent such as ether, and a drop of this solution is applied to one end of a specially coated absorbent plate where it is allowed to dry. A spot of a known substance, in this instance nitroglycerine, is applied alongside it. The plate is then stood upright, sample end downwards, in a dish of working solvent, described in this part of the test as an "eluent". The solvent in the test used was toluene. This solvent is drawn up the absorbent plate like water up asheet of blotting paper. As it rises it carries with it the known and unknown substances, and their final positions are revealed in a coloured spot by spraying a developer onto the plate. In the test the developer was called Greiss's reagent. The performance of the tested substance in terms of colour and their final position on a scale between 0 and 1 is compared with that of the known substance, nitroglycerine.There were two spots appearing on the tray. The position at which they appeared and the degree of colour – pink – they now adopted was measured on that scale and compared.

The results would indicate whether the unknown substance swabbed from the suspect's hands was the same as the standard spot of nitroglycerine. However, the prosecution and the defence disagreed on one point: if the unknown sample reacted in the same way as nitroglycerine then it followed that the sample must be nitroglycerine and was not some other substance.

The prosecution expert, Mr Higgs said he had received back well over 900 hand test kits and of these it was possible to test the contents of 916 kits by the TLC/toluene technique. Mr Higgs then told the jury – the defence objections to this were over-ruled – that all 916 kits had proved to be negative for the presence of nitroglycerine or for any other substance which might have closely resembled, or mimicked, nitroglycerine.

Bob Woffinden, in his book *Miscarriages of Justice*, comments on these 916 random tests[95]: "However, at no stage was the defence allowed to scrutinise the results of these tests, nor to have them independently examined." If that decision was made, the responsibility for it rested entirely on the shoulders of Sir Michael Havers, Mr Elliot Michael Hill, and Mr Paul Oliver Purnell. The conduct of the prosecution was at that stage theirs alone.

Whether these three knew it or not, the evidence Mr Higgs gave to the trial court that all 916 test were negative was economical with the truth, for when the RARDE notebooks were examined by the May inquiry they showed that in fact a few "rogue" positive results had shown up. When this was raised by the inquiry it transpired that Mrs Brooker's evidence was to the effect that any interpretation of the TLC results were not made by her but by one of her superiors who was present when she carried out the test.

Mr Higgs had only been allowed to give evidence on the basis that the 916 kits had been tested either by him personally or at least under his direct supervision. In fact what happened was that the TLC tests were carried out by junior staff at RARDE, and not under the direct supervision of Mr Higgs at all. They told him what they had found, and he repeated what he had been told to the jury at the trial. Even Mr Philip Havers, drawing on all his fourteen months experience as a barrister, could have been expected to understand that Mr Higgs' repetition of a statement of another person was inadmissible in law, as offending against the rule against hearsay evidence.

There was another objection which was taken at the trial to the admissibility of this evidence. No evidence was available to the court about how the scenes of crimes officers had taken the swabs before they were returned to RARDE. As Sir John May states[96]: "Without such evidence, the 916 test kits could have been returned to RARDE without any of them being used at all, when it would not be surprising that the results of the TLC / toluene tests upon them proved negative."

Robert Kee notes[97] that the trial judge reminded the jury of these tests where swabs taken from the hands of ordinary people in the Home Counties going about their everyday business failed to produce a single result identical with nitroglycerine. Mr Kee says: "On the other hand there was something scientifically suspicious about the results of these tests. nitroglycerine is a chemical constituent of a wide range of medicines used for apparent heart pain. Some can be bought without prescription. For others, doctors issue over 800,000 prescriptions a year. A single tablet contains enough active nitroglycerine to register positively on a whole series of TLC tests. A claim for the TLC test made at the trial was that it was capable of registering a quantity of nitroglycerine ʿequivalent to one millionth of a lump of sugar. The chances of nitroglycerine showing up on a random sample of the adult population may, therefore, be reckoned at about 100–1 against. And yet here were about 900 adults taken at random without a single one registering positive to nitroglycerine."

In his summing up to the jury, the trial judge did not remind them of the use of nitroglycerine in medicine. As already noted, no one at the Maguire house at Third Avenue was saying that they had a heart tablet in their hands for any period of time, let alone up to three and a half hours. But what about those in the 916 test cases? Did not one of them take tablets for a heart condition? In Mr Kee's words, the 916 results might have been impressive but, "It was one more example of the jury being impressed scientifically with evidence that was not scientifically sound." And of course, Mr Kee did not know at the time he wrote *Trial and Error* that, contrary to the evidence given to the trial court, there were in fact a few positive "rogue" results. From heart patients, perhaps? The defence counsel did not see the note books which disclosed these rogue results. If the prosecution counsel did not, one might ask, why did they not?

It cannot be emphasised too strongly that the case against the Maguire Seven rested fairly and squarely on the scientific evidence. The trial judge recognised that, for he told the jury, "Unless you are satisfied by the scientific evidence that nitroglycerine was present on those people's hands (or gloves) it would be quite unsafe to convict any of them. If you have any real doubt as to whether the material which was analysed was nitroglycerine, that must be the end of the case."

When Mr Peter Archer Q.C., who was the Solicitor General and junior Law Officer to Mr Samuel Silkin, gave evidence, both oral and written, to Sir John May on 9 September 1991, he was asked by counsel for the inquiry if before the Maguires' case there was a policy of not prosecuting cases brought solely on the basis of forensic evidence. Counsel said that the Maguires' prosecution was believed to be the only such case brought without corroborating evidence. Mr Archer said his recollection was that no such policy existed but that each case was considered on its merits.

Counsel cited to the inquiry several other cases where hand swabs had tested positive for nitroglycerine but no charges had been brought. In one such case, an extract from a police report said: "It will be appreciated that positive traces of explosives on hands and nails alone is not sufficient evidence of handling explosives due to contamination which could be caused by other means." It follows from the example that others had not been charged when the evidence against them was the same which caused the conviction and imprisonment of the Maguire Seven.

Mr Archer told the inquiry in a written statement that he was aware of the concern about the scientific evidence expressed by Mr Roger Maitland. In the light of Mr Maitland's concern, it was agreed that the scientific literature should be studied further. He said, "To have required a further scientific opinion would have been construed as a criticism of the scientists whose statements we were given."

In his oral evidence, Mr Archer told Sir John May that each time the doubt was raised with the Director of Public Prosecutions office, the response was that the TLC test was satisfactory.[98] There was clearly a determination in that department, perhaps shared by prosecuting counsel, that the trial of the Maguire Seven was going to proceed. One wonders why the Maguire Seven were apparently singled out for special treatment when no prosecutions had been launched against others where the incriminating evidence was exactly the same.

If this answer is to be found in the statements of Paul Hill and Gerard Conlon, then it should be noted that, following their arrests, over forty people were arrested under the Prevention of Terrorism (Temporary Provisions) Act, 1974. Twenty came from the Kilburn squats, fourteen of whom were released fairly quickly. Most of the rest were either relatives of the Guilford Four or named in their statements.[99]

Three other entirely innocent men – Paul Colman, Sean McGuinness and Brian Anderson – were charged with murder on the strength of nothing more than unsupported allegations of those two whilst in police custody. The murder charges against the three were later withdrawn, there was simply no evidence against them. The statements of both Conlon and Hill were therefore shown at an early stage not to be reliable.

There was an added difficulty for the prosecution if they only faced up to it. On 12 December 1975, one month before the trial of the Maguire Seven began, four members of an IRA active service unit – Joseph O'Connell, Edward Butler, Harry Duggan and Hugh Doherty – were arrested after a siege at Balcombe Street in London. Butler and O'Connell made admissions of responsibility to senior officers of the

London Metropolitan Police concerning the bombing of the public houses at Guildford and Woolwich, for which offences the Guildford Four had already been wrongly convicted.

At this stage, did the prosecution doubt the validity of the case against the Maguire Seven? At least two of the prosecuting barristers, Havers and Hill, had given emphatic assurances to the Attorney General about the safety of the scientific evidence. Mr Roger Maitland had expressed his unease to the AttorneyGeneral about the tests and about RARDE before the consent to the prosecution was signed. He again detailed his doubts two weeks after the meeting between prosecution counsel and Mr Silkin, and in the event those doubts proved to be correct.

One of the sources of doubt, which must have troubled the RARDE scientists if they had been open-minded and fair, was the result of the swabs taken from Paddy Maguire. That result was most unusual, especially when compared with the results of the tests on Sean Smyth and Guiseppe Conlon.

Sean Smyth was the most heavily contaminated of all the Seven. He had been working all day on Tuesday, 3 December 1974. He had returned to the house in the evening, arriving just before Paddy Maguire's return from the police station. Both Sean Smyth's hands, and the scrapings under his fingernails, were positive. However, of the Seven, he had the least opportunity, in the shortest period of time, in which to handle nitroglycerine.

The next most heavily contaminated was Guiseppe Conlon. All the swabs were positive for him, except for the dry swab on his left hand. The nail scrapings for both hands were positive as well. He was a very sick man, suffering from extensive tuberculosis in both lungs, which had caused him to give up employment eleven years previously. His condition had been stabilised by a rigorous course of anti-TB drugs, but he had extensive fibrosis and calcification of both lungs. In fact, he really was, according to his general medical practitioner in Belfast, Dr Joe Hendron, too ill to travel from Belfast to London at all, " . . . but he was terribly worried that his son had been arrested and he was determined to go."[100]

Yet, if the forensic evidence was right, Conlon had "kneaded and manipulated nitroglycerine" to a greater extent than anyone except Sean Smyth. Guiseppe Conlon died in prison on 23 January 1980. According to his son, Gerard, the day after his father's death his mother received a letter from the Home Office. "It said that, taking into account the many representations which had been made to the Home Secretary regarding my father's state of health, Mr Whitelaw had now decided to arrange for his speedy release into her custody. The decision was made purely on compassionate grounds. It was signed by an official."[101]

In Paddy Maguire's case the test results were so unusual that they caused Mr John Yallop to reconsider the force and validity of the TLC test which he had developed.

The test is done in this way: A first dry cotton wool swab is applied to the hands to remove material from the surface of the skin. Any recent handling of explosive will be picked up on the swab unless the hand has been very thoroughly washed. Since nitroglycerine will become absorbed thought the skin into the bloodstream within twenty minutes of handling, a second swab, soaked in ether, is applied to the hand to draw out materials that have penetrated the skin.

In Paddy Maguire's case, the dry swab on his right hand (but not his left) proved positive. However, the ether swab on both hands proved to be negative. Mr John Yallop, who had thirty-four years experience as a scientist, a former Principal Scientific Officer at RARDE, working threfore in the Government Service, told the jury in his evidence given for the defence at the trial that the dry swab was no more than a preliminary test; if nitroglycerine were present in the dry swab it would be highly irregular for it to be absent in the ether-soaked subcutaneous swab, as it had been in Paddy Maguire's case. Mr Yallop told the court: "At the end of three to four hours he apparently had sufficient [nytroglycerine] still on the surface to come off on a dry swab but none at all came off on an ether swab, and this is just not how nitroglycerine behaves." He explained to the jury that since the dry swab had been positive the process of absorption would still have been continuing. It was, he said, "an extraordinary anomaly."[102]

It must have taken enormous personal and professional courage for a man in Mr Yallop's position to give this evidence for the defence at the trial. He was retired after thirty-four years of distinguished public service. As well as having to endure the ridicule of Sir Michael Havers during cross-examination, with emotive terms suggesting retreat and hinting at professional cowardice, he had to face a damaging accusation. At one stage Havers put to him: "It is on one result of the seven accused, or six accused whose hands were positive, that you turned round and *started running back down the road* [emphasis added] you have been travelling for years."[103] Mr Yallop had to face a final slight on his competence and qualifications in the Court of Appeal where Lord Justice Roskill made reference to "certain allegedly scientific evidence of a Mr Yallop."[104] If he had been a witness for the prosecution it is doubtful if either he or his evidence would have been treated in such a high-handed and dismissive manner.

Mr Yallop's treatment both at the trial before the jury and in the Appeal Court must have given many expert witnesses pause for thought, if they were approached to give evidence for the defence in any case involving terrorism. After such treatment, who would blame anyone who valued their professional reputation and integrity and therefore declined to give such defence evidence, even in cases where their absence from the witness box might result in the conviction of the innocent?

Such caution has not only to be exercised by expert witnesses, for there are others. Who can forget, for example, the vitriolic smear campaign directed by the British tabloid press against Mrs Carmen Proetta in 1988. She was an eye witness to the shootings in Gibraltar, on 6 March of that year, of three members of the IRA by soldiers of the SAS. *The Star* newspaper headline was: "Shame of SAS smear girl". *The Daily Express* stated, quite falsely: "Trial by TV Carmen is Escort Girl Boss". Not unexpectedly, *The Sun* called her "The Tart of Gib." The very substantial libel damages for these foul lies which were awarded to Mrs Proetta might help to restore her reputation, but the underlying message in her case, as perhaps in the case of Mr Yallop is, in Paul Foot's striking phrase: "Stand up, tell the truth and be maligned. "

In the event, Mr Yallop's reservations about the force and reliability of the TLC test was recognised by the Home Office who declared, in a letter dated 21 April 1986, " . . . it would now be standard practice to establish the presence of nitroglycerine through confirmatory tests."[105] Mr Yallop would have regarded the findings of a mechanical sniffer – a hand-held explosives detector –as a confirmatory test in 1974.

In fact the sniffer had failed to register the presence of any explosive materials in the house. "This is a reasonable condition under which to use a sniffer and to expect to get a positive response. The fact that it gave a negative one is, to my way of thinking, another factor to add to Mr Maguire's hands pointing away from the interpretation of nitroglycerine."[106]

Sir John May said[107]: "In my opinion it has been shown that the whole scientific basis upon which the prosecution was founded was in truth so vitiated that on this basis alone the Court of Appeal should be invited to set aside the convictions." The Court of Appeal did quash the convictions against all the Maguire Seven, in June 1991.

In spite of this, when the May inquiry resumed its second set of hearings in September 1991, Mr Elliot Michael Hill, who had asked the Attorney General to give his consent to the prosecution of the Maguire Seven, had the effrontery to suggest that they were in fact guilty as charged. He said in a written statement to the inquiry that, although there were not traces of nitroglycerine in the house, "the participation of the accused is not inherently unlikely."[108]

After hearing Mr Hill's comments, Mrs Anne Maguire approached him and said: "You're wrong. After seventeen years you're still wrong, and my family have suffered." If Mrs Maguire was angry and distressed, she had every right to be so. She had been sent to prison for fourteen years; she spent eight years of the ten years she actually served in prison in "H" Wing of the maximum security prison in Durham; she had seen her husband and two of her children sent away as well; she was carried from the dock at the Old Bailey screaming her innocence. Her daughter Ann Marie, aged 9, and her son John, aged 15, were without their parents and their home. When she was released from prison everyone who saw her could not fail to be impressed by her dignity, lack of bitterness and her simple faith that one day justice would be done to her and her family. She tried to resume some semblance of normal family life, labouring under the stigma of being "a vitally important cog in the provisional IRA operating in London."

Courageously, Mrs Maguire continued to live in London. She found a job as a meals assistant in a primary school. It is now accepted that she and her family would not have been put on trial in 1992 on the basis of evidence which convicted them in 1976. Yet even now a senior member of the Criminal Bar in London, Mr Elliot Michael Hill, Q.C., implied that one, or more than one, if not all of the Maguire Seven is in fact guilty.

The May inquiry is not concluded. At some date in the future, probably after the end of the trial of those presently charged with conspiracy to pervert the course of justice in connection with the Guildford Four case, Sir John May will inquire into the circumstances which led to the conviction of the Guildford Four. In that inquiry the conduct of Mr Elliot Michael Hill of Counsel, together with that of the three other prosecuting barristers, will come under examination. The allegation they will have to face is that they made a concious and informed decision to conceal material evidence from the trial court, and which evidence was relevant to the defence of Gerard Conlon.

Conlon, Paul Hill, Patrick Armstrong and Carole Richardson were charged with and convicted of bombing two public houses at Guildford,Surrey. Five people were killed and fifty-seven were injured when a bomb exploded in the "Horse and Groom" public house. The four were convicted of the five murder charges laid against them as a consequence of that bombing. The prosecution case against them consisted almost entirely of confession evidence in respect of all the charges for which they were convicted.

The Guildford bombings took place on the evening of Saturday, 5 October1974. Solicitors acting on behalf of Gerard Conlon served a notice of alibi, as they were required to do under the provisions of the Criminal Justice Act, 1967, stating that on 5 October he was not at Guildford but in a hostel for young men at Quex Road in Kilburn. He was unable to call any witness in support of that alibi. However, his three co-defendants had eleven alibi witnesses between them. Since they were all convicted it followed that none of those witnesses were believed by the jury.

What Gerard Conlon and his solicitors did not know was that the police had obtained a statement from a man called Charles Burke, who said that he had seen Gerard Conlon asleep at the hostel at Quex Road on the Saturday evening when the bombs were being planted. Although his first name was Charles he was known to Conlon as "Paul the Greengrocer" probably because he worked in a greengrocer's shop. He had shared the same room, the S. Louis, at the hostel with Gerard Conlon and Paul Hill.[109] He left on Saturday, 5 October.

On 13 December 1990, the BBC Panorama programme presented *Guildford – the Untold Story*. It contains the following scene: an actor's voice says Burke's words "I got back to Quex Road at about 7 p.m. I packed my gear and Gerry was in his bed. He was the only other person in the room. He said he was broke and asked to borrow a quid, but I never let him have it. When I left he was still in bed." If that evidence was right, then Gerard Conlon could not have been a member of the team that bombed the "Horse and Groom" in Guildford.

In his book *Proved Innocent*, Gerard Conlon maintains that a solicitor acting on his behalf discovered amongst the bundles of statements disclosed by the Somerset and Avon police who were inquiring into the case, one statement of particular relevance. It was a witness statement made by Charles Burke about the events of 5 October 1974, and it was dated January 1975. The defence at the trial had not been told of the existence of this witness statement; someone had concealed it from the defence and from the court.

The law relating to material evidence was at that time governed by a decision of the Court of Criminal Appeal, Regina versus Bryan and Dickson.[110] In that case the Court decided that "where the prosecution have taken a statement from a person they know can give material evidence but decide not to call him as a witness, they are under a duty to make that person available as a witness for the defence, but they are not under a further duty of supplying the defence with a copy of the statement which they have taken."

The Panorama researchers found that the statement of Charles Burke was known to three of the four prosecuting barristers: Hill, Purnell and Philip Havers. On 16 May 1975 all three counsel "signed a lengthy note about alibis in which they mentioned Burke's statement. The note also mentions a statement from another witness, Peter Vine, which the barristers said, destroyed Burke's alibi evidence because Vine said Burke was wrong about the date he'd seen Gerry Conlon."

As the programme pointed out, it is for the jury, not for the barristers prosecuting the case, to decide which witnesses they believe and which they reject. It is the duty of the prosecution to put before the court all the material, relevant credible evidence, and if they do not propose to call any witness who can give material evidence, then they must tell the defence of the existence of that witness, so they can decide if they wish to call him. In the Guildford Four case the defence never had this chance, for they were never told about this witness statement. It is not for counsel in the case to make a subjective assessment on the strength or weakness of the evidence and then, having rejected it, to conceal it. If Hill, Purnell and Philip Havers thought that the evidence of one witness was destroyed by another, they should have informed the Director of Public Prosecutions to tell the defence of Burke's existence, and if he was called, to cross-examine him in accordance with what Peter Vine alleged.

But conceal that evidence they did, according to Panorama. "That same month [May] the barristers drew up a list of all the witnesses they were prepared to disclose to the defence."This would be in accordance with the direction given by the Court of Criminal Appeal in the Bryan and Dickson case. "There were two thousand and fifteen names on it – Charles Burke was not one of them. At the end of July, with the trial not just two months away, the barristers decided to do a final check of what was being disclosed to the defence. They asked the DPP to send them everything that hadn't been disclosed so far to see if anything had been missed. Once again Burke's statement was among the papers – so was Vine's, the statement that contradicted Burke, but this time the barristers were given a vital piece of new evidence. A third witness who showed that Burke was correct about the date he left the hostel and had seen Conlon. This statement was from a nun, Sister Power, who was an assistant at the Quex Road hostel. She had told the police that 'my records show that Charles Burke left the hostel on the fifth of October and that his bed was left vacant until the end of the week'." Sister Power is now dead but a contemporaneous documentary record confirming that information, clearly proving that Burke left on the night of the bombings, still exists.

That was not the end of the matter. There was a third and final opportunity to disclose the existence of the statement of Charles Burke. During his closing speech to the jury, Sir Michael Havers said that

Gerard Conlon had not got an alibi. That statement was false. He did have an alibi, and he gave evidence on oath in support of that alibi. What he did not do was to call evidence in support of his alibi. The witness who he did expect to call, Paddy Carey – another room-mate at the Quex Road hostel – failed to attend court to give evidence. He had returned home to Northern Ireland, and clearly did not relish the thought of giving defence evidence at such a trial.

When summing up the evidence to the jury, the trial judge said: "Sir Michael has quite rightly on two or three occasions, corrected me during my summing up, and I can get my own back on him now, and correct him. He said that Conlon had not got an abili. That is not true. Conlon has got an alibi. What he has not got is independent witnesses to support him." The Panorama presenter, the journalist John Ware, added this comment on the film soundtrack: "As we now know, that wasn't true. But none of the junior barristers present, or those representing the DPP, or the Surrey Police, intervened. The junior barristers don't wish to comment publicly until the May inquiry. For his part Sir Michael Havers says he's no recollection of seeing the alibi witness statements."

The importance of this evidence cannot be overstated. If Charles Burke had given evidence for the defence and that was believed – and of course it might not have been – then if the case against Conlon failed, the jury might have given greater weight to the evidence called by the other three defendants. If Conlon was acquitted, the acquittal of the others must surely have followed since the cases against the four, based almost exclusively on confession evidence, stood or fell together.

The responsibility for the failure to disclose the name and address of Charles Burke, a vital defence witness, cannot be attributed to the police. They had done all that they were required to do: they had interviewed a witness and recorded his statement and passed that statement to the department of the Director of Public Prosecutions. No one in that department can be blamed either. It was the invariable practice of the Director at that time to send specific instructions to counsel and ask, in accordance with the decision of the Court of Criminal Appeal in the Bryant and Dickson case. That authority was quoted in the bundle of papers, for a list to be drawn up of those witnesses whom the prosecution did not propose to call, so that the defence could be informed. The defence were never told that the police had taken that vital statement.

There is no doubt that Sir Michael Havers, as the leading counsel in the case, would have followed the normal practice in leaving his junior counsel to decide which witnesses should be "given away" or tendered to the defence, and for that counsel to draw up a list to be sent to the DPP.

That, as has been noted, had been done in May 1975 when Burke's name was left off the list. Neither Hill nor Purnell were enthusiastic amateurs doing their incompetent best; both were senior members of the Criminal Bar. They knew exactly what their duty and responsibility in law amounted to in relation to a witness. Their explanation to the May inquiry for the failure of the prosecution to disclose to the defence the name and address of a material witness, whom they do not propose to call, will be awaited with considerable interest.

Both those barristers must have realised that if the case against the Guildford Four had resulted in acquittals, then the prosecution against the Maguire Seven could hardly have continued. If Paul Hill and Conlon were really innocent, and had nothing to do with the Guildford bombings, then could they have possibly pointed the police to "the bomb factory" at the Maguire house? Would that have meant another delegation consisting of Havers and Hill going to see the Attorney General again, and explaining on this occasion that the prosecution against the Maguire Seven, which they had previously asked should go ahead, should now be discontinued?

When the Court of Appeal quashed the convictions of the Guildford Four on 19 October 1989 they did so under the most unusual circumstances. There was no evidence before the court. The decision not to oppose the appeal had been made in advance of the hearing by the Director of Public Prosecutions. Mr Roy Amlot, Q.C., told the Lord Chief Justice Lord Lane and two other Appeal Court judges that, since the Home Secretary's decision in January to refer the case back to the Court of Appeal, evidence of great significance had come to light.

The evidence threw "such doubt upon the honesty and integrity of a number of Surrey officers investigating the case in 1974, that the Crown now feels unable to say that the convictions of any of the four are safe or satisfactory." Mr Amlot told the court that officers of the Avon and Somerset police started a close inspection of the vast amount of documentation generated by the Guildford case, the Balcombe Street case and the application to the Appeal Court in 1977.

Close scrutiny of the papers led to the discovery of rough draft notes of each of three interviews with Patrick Armstrong. The notes were typewritten with a large number of alterations in manuscript and had been identified by the three Surrey officers concerned. Mr Amlot said: "In their altered form they match almost word for word the manuscript notes of the interviews used by the officers in the trial".

At the trial, the officers claimed that the manuscript notes were made during each interview, but if that was so it was difficult to see why draft notes were ever made. It was impossible to say why the draft notes took the form they did, unless they were made before the manuscript notes. If they were, the manuscript notes could not have been made during the interviews.

The officers concerned could not offer a satisfactory explanation. "The inescapable conclusion was that no comtemporaneous notes were made of each interview as was suggested during the trial, and that the officers seriously misled the court."

During the trial, Mr Armstrong's counsel – John Leonard Q.C, now Mr Justice Leonard – had suggested that the interviews had been made up. The first of the officers maintained that the notes were contemporaneous and that there was such an interview. Mr Amlot told the court that not only did the three officers involved in the interviews mislead the court, but because of the notes, preparation and statements they gave, they clearly agreed to present their notes in this fashion. At the trial the prosecution suggested Mr Armstrong's version of events could be regarded as nearest to the truth amongst the substantially different accounts given by the defendants.[111]

That version was fully reported in *The Times* on 18 September 1975, at the beginning of the trial of the Guildford Four, under the headline: "Defendant said to have taken bomb into Guildford pub because companion threatened him with death." The report states: "In an alleged statement, made on 4 December, Mr Armstrong said: 'I'm pleased I've been caught. It's nice to tell someone all about it. I'm going to tell you everything I've done right from the beginning. I joined the IRA in 1969 and did my training in Dundalk . . . Patrick Docherty was my commanding officer and Gerry Conlon was a lieutenant and a man called Hill was also a lieutenant in the Provisionals."

By the time Lord Rawlinson Q.C., wrote in *The Tablet* about this case, on 6 December 1986, these two seem to have been reduced to the ranks, because he refers to the recruitment of "footsoldiers" by the IRA, and the carrying and placing of the bomb carried out by amateur auxiliaries.

The report of the statement continues: "The next Saturday I went as arranged.Conlon was already there. This time he was with Hill. I was surprised to see him. I didn't know he was over in this country.Hill, Conlon and me went and sat at a table. Conlon showed me some photographs of the two pubs. There was about eight photos, four of each pub. There was one of the outside, one of the inside and one of each side street."

These photographs were never found.

"Conlon showed me one set of photographs and told me I was going with him, Carole and Hill to bomb it. He told me it was a military target.

I said 'OK, so long as there's no civilians in it.' He told me it was just used by soldiers and that he wanted to kill them. This didn't worry me because it was a military target and I was under orders. I wasn't told the name of the pub or any other details.

Mr Armstrong, it was alleged, said that on 5 October he was picked up at Kilburn at about 3 p.m. "As we started to drive off, Conlon said we were going to that place he had shown me on the photograph. In between Carole and me was a parcel. It was about 18 inches by 12 inches by 6 inches. it was in the shape of a box wrapped in brown paper with Sellotape and string on it. I asked Conlon what it was and he replied 'It's a bomb.' I got a bit worried about having it so close to me, but Conlon said it was alright. I asked him how it worked. He told me it consisted of gelignite or dynamite sticks with a detonator attached to it with a timer wire on to it. There was nothing showing on the outside and I thought it must have already been set."

The next day Mr Armstrong was alleged to have made a further statement in which he said: "I've been thinking there's something else I want to tell you. I went into the pub with Carole and it was me that planted the bomb under the seat. The story I told you before was dead right up till the time we pulled up at the pub. For some reason Conlon changed his mind and said I was to go in. I had an argument with him about it. I didn't want to go in. He told me that if I didn't do it I would be shot. So me and Carole got out of the car with the bomb. I was carrying it under my arm. I gave Carole the bomb and went up to the bar and bought some drinks.

"As I had gone to get the drinks Carole had gone over to an alcove by a fireplace. It had a jukebox and tables in it. When I got the drinks I went over and sat by Carole. The pub was quite crowded and the alcove as well. At first Carole and me sat right at the end of a bench seat opposite the fireplace. The bomb was on the seat between us . . . After a few minutes some people came and sat by Carole, and both me and Carole shifted round the seat so that both of us had our backs to the outside wall. I decided to put the bomb under the seat where I was sitting. Because it was so crowded Carole leant forward and bent down in front of me. I got hold of the bomb with my right hand and slipped it under the seat. I pushed it under as far as it would go. After that we sat there having our drinks and I saw Conlon come in and stand by the bar. I saw him look at us. Carole and me started necking . . . After about twenty minutes I decided to go and we left."

The most striking facts that seem to spring up from this report are that Armstrong seemed not to have asked any questions about either why the bomb was primed before driving from London to Guildford and the dangers that might follow from that, or when it was timed to go off, for he and Carole apparently remained for no less than twenty minutes with a primed bomb underneath the spot where they sat.

Although Armstrong told the police in the statement that "Carole and me started necking," Private Jonathan Cook who had been in the public house before the explosion told the court that he had seen a young couple sitting in the alcove earlier. "They were leaning forward to talk to each other. I cannot remember them laughing or smiling. To my mind they didn't seem to be hitting it off."[112] That evidence seems irreconcilable with Armstrong's statement.

It was not only in relation to the interviews and statements of Patrick Armstrong that Mr Roy Amlot told the Appeal Court that the Crown could not support the convictions of the Guildford Four. For "Avon and Somerset officers also discovered a set of manuscript notes relating to an interview with Mr Hill. The interview was not entered in evidence and was not disclosed to the then DPP, Sir Norman Skelhorn, or the prosecution, but it related to "relevant and significant matters." It was clear from the contents that it took place two days after Mr Hill was charged and it led to his fifth statement.

"It is clear those officers also misled the court. The contents of the notes bear no resemblance to the evidence given by the officers about the way Hill volunteered the interview. The true interview was suppressed and false evidence given in court in order to circumvent the rules that a prisoner must not be interviewed after being charged."

The fifth statement was significant because it was the first time Mr Hill identified Miss Richardson as the bomb-maker he had earlier described as Marion. During the trial, the officers denied Mr Hill was interviewed that day but it was clear that he was, and this was supported by the detention records which showed he was twice taken from his cell ostensibly for fingerprinting.

It was the view of the Crown that newly discovered interview notes for Mr Armstrong and Mr Hill show "clear prime facie evidence that a total of five officers seriously misled the court in relation to two of the four appellants."[113]

The list of alleged criminal offences disclosed in this summary of the Crown's case is a very substantial one. It includes perjury, forgery, conspiracy to fabricate evidence and conspiracy to pervert the course of justice. They were discovered in the course of the investigation into the case documents by the Avon and Somerset Constabulary. Not everyone believes what those documents clearly show. When the Recorder of London, Sir James Miskin Q.C., one of the senior judges at the Old Bailey, retired on 26 July 1990, he said on BBC South East, in reply to a question whether he supported capital punishment in the light of the Guildford Four case:

"That was a mad decision, was it not?"[114] He said the IRA may have collected money and offered it to a policeman to cook up documents. "I'm not saying that it did happen . . . but there should have been a full inquiry."[115]

If Sir James Miskin had read a report of the Crown's case in the Court of Appeal, he had not understood it. Mr Amlot had made it perfectly clear to that court that the typewritten notes with the large numbers of alterations in manuscript had been identified by the three officers concerned, and they could not offer a satisfactory explanation. Miskin's vivid imagination fails to consider the evidence that a true interview with Paul Hill was suppressed and false evidence given in its place, so that the defence would not know that there had been a breach of the Judges' Rules, prohibiting the interrogation of a suspect after charge, so that he cannot be questioned further about matters relating to that charge.

In the case of the Maguire Seven as in the case of the Guildford Four, important evidence was concealed from the court. In the latter case there is strong and compelling evidence discovered by the police themselves of fabrication in order to convict at least some if not all the defendants. In the case of Mrs Maguire, her family and their friend, Patrick O'Neill, was there fabrication of evidence as well, by tampering with the forensic swabs? How unfortunate it was that the forensic evidence should have been sent to the Government laboratories at Woolwich for forensic examination, in the light of the Woolwich public house bombing – for which Armstrong and Hill were convicted – in which two people died and more than fifty were injured.

Anne Maguire has always maintained that she was told that if she confessed to the Guildford pub bombings, with which she was originally charged, her two children Vincent and Patrick would not be charged. She refused to confess to murders she had not committed. On the very day that charge was withdrawn against her, 24 February 1975, Vincent and Patrick were charged with the unlawful possession of nitroglycerine. Patrick, who was 13 at the time of his arrest, was convicted by a majority verdict of the jury. That juror was acting illogically, for the evidence against Patrick was identical to that against Vincent, so a not guilty vote in respect of the younger should have meant a similar vote for the older brother. That never happened; the remainder of the family were convicted unanimously.

However, the conduct of this juror may throw a slightly different perspective on a matter of considerable importance which was dealt with in the summing up of the trial judge to the jury, at the end of the evidence. No one, apart from themselves really knows how a jury goes about determining and deciding their verdict, even where and at what point they start their deliberations and consideration of the evidence in the case. Do they start in chronological order, with the prosecution evidence, or with the defence case, and consider what, if anything, a defendant may have said on oath in his own defence?

In the Maguire Seven case, everything turned upon the forensic evidence against each one of the accused. If the prosecution failed against one, then it would be inconsistent, both on the facts and as a matter of law, to convict any one of the remainder.

Suppose then, that the jury decided to consider the case against Vincent Maguire at the very outset of their deliberations. Notwithstanding the finding of traces of nitroglycerine under the fingernails of his right hand, he was not charged with any offence until 24 February 1975. In fact he had been released without charge together with his two brothers Patrick and John (who was never charged) on 4 December 1974, the day after their arrest. His movements on the relevant day, 3 December, have already been examined in detail. He had gone to work on the morning of December three hours before the arrival of his uncle Guiseppe Conlon at the Maguire home, and he had returned from work early in the afternoon whilst his father and uncle were at the public house. When he finished his studies in the evening at the Technical College, he went home and found police officers at the house. The prosecution never attempted to pin-point the time and place when they alleged he handled the nitroglycerine. If the verdict, in Vincent's case was not guilty, then the jury would be virtually bound to acquit the others as well. The prosecution case against him was given a helping hand from a somewhat unexpected quarter: the trial judge, Mr Justice Donaldson.

Sir John Francis Donaldson, Baron Donaldson of Lymington, became the Master of the Rolls, the head of the civil division of the Court of Appeal. He was educated at Charterhouse and Cambridge University, where he was chairman of the Federation of University Conservative Associations. He served in the British Army, being commissioned in the Royal Signals in 1941, and served with the Guards Armoured Divisional Signals during World War Two.

In a not unfriendly profile of him by the journalist Alan Watkins in the *Observer* of 28 February 1988, he was referred to as Mrs Thatcher's favourite judge. He had been appointed to the High Court Bench in 1966. It is a fact that she was appointed Prime Minister in May 1979, and in July 1979 Mr Justice Donaldson was promoted from the High

Court to the Court of Appeal. Mrs Thatcher's admiration of him was not shared by some members of the Labour Party. Donaldson had aroused their anger in October 1973 when he, as chairman of the Industrial Relations Court, had made an order exercising the power of sequestration against the assets held in the so called political fund of the Amalgamated Union of Engineering Workers, which had refused to obey an order of the Court. As a result 187 Labour Members of Parliament signed a motion put down in Parliament calling for Donaldson's removal from office, on the grounds, amongst others, of his political prejudice and partiality. In the event the motion was never debated in Parliament, for parliamentary time to do so was not available, and it fell into abeyance when the House of Commons rose for the Christmas recess in December 1973.

Sir John Donaldson returned to the High Court Bench in 1974 after the abolition of the Industrial Relations Court by the incoming Labour Government which won the General Election in that year.

Before he tried the Guildford Four at the Central Criminal Court in London, the Old Bailey, Sir John Donaldson had never sat there as a judge. It is highly unlikely that he ever appeared there whilst practising as a barrister. His area of expertise was commercial law, especially insurance, and maritime law. It has not been possible to find any case in which he acquired any experience of criminal law in any capacity before the Guildford and Maguire trials.

His helpful intevention in the Maguire case – helpful to the prosecution that is – arose in this way: the defence evidence was that Vincent Maguire had found a long, thick piece of chalk under Sean Smyth's bed in the house at Third Avenue on 3 December whilst he was looking for some playing cards. He knew very well it was chalk; it had been brought to the house from a school. While Vincent was being questioned by Police Constable Bray he said he could hear his brother Patrick, then aged 13, crying in the next room.

It was stated in the Home Office's Administrative Directions on Interrogation and the taking of statements, appended to the Judges' Rules that, "As far as practicable children and young persons under the age of 17 years (whether suspected of crime or not) should only be interviewed in the presence of a parent or guardian, or in their absence, some person who is not a police officer and is of the same sex as the child." Clearly neither of the parents could be present at the interview, but the absence of an independent adult to safeguard Patrick's interests, and this breach of the Home Office's directions, were apparently not canvassed by the defence or anyone else at the trial.

What may be of some importance was why Patrick was crying at all, and the effect it had on his sixteen year old brother, Vincent. He must have been greatly distressed. He described the chalk "it was like a big candle, really." The police evidence was that Vincent had described the object "like a candle, about eight inches long and smooth like a sort of wax."

When the full description of the object was read to a prosecution witness from RARDE he was allowed to comment that this didn't suggest a candle, but more aptly fitted the description of a stick of gelignite. It was a false point to make. The witness accepted in cross-examination that the object, in reality a piece of chalk, could not possibly have been gelignite because the mechanical device, the sniffer, would have detected it in the course of the search of the Maguire house. Worse still, however, was the fact noted by Robert Kee that when the police drove Vincent home to Third Avenue from Guildford Police station in December 1974, he said that the police officers were shown the candle-like object by him. The defence did not adduce this evidence at the trial, and did not put the facts and events to any of the prosecution witnesses whilst they gave evidence, probably on the ground that they thought the point was disposed of, and laid to rest, in cross-examination when the forensic scientist admitted the object could not have been gelignite. The defence could not have foreseen that the trial judge would have raised it, and dealt with the point again, in the following way, and which the jury might have found extremely unhelpful, for Donaldson interwove two separate and distinct points.

He read to the jury his note of Vincent's evidence given on oath from the witness box. "I was hit and threatened. I heard Patrick screaming . .

Harvey ran at me with his forearm against my throat up against the wall. He twisted my head. He hit me in the stomach. It hurt and I cried. There was no other violence. I decided to tell the story about the candle when I heard Patrick scream."

The judge then posed the following questions: "Do you think the police officers really have got it wrong? Do you think they are lying? If, of course, you think that Vincent really did talk about a candle and wax, do you think that he was beaten up, and do you think he said it because he was beaten up? You, no doubt, will consider whether, if he was really beaten up like that, he would have complained to someone at the time . .

But really, in the end, of course what you will want to make your minds up about is this: was it true that Vincent handled something which Mr Higgs says is a good description of gelignite? It was young Patrick who was asked about the stick of white material and he said 'It is chalk. I got it from school. The gym master gave it to me.' And young Patrick, you know, he also alleged that he was beaten up . . . If it is

104

untrue why is he lying? Is young Patrick simply supporting Vincent in a lie? And what about Vincent? Is he lying because he regrets having told the truth *about this stick of gelignite* [emphasis added]? Well, it is matter for you."

In what passes for a circular argument, Donaldson made a number of errors. At no stage, either in the course of police interrogation or in evidence at the trial, did Vincent Maguire even admit that the object which he found under the bed was a stick of gelignite. As a point of fact it was shallow, but above all it was an error of fundamental importance for the trial judge to invite the jury to draw the inference that if Vincent lied about the assault by the police, then the aim, the object and the purpose of the lie was to conceal the fact that there had been gelignite in the house, and that he had handled it.

On the basis of Donaldson's posed questions, did the jury find themselves in the position of having to decide first: did the police assault two boys aged 13 and 16 as they alleged, and if they rejected their allegations and no assaults took place, did it then follow because one or both boys lied on that issue, the separate issue of possession of an explosive had been proved against one of them? And if that was proved against Vincent, since the forensic evidence against him was identical to that against the other six accused, was guilt not proved against them all?

Anyone with even an iota of experience in criminal cases would have realised that the Maguire Seven had nothing whatever to gain by making these allegations against the police, and everything to lose, more especially any sympathy the jury might have had for any one of them. Such suggestions of police brutality were then frequently made in jury trials, but made in the most part in cases where an accused person wished to explain away the existence of a confession statement admitting guilt. There was no such evidence in the Maguire Seven case. Therefore, from the defence point of view, since the allegations of assaults and abuse had no relevance either to the prosecution or the defence case in answer to it, it would have been better if the allegations had never been made. However, what is most regretable was the failure of the trial judge to remind the jury that the forensic scientist from RADRE had accepted that the object, what ever it was, was not gelignite. Of course if he had done that the jury might have wondered what point was the judge trying to make at all, for without an acceptance of the object being an explosive, the entire episode of the treatment of Vincent and Patrick Maguire in the police station was wholly irrelevant. For some reason, which will probably never be explained, the trial judge returned to this spurious point several times as if to improve upon it by repetition. The damage done to the defence case must have been immense.

Yet, who could tell what weight the jury might have given to it? Could a jury really bring themselves to believe that one of Her Majesty's Judges, learned in the law, would descend into the arena and make a point against an accused person, a point which was utterly false and without foundation? Did they remember the fact that in the course of the trial the prosecution witness had accepted that the object that Vincent found under the bed could not have been, and was not, nitroglycerine?

There can be no doubt that Sir John Donaldson considered that the Maguire Seven were guilty as charged. He clearly regretted that, in the case of Paddy and Anne Maguire, he could not send them to prison for longer than the fourteen years term he passed on them both. Passing sentence he said, "You have all been convicted and, in my judgement, rightly convicted, of possessing nitroglycerine for an unlawful object. On the evidence that object could only have been terrorism, and therein lies the extreme gravity of your offence. Terrorism involves the obtaining of arms, ammunition, explosives, detonators and timings devices. Bombs have to be made. All these have to be hidden. They have to be moved about and finally used against a target. This involves more than one person; it can, indeed, involve small teams. And let it never be forgotten; it is not only the man or woman who pulls the trigger or plants the bomb who is the terrorist. Anyone concerned at any stage shares the guilt of using violence for political ends. There can be no greater offence than this, for it strikes at the very root of the way of life which generations have fought and,indeed,died to preserve. The maximum sentence for possessing explosives is fourteen years. There will be those who think that such a sentence is inadequate where the crime is committed in furtherance of terrorism. They may well be right, but the duty of this court is to administer the law. It is up to Parliament to fix or vary the maximum penalty."

Mrs Anne Maguire was carried screaming and kicking from the dock at the Central Criminal Court with those words ringing in her ears. Of all the homilies delivered on the passing of sentence in that court or elsewhere, the one addressed by Sir John Donaldson to the Maguire Seven must rank as one of the most worthless.

In both the cases of the Maguire Seven and the Guildford Four, justice has clearly miscarried. Now, nearly two decades later, nothing short of a unanimous and unequivocal statement accepting the total innocence of all eleven people involved will satisfy the interests of justice. That statement must contain the views and regrets of all those,

106

whoever they are and whatever position they held then or hold now, whose conduct contributed to the wrongful conviction of eleven innocent people. Unless and until that happens, British justice will not be able to even begin repairing the damage done to its reputation by these two cases.

Postscript

On 4 June 1992 the Criminal Division of the Court of Appeal (Lord Justices Glidewell, Nolan and Steyn) delivered a written reserved judgement in the case of Judith Ward, now aged 43. She had spent eighteen years in prison following her conviction on 4 November 1974 for fifteen counts relating to bomb explosions in 1973 at Euston Station and in 1974 on a coach on the M62 motorway and at the National Defence College, Latimer, Buckinghamshire. Twelve people, including four members of the same family, two of whom were children, died in the coach bombing. Miss Ward was convicted of murdering all twelve victims. The prosecution case against her was based on three grounds. First, there was confession evidence based on police interviews in the time between her arrest and trial, and during which she was alleged to have admitted the offences with which she was charged. Second, there was expert scientific evidence to the effect that after both the Euston and Latimer explosions traces of nitroglycerine were found on Miss Ward's person, and that after the M62 coach explosion traces of nitroglycerine were found in a caravan in which she had been staying and on various articles belonging to her.

She was sentenced to life imprisonment on the counts of murder and a determinate sentence of thirty years on the other charges. She did not appeal against her conviction or sentence in 1974. However, on 17 September 1991, the Home Secretary referred Miss Ward's case to the Court of Appeal. He has the power, sparingly used, to refer a case to that Court under the Criminal Appeal Act 1968 if he is satisfied that there is new evidence or considerations of substance that may cast significant doubt on the correctness of the conviction.

The Court of Appeal quashed the convictions on all fifteen counts. The whole case against Miss Ward was a complete sham. The Court was told that, in the course of the investigation into the motorway bombing, West Yorkshire police took statements from more than 1700 people, yet only 224 were forwarded to the Director of Public Prosecutions for his consideration. The relevance of those statements and interviews with Miss Ward lay in their bearing on her proclivities for attention-seeking, fantasy and of making and withdrawing untrue confessions. In addition, interviews with police and medical reports were not disclosed. The Court heard that a psychiatrist who treated Miss Ward, while she was on remand for ten months at Risley Remand Centre near Warrington, had failed to tell the prosecution team that Miss Ward had twice tried to commit suicide by cutting her wrists. His medical report noted only one suicide attempt, and if it had been passed to her defence lawyers it might have alerted them to the mental disorder from which she suffered. That report was not passed to the defence. Nor was Miss Ward's family told of these attempts on her own life.

Most tragic of all, not only for Miss Ward but also for the Maguire family, was the repetition of one name, that of Mr Douglas Higgs of RARDE; he was mentioned again and again. In 1992 the Court of Appeal branded Mr Higgs a liar. Yet he had been at the forefront of the witnesses whose evidence convicted the Maguire Seven. If the evidence before the Appeal Court this year had been known to the trial court in 1976, seven innocent people would not have been convicted for a crime which had never in fact been committed by anyone. In Miss Ward's case someone had bombed Euston Station and the Defence College at Latimer. Someone had mercilessly murdered twelve innocent people, but that someone was not Miss Ward. After her conviction was quashed, the assistant chief constable of the West Yorkshire police had the good grace and sound common sense to say "I wish to express regret, on behalf of the force, that Miss Ward has spent so many years in prison for offences . . . she did not commit."

In the Maguire Seven case, on the other hand, no one had handled nitroglycerine at the family home in North London. There was none there to handle and the so called forensic evidence against them, purporting to establish its presence in the house, was totally worthless.

At the Appeal Court hearing, Miss Ward's counsel Michael Mansfield Q.C., directed his criticism at the conduct of three senior officials at RARDE, namely Mr Douglas Higgs, a principal scientific officer at the establishment and head of the forensic section, and Mr Walter Elliott and Mr Berryman, both higher scientific officers. The starting point was the evidence relating to the swabs taken from Miss Ward's hands following the Euston explosion. The chemical analysis sheets showed only two faint traces in respects of both hands; two other people who were seen with Miss Ward at Euston station shortly after the explosion both provided swabs which were more positive. Despite that, the Crown accepted that neither of these two were involved in the bombing.

In respect of the Euston test, Mr Elliott simply stated: "All gave positive results for nitroglycerine and dinitrotoluene." This, said the Appeal Court, was a misleading statement for which Mr Elliott was responsible, for the statement failed to distinguish between the test results for Miss Ward and the other two persons, and it was an overstatement in her case to describe "a faint trace" simply as a "positive".

It was wrong, in addition, for the prosecution to serve such an uninformative witness statement on behalf of a forensic scientist. It was calculated to make it more difficult for the defence experts to probe the matter. Three different judges in the Appeal Court who decided the Maguire Seven Appeal made no such criticism against either the prosecution or the scientists, and yet their conduct had been exactly the same in both cases. The prosecution teams may have been different, but the scientists Higgs and Elliott, who failed to make full and proper disclosure of their findings, were the same.

In relation to the forensic evidence obtained from the samples from Miss Ward's caravan, Mr Higgs said that one of the samples gave "a positive result for nitroglycerine" on a TLC test. Mr Elliott's witness statement is equally economical. He referred to the tests on the samples which he took and said, "From these results it is my opinion that explosive material has been present in the vehicle." On any view, said the Appeal Court, both statements overstated the position. The chemical analysis sheets recorded the result as "v. faint", "v. faint trace" and "faint". If the statements had disclosed the true position it is likely that the defence experts would have probed this aspect.

If therefore this was the quality of the work of these two scientists, small wonder that in the Maguire Seven case the Director of Public Prosecutions did not reply to the defence solicitors request for information about the tests and how they were carried out, as opposed to a mere conclusion, and perhaps explains in greater detail the "prosecution hedge" attitude of Paul Oliver Purnell, the junior counsel in the prosecution team against the Maguires. If full disclosure had been made the prosecution case would have collapsed like a house of cards. The judges in the Ward Appeal were unstinting in their condemnation of Mr Douglas Higgs. They said: "The statements were calculated to discourage investigation . . . We find that Mr Higgs did not wish to reveal anything which might encourage investigation by the defence."

There was more to follow. Counsel at Miss Ward's trial had contended that a TLC test can only be regarded as giving a positive result if the suspect spot matches the known nitroglycerine spot in position on the plate and is identical in colour. It followed from that that there might be a substance which produces a point in the right position for nitroglycerine but which does not have the right colour. The defence called an expert who said that there could be such a substance, but for

Miss Ward's case he was unable to name one. The trial jury must have regarded this as a fundamental weakness in the defence case. Mr Higgs, Mr Elliott and Mr Berry knew the truth but they supressed it.

In 1973 Mr Elliott had carried out control tests at the RARDE laboratory at Woolwich on samples of ten boot polishes to determine whether dyestuffs present in black boot polish could interfere in the detection of nitroglycerine and dinitrotoluene in the TLC test. The result of those tests was that the dye described as "solvent yellow 56" was found in some types of black shoe polish. Such a dye can be found not only in shoe polish and in floor polish, but in other everyday items such as soap and cosmetics. This information was known to the RARDE scientists before Miss Ward's trial began on 3 October 1974. Despite a RARDE memorandum signed by Mr Higgs, in answer to a series of questions posed by prosecuting counsel, who included the present Lord Chief Justice, Lord Taylor,Mr Higgs maintained that there was no commodity which could, on a TLC test, mimic the reaction for nitroglycerine in respect of colour, position and time of colour development. In that memorandum, delivered to counsel between 3 and 11 September 1974, Mr Higgs added: "These three factors constitute an absolute test, in our opinion, for nitroglycerine."

The appeal court judges thought that it is probable that the memorandum was the combined work of Mr Higgs, Mr Elliott and Mr Berryman. Because he supervised the boot polish tests in 1973, Mr Elliott must have known that the advice to prosecuting counsel in September 1974 was incorrect and misleading. Mr Higgs told the court in evidence at Miss Ward's appeal that, although he became head of the Woolwich laboratory in 1973, he was unaware of the experimental data. The appeal court judges did not believe this piece of evidence. They found he was an experienced chemist. He was the head of a closely knit team of five forensic scientists. The court said' "It is inconceivable that Mr Higgs was not aware of these experimental data. We reject Mr.Higgs' evidence and find that he was fully aware of these data. But Mr Higgs did not want the prosecution and defence to know about these experiments. In short Mr Higgs's attitude was that he was not going to reveal data which might weaken the prosecution case."

Mr Berryman also denied that he was aware of the boot polish tests. The judges were satisfied that he too was aware of these experimental data.

It was in relation to further scientific evidence that the judges had the strongest criticisms of the RARDE scientists, branding both Higgs and Elliott as liars.

Following Miss Ward's arrest, and while her defence was being prepared for the trial hearing, it was known to Mr Higgs, Mr Elliott and Mr Berryman that the defence might raise the issue that, in respect of the TLC tests relating to the Euston station bombing, Miss Ward might have become contaminated by touching debris or as a result of physical contact with a companion. Accordingly, in order to deal with this issue, a firing cell experiment was conducted at RARDE on 26 February 1974. A RARDE notebook which had been concealed from Miss Ward's defence at the trial, from the Maguire Seven trial and appeal and even from Sir John May's inquiry, surfaced during Miss Ward's appeal. That notebook showed that a member of staff recorded a faint positive from one swab taken during the tests. The fact that this experiment had been conducted was not disclosed to anyone before the trial, but while giving evidence for the prosecution against Miss Ward Mr Higgs relied on it. He told the jury that a test had been done as to whether a person's hands could be contaminated by picking up debris and brazenly told the court "the results were all negative." He was clearly prepared to disclose the existence of the experiment but lied when he said all the results were negative.

Even then he concealed more material information which would have greatly assisted Miss Ward's defence, for as the RARDE notebooks now disclose, between 20 September and 4 October 1974, in a firing cell at RARDE a series of further experiments were conducted. These experiments resulted in a number of positive results for the presence of nitroglycerine on the hands of staff members who had touched objects in the firing cell. Indeed one such result related to the hands of Mr Higgs himself. The positive results for nitroglycerine contamination varied from "very heavy" to "extremely heavy". The purpose of the firing cell tests was to deal with the question which Miss Ward's defence might raise that she was innocently contaminated by touching debris or by physical contact with a friend to explain the positive TLC test following the Euston station bombing. The chemical analysis sheets showed only two faint traces in respect of hand swabs taken from Miss Ward. Yet, when her trial began on 3 October 1974, these scientists colluded to conceal not just the results but even the very existence of tests which showed very heavy or extremely heavy contamination in cases of swabs taken from innocent persons not involved in explosive offences.

Mr Higgs had no alternative but to admit that the experiments and their results ought to have to have been disclosed to the court, the prosecution and Miss Ward's defence team at the trial, but he nonetheless sought to distance himself from the results. He told the appeal court he had not been involved in the other tests. And he said that when he testified at the trial he had forgotten about the tests in

September and 4 October.

The appeal court judges said that bearing in mind two things, first that Mr Higgs was head of a vary small team who conducted firing cell experiments with a view to using the results in evidence in the case against Miss Ward, and further that he was to be the senior RARDE witness at her trial "we reject Mr Higg's account as a deliberate falsehood." How strange it was that Mr Higgs could remember the undisclosed existence of the test on 26 February 1974, when he misrepresented the results, but he forgot the conduct of the tests carried out within the thirteen days prior to the commencement of Miss Ward's trial, and which continued until the day after that trial began.

Mr Berryman did not escape detailed criticism either. He had set up the cell firing tests. He knew what the results were. In evidence to the appeal court at Miss Ward's appeal he attempted to deny the relevance of the tests. The judges thought that approach was "wholly implausible". He had made a statement on 4 October, 1974, that is on the second day of the trial, in which he described – or more accurately misdescribed – the results of the cell firing tests on 26 February. Of the tests which had been going on in September up to October there was not a single mention. The judges said "we reject Mr Berryman's evidence as untrue." They identified the consequence of this shameful behaviour.

"The consequence is that, in a criminal trial involving grave charges, three senior government forensic scientists deliberately witheld material experimental data on the ground it might damage the prosecution case. Moreoever, Mr Higgs and Mr Berryman misled the court as to the state of their knowledge about the possibility of contamination occurring from the debris of an explosion. No doubt they judged that the records of the firing call tests would forever remain confidential. They were wrong. But the records were only disclosed about seventeen years after Miss Ward's conviction and imprisonment . . .

"In Miss Ward's case the disclosure of scientific evidence was woefully deficient. Three senior RARDE scientists took the law into their own hands, and concealed from the prosecution, the defence and the court, matters which might have changed the course of the trial. The catalogue of lamentable omissions included failures to reveal actual tests results, the failure to reveal discrepant Rf values, the suppression of the boot polish experimental data, the misrepresentation of the first firing cell test results, the concealment of subsequent positive firing call tests results, economical witness statements calculated to obstruct inquiry by the defence, and most importantly of all, oral evidence at the trial in the course of which senior RARDE scientists knowingly placed a false and distorted scientific picture before the jury. It is in our judgement also a

112

necessary inference that the three senior RARDE forensic scientists acted in concert in witholding material evidence."

All these comments relate to the conduct of forensic scientists, two of whom, Higgs and Elliott, were in the van of the prosecution scientific evidence against the Maguire Seven. Much of the evidence which they gathered had a direct relevance in the case not only against Miss Ward, but also against the Maguire Seven. She was convicted on 4 November 1974 because senior forensic scientists knowingly placed a false and distorted scientific picture before the jury. Just a month later, on 3 December 1974 the Maguire Seven were arrested at the family home in North London. They were never going to have the semblance of a fair trial either.

There were other factors common to both cases, besides the scientific evidence. At Miss Ward's appeal the judges made a request to hear evidence from Brian Walsh, now a Queen's Counsel. He had been junior counsel, led for the prosecution by John Cobb Q.C. and Peter Taylor Q.C., now Lord Taylor, the Lord Chief Justice. He was generally responsible for advising the Director of Public Prosecutions on which evidence should be disclosed to the defence. The Crown declined to call Mr Walsh to give evidence at the appeal. The judges said a letter drafted by Mr Walsh and adopted by the DPP was "wholly wrong" and "seriously misrepresented the position" about police interviews. "It was calculated to give the impression to the defence that the interviews were of no material significance, and that is precisely what it did."

Whether Mr Walsh will ever have to explain and justify his conduct to the Bar Council which is responsible for any appropriate disciplinary action remains to be seen. If he is invited to appear before the Bar Council, then Mr Elliot Michael Hill, Mr Paul Oliver Purnell and Mr Philip Havers should not be far behind to answer for their advice in the Maguire Seven case. It seems a matter of regret that they were not invited by the court to give evidence at the Maguire appeal hearing. However in that case too, it may be that the Crown would have declined to call them. The grounds for failing or refusing to do so can only be guessed at, as happened in the case of Mr Brian Walsh. As so often happens, a civil servant, Mr Michael Bibby, now a member of the Crown Prosecution Service, was called by the Crown at Miss Ward's appeal, for he had drafted at least one letter from the Director of Public Prosecutions to the defence in accordance with advice given to him by Mr Walsh. He had to explain, as far as he could, what was the purpose and meaning of that letter, when in fact the fuller explanation could and should have come from the person upon whose advice Mr Bibby was relying.

Judith Ward's case was the last to be uncovered, but she was the first of eighteen innocent people to be convicted. If the case against her in 1974 had been demonstrated to be based on fundamentally false premises, of false confession statements and worthless forensic evidence, then the Birmingham Six, the Guildford Four and the Maguire Seven might not have been prosecuted at all, let alone convicted and sent to prison for substantial periods of time. It took years of endeavour to establish the truth. Those who concealed it have much to answer for.

Chapter 3

THE HACKNEY ARMS TRIAL

On the morning of Monday, 15 November 1971 a building in Sidcup used by the Kent Sea Cadets as an armoury store was broken into, and eleven .303 rifles and eight bayonets were stolen. The rifles were useless as weapons because the firing pins had been removed and the barrels had been drilled.[1] The letters "DP" – for drill purposes – were stamped on the rifles' butts.[2]

Two days later, on Wednesday, 17 November 1971, about twenty armed police officers raided a shop at 257 Wick Road, Hackney, in the East End of London. In a flat above the shop, officers of the Special Branch of the Metropolitan Police found the eleven stolen .303 rifles, together with three automatic pistols. They arrested four men and a woman at the premises.[3] They were Edmund Pettigrew, aged 37, a painter, of Wick Road, Hackney, London; Majorie Allen, aged 30, his common-law wife; Patrick Martin O'Sulliven, aged 20, unemployed, of Barrack Street, Cork; Lawrence McGrandles, aged 24, a bricklayer, of Wellsley Road, Chiswick, London; Donald de Faoit, aged 25, a hairdresser, of Botarourit, County Cork.[4]

On Tuesday, 6 june 1972 the five were arraigned at the Central Criminal Court in London on an indictment containing two counts, the first alleging a conspiracy unlawfully to possess firearms and ammunition, and second, unlawfully possessing eleven .303 Lee Enfield rifles, eight bayonets, three automatic pistols and fifty-six rounds of ammunition.[5] They were joined in the dock by Martin Joseph Christopher Crawford, aged 20, unemployed, of Ladbroke Terrace, Belfast, who was accused of being concerned in the conspiracy alleged against the others in count 1 of the indictment. He had flown home from London to Belfast on Monday, 15 November 1971 (the day of the raid on the sea cadet armoury) and had been detained early in the afternoon of the same day by an army unit in Belfast and questioned by RUC Special Branch officers at Girdwood Barracks.[6]

The trial began with a voir dire – or legal argument – in respect of the admissibility of evidence against Mr Crawford. He alleged that a confession statement that he had made whilst in custody at Girdwood Barracks was not voluntary. Of course, no details of the evidence given at the voir dire could be published at the time, since that evidence was received by the court in the absence of the jury. No report of what was alleged in court by the defence seems to have been published subsequently. In his book[7] *The Branch – The History of the Metropolitan Police Special Branch 1883-1983*, Nigel West (the pen-name of the Conservative member Of Parliament Rupert Allason) writes: "Crawford, who later alleged that he had been beaten by his interrogators, signed a confession in which he admitted his part in the raid."

In fact, Mr Crawford alleged far more than just a beating. In a statement sworn to on 25 November 1971 at Crumlin Road Jail in Belfast and given to Amnesty International, he stated that he had been arrested by British soldiers at 1:55 p.m. on Monday, 15 November 1971 and taken to Girdwood Barracks. There he was made to sit facing a white wall for four to five hours, then questioned. He said that if he did not answer questions he was punched, with a half-closed fist, on the chest. During questioning, which went on for an hour, he was kept standing with his hands by his sides, beside the table at which his interrogators sat. He was threatened with a hypodermic syringe containing a red liquid, which he was told was a truth drug; his arm was just pricked by the needle but nothing was injected. After this he was made to sit facing the wall until about 4:30 a.m. on 16 November. He was then allowed to sleep on a camp bed for three hours.

On the following day he was again made to sit facing the wall. There was further questioning, during which he was "banged about". This treatment continued for the rest of the time he was at Girdwood Barracks[8]. It may be difficult to comprehend that this gestapo-type treatment was being administered to a young man, in a part of the United Kingdom which at least one politician constantly proclaims is as British as Finchley. But perhaps most chilling and most frightening of all for Martin Crawford was a form of mock execution perpetrated upon him. He said in his sworn statement: "At one stage a pistol containing live ammunition was put into my mouth; the breach was in the firing position."[9]

It is highly probable that Mr Crawford gave evidence at the voir dire in accordance with his sworn statement, setting out the same sequence of events and allegations of assault, sleep deprivation and mock execution. *The Sunday Times*[10] reported that "Crawford says that he was in a very bad physical and mental shape when the Special Branch men took his statement. He does not recall making the "confession or signing it." In any event the trial judge – Bean J. – ruled that the prosecution had not proved that the confession was voluntary and excluded it. That being the case, and there being no other evidence against him, the learned judge directed the jury to find Mr Crawford not guilty and he left the court a free man, after some months in custody.

The trial in respect of the remaining five accused then began. It was "expected to last four weeks".[11]

Mr Brian Leary, for the prosecution, told the jury that at the time of the conspiracy the accused were in Britain to get firearms for use in Northern Ireland. The four male defendants, it was alleged, were supporters or members of Sinn Fein or Saor Eire (Free Ireland), branches of the Irish Republican movement. Mr Leary said that on 17 November the year before police officers were keeping watch on certain of the defendants and on a shop at Wick Road, Hackney. When the premises were entered the weapons and ammunition were found in a locked storeroom. The rifles and bayonets were stolen from a drill hall at Bexley, Kent, and the pistols, which were in excellent working order, *"were stolen in Birmingham three three years ago."*[12] [emphasis added].

The defence case was simple. They claimed that they had nothing to do with the weapons. They were, they said, simply setting up a clothing and toy shop in the Hackney premises with the intention of sending the profits to Northern Ireland to help needy Catholics in Belfast and Derry.[13]

One of the accused, Edmund Pettigrew, a native of Belfast, had met another Belfast man, Peter Farron, in a London public house, sometime in early November 1971. Mr Farron had worked distributing clothing and food for the Northern Aid Society in Belfast, and whilst discussing that work, a man in the public house joined in their conversation. He was John Parker, a man in his forties, with a criminal record. He was also a Special Branch informer. The three man talked of the troubles in Ulster. Mr Parker gave the men his telephone number. When they met again, Mr Parker was accompanied by a man who gave the name "Dave Lee". That name was false. He was in fact a Special Branch detective constable stationed at a police station not very far from Mr Parker's former home in Whitechapel.[14] Mr Parker, "Mr Lee", Mr Farron and the five accused, together with Mr Crawford, met in various public houses in the London area. According to the defence, the Special Branch surveillance had begun at this stage, for Mr Crawford maintained he was shown photographs of an early meeting of some of the group at the station buffet at Euston railway station.[15]

Mr Parker said he could arrange the letting and stocking of the shop. Suitable premises were found at 257, Wick Road, Hackney[16]. The defence discovered, during the trial, that Mr Parker negotiated the lease on the premises.[17] According to him, the Special Branch arranged the installation of a telephone and were tapping the line from the start.[18] Concealed cameras were allegedly used to photograph the defendants. A detective who gave evidence was asked in court about photographs which were allegedly shown to some of the defendants after their arrest. "I may not tell you whether I know or not," he replied.[19]

On Sunday, 14 November 1971 everyone involved in the case turned up at the shop to help with the cleaning prior to opening. It was in the early hours of the next day, the Monday, that the sea cadet premises in Kent were broken into and the useless rifles were stolen. If any attempt was made to fire them, they would probably cause more danger to the user than to anyone else.. According to Mr Pettigrew, at 7:30 a.m. that Monday, Mr Parker and "Mr Lee" arrived at the shop and carried some stuff into the boxroom at the back of the flat.

Mr Parker was alleged by the accused Mr O'Sullivan and Mr De Faoit to have offered to sell them some rifles and some pistols on Tuesday evening. They were not interested. Both men told him that they considered their job was finished and planned to return to Ireland the next day, but Mr Parker told them there were still some more papers to sign for the shop, and he asked them to meet him there at about 3:30p.m. on Wednesday afternoon.[20]

In the meanwhile Mr Pettigrew, who had been given the key to a box in which the firearms were locked and left at the shop by Mr Parker and "Mr Lee", telephoned Mr Parker. He was anxious about the guns, so would Parker please remove them from the shop? Of course, said Parker, he would pick them up at 4 p.m. that very afternoon. Would Pettigrew make sure he was present with the key to the box? When the men arrived at the shop they were arrested, with the others, by armed police officers.[21] Of Mr Parker and "Mr Lee" there was no sign.

Nor was there any mention of these two men in the police statements served upon the defence.[22] The defence claimed at the trial that it was Parker and "Lee" who actually planted the guns and ammunition at the Hackney shop before the police raid. Mr John Platts-Mills Q.C. said, "I intend to show that this whole case has been engineered by the Special Branch through a man, Parker, to plant these guns on my clients."[23] But every attempt to obtain any information about Parker and "Dave Lee" – their whereabouts, their antecedents, their relationship with the police – proved in vain. Two Special Branch detectives from the arresting squad who gave evidence refused to answer all such questions on the ground "that it would prejudice the security.of the State." One said he knew Parker; the other said he knew "Lee"; neither knew both men.[24] Just how the security of the State was endangered by the disclosure of the truth was never explained either at the time or at any time since.

On the morning of Monday 12 June 1972 the prosecution suddenly collapsed. Mr Brian Leary told the trial judge: "After considering the evidence over the weekend it has been decided that it would not be proper for the prosecution to continue."[25] He gave no reason for the decision,which was apparently a joint one involving Mr Leary, the Director of Public Prosecutions, Sir Norman Skelhorne Q.C. and the Attorney General, Sir Peter Rawlinson Q.C.[26] Mr Justice Bean, the trial judge, was clearly not greatly impressed by the decision and the lack of explantion for it. He said to the jury: "For reasons known only to themselves, the prosecution have decided to offer no further evidence against the accused. In these circumstances my duty is to direct you to return formal verdicts of not guilty."[27] After the jury had done so the accused left the dock, after some eight months in custody.

The next day a statement was issued about the case. *The Sunday Times Insight* team attribute it to the Attorney General, Sir Peter Rawlinson Q.C.[28] Geoffrey Robertson attributes it to the Home Secretary, Mr Reginald Maudling.[29]

There may have been two statements, but if there were, they were remarkably similar in wording and format. Reference is made to "a need to protect the identity of certain persons in the interests of their own personal safety . . . the full facts could not be put before the jury, and it was agreed that the prosecution should not, in the interests of justice, continue." Of course, if Mr Parker was not merely continuing his practice as an informer for the Special Branch, but had extended his activities to committing an offence in order to involve entirely innocent people, and the prosecution knew it, that fact could hardly be put before the court. The *Insight* version of the statement – but not Robertson's – states: "The ruling about Crawford's confession 'necessarily affected the course of the case'."

This is difficult to follow. First, Crawford's confession, as a matter of law, was the only evidence against him, the maker of it, and it's admissibility in, or exclusion from, evidence could not affect the course of the case against the co-accused. Second, assuming that is wrong in law, why did the trial continue for three full days against the remaining five accused after the trial judge's ruling on the first day of the hearing that the Crawford confession was not voluntary? Third, in that confession Mr Crawford gave a detailed description of the raid on the sea cadet armoury; Parker and "Lee", he said, were also on the raid.[30] Just how would the prosecution have explained Parker's and "Lee's" absence from the courtroom if that confession had been admitted in evidence? If they were not involved in the commission of the offence at the outset, why did they not give evidence for the prosecution? All these questions pale into insignificance in the light of Robertson's statements about the three pistols found in the raid on the Wick Road flat. He says[31] that journalists traced the origin of the three pistols and, "They had last

119

been seen at Birmingham law courts in December 1969 – in police custody. The man who pleaded guilty to stealing them from a Birmingham gunsmith subsequently had his sentence reduced by the Court of Appeal on the grounds that the offence was less serious because all the stolen guns had been retrieved by the police."

If this is true then a new and sinister element is added to the distasteful and unlawful conduct which had already taken place. These pistols were in working order. If Parker and "Lee" were really dealing with an active service unit of the IRA were they not providing them with three most dangerous and useful weapons for use in the course of terrorism? But a question of equal importance that must be asked was: how did the pistols get from police custody in Birmingham to the flat in the East End of London? It must have been asked by the subsequent inquiry which was set up following a statement issued by Scotland Yard on Friday, 16 June 1972.[32] The statement said: "The Commissioner of Police of the Metropolis, with the approval of the Home Secretary, has arranged for the investigation of the circumstances so far as Metropolitan Police Officers are concerned, which led to the discontinuance of a prosecution at the Central Criminal Court on June 12."

The investigation was to be carried out by Mr W. Kelsall, Deputy Chief Constable of Cheshire and Detective Chief Superintendent Horan, Manchester and Salford Police. Those officers " . . . sat in secret for six months. They reported that no criminal charges should be brought against police or their agents. Their report was never made public."[33] The mystery of how the three pistols commuted from Birmingham to London remains unsolved so far as the public is concerned.

There are a number of conclusions to be drawn from this case. First, so far as is known, there were no prosecutions against anyone in respect of the assaults upon Mr Crawford whilst he was in custody in Girdwood Barracks. The trial judge did not disbelieve Mr Crawford's evidence about his treatment there, otherwise he would have admitted the confession in evidence, yet he failed to initiate a police inquiry into what had happened at Girdwood by sending the papers, with his comments, to the Director of Public Prosecutions. The Commission of Amnesty International, having considered Mr Crawford's affidavit and the evidence given by a doctor, accepted the substance of his allegations.[34] Thus there was clearly a case for the police to investigate and the Special Branch officers to answer. Second, Mr Crawford was alleging a form of mock execution at a trial at the Central Criminal Court in June 1972.

Just over three years later, at Lancaster Crown Court, one of the six men wrongly convicted of the Birmingham public house bombings – Mr Richard McIlkenny – was alleging that he too was subjected to a form of mock execution by police officers whilst in custody[35] when a pistol was pointed at his head, or just below, although in his case the trigger was actually pulled. The trial judge – Bridge J. – is quoted as saying that this " . . . represented a gruesome pantomime, he told the jury. The allegations of death threats had reminded him of Hitler's Gestapo and the rack and the thumbscrew under Tudor monarchs, he said."[36]

In the light of the quashing of the convictions of the Birmingham Six, it may be that the language of Lord Bridge of Harwich (as he is now) was a little more accurate and the comparison a little more appropriate then he realised at the time.

Thirdly, in opening the case, counsel for the prosecution had told the jury that the three pistols were stolen in Birmingham. That was a perfectly true statement, but it was incomplete. They had been stolen from a Birmingham gunsmith, and recovered – by the police. Had they been stolen thereafter from the police, and if so when and in what circumstances and by whom? An examination of the witness statements in the case will quickly clear up that point. It is inconceivable that Mr Brian Leary, a respected member of the Bar, would have misled the court. Could it have been that the police failed to tell prosecuting counsel the truth about the origin of those pistols ?

When the defendants were discharged from the dock, after eight months in custody, the defence solicitors, Messrs Simon & Co., issued a statement to the press. They said: "During the trial it was alleged as part of the defence that weapons have been planted at Wick Road, Hackney, by two men whose names were given in court. It was alleged that these two men were police informers and had been working in collusion with Special Branch. It was alleged that the purpose was to frame the accused, who were innocent . . . "[37]

If there was any public reaction to that statement, it was very low-key and muted. However, for the police in Northern Ireland, in the London area and in Birmingham, the message from the authorities must have been clear and unequivocal. In the event of a suspect being ill-treated whilst in custody and evidence being planted upon others, then even when that is disclosed to the court and to the public, there is nothing to fear; there will be no prosecutions, just a drawn-out secret inquiry the results of which will not be disclosed. Was it not such a signal that led to the miscarriages of justice, within the space of three years in the cases, sometimes called the Irish cases, of the Guildford Four, the Maguire family, and the Birmingham Six? The defendants in those cases, like those in the Hackney trial, were linked by their

Catholic religion and their membership of the so called minority community in Northern Ireland.

There is another factor common to all four cases. At all the committal proceedings and at the trials there were heavily armed escorted vehicles speeding amongst the stationary traffic on the streets of London. Armed police were everywhere: they were positioned on rooftops, they surrounded the court building, there were alsatian dogs and the pat-down searches of all who entered the court. All those high profile security arrangements were quite inconsistent with the presumption of innocence. To the disinterested bystander it must have appeared that only the guilty attract such measures. That is an issue which must surely be addressed by the Royal Commission chaired by Lord Runciman, on how best to avoid pre-trial prejudice while at the same time protecting the public.

There can be no innocent explantion for the planting of three pistols from police custody in Birmingham on those entirely innocent people at Wick Road in London. Such conduct goes far beyond what the former Commissioner of the Metropolitan Police said in his evidence to the Royal Commission on Criminal Procedure: "Many police officers have, early in their careers, learned to use methods bordering on trickery or stealth in their investigations because they were deprived of proper powers by the legislature." [38] If those responsible for that criminal conduct had been prosecuted, would lessons have been learnt, and the double obscenity of the conviction of the innocent while the guilty walked free in the Irish cases in 1975 and 1976 have been avoided?

122

Chapter 4

THE CASE OF EDWARD MANNING BROPHY AND
THE LA MON HOUSE HOTEL

On 10 September 1976 Mr Roy Mason, a former coal miner from Barnsley, England, was appointed Secretary of State for Northern Ireland. His appointment was welcomed by Unionist politicians, but Mr Gerry Fitt of the mainly Catholic SDLP expressed "strong objections" to the appointment.[1] There were other important changes in the Security Forces in that year; Sir Kenneth Newman, a former London Metropolitan policeman, had been appointed Chief Constable of the Royal Ulster Constabulary, in place of Sir Jamie Flanagan, on 30 April 1976[2], and Lieutenant-General Sir Timothy Creasy had been appointed General Officer Commanding, Northern Ireland. He was at soldier of substantial experience for he had served in Burma, Iran, Iraq, Italy, Greece, Kenya, Aden and Oman. Only a nation as uninquisitive as the British would fail to question the presence and purpose of Britain's army in such far flung outposts, many of which fall within the former Empire, and fail to wonder who the beneficiaries of such armed military presence might be.

The television journalist Desmond Hamill, in his widely admired study of the army in Northern Ireland 1969-1985, quotes an instance which must cause some anxiety amongst civil liberty campaigners who regard the army as being subject to the restraints of the ordinary criminal law. Hamill states that, after a very short time in Northern Ireland, Creasy was making his views known. A guest at one reception he attended remembered him talking at length about the need to "stop messing around and take out the terrorists." Asked how he had dealt with the matter in Oman, he said they "just disappeared." It was apparently pointed out to him that the disposal of bodies might be easier in the sand of the endless deserts of Oman than in the tarmac streets of Belfast.[3] Such an attitude displayed by a very senior army officer, indicating that they might on occasions operate outside the rule of law, might come as a severe shock to those who have always considered that those who enforce the law must also comply with it.

The new Secretary of State Mr Mason had the responsibility of continuing the policies of the Labour Government of "Ulsterisation" and "criminalisation" in the Province. The policy of releasing those interned without trial, which had been introduced on 9 August 1971 under the

Civil Authorities (Special Powers) Act (Northern Ireland) 1922 had recently ended and was replaced by a determination that the paramilitaries' claim that they were engaged in a political struggle should be denied. Internment by its very nature was a recognition that the problems of Northern Ireland were not the result of the conduct of ordinary criminals, and its abolition meant that emphasis could be returned to police investigation of criminal offences which would then be dealt with by the criminal courts, albeit without the right of trial by jury. Such a move meant an end to the "special category status" or political status, which the Northern Ireland Secretary of State (Mr William Whitelaw) had conceded to the paramilitaries in 1972. Such status was ended for those sentenced for crimes committed after 1 March 1976. New prison rules were introduced. The remission of sentence for good conduct was increased from one third of the sentence to one half, and this allowed 450 special category prisoners to be released on licence. Existing special category prisoners kept their status and remained in the compound of the Maze prison. A new complex, the Maze (Cellular), to become infamous as the "H" Blocks, so named because of their shape, was opened up to house new inmates.[3]

The major responses to these changes did not come immediately. One was in September 1976, when Kieran Nugent, aged 19, a member of the Provisional IRA, was sentenced for his part in bombing missions, and he "went on the blanket", i.e. he refused to wear prison uniform and covered himself with a blanket.[5]

Various paramilitary groupings had begun a campaign of bombing in both the North and the South of Ireland. On 3 July four people were injured in bomb attacks on four hotels in Dublin, Rosslare, Limerick and Killarney in the Irish Republic. An advance warning was given by the Ulster Freedom Fighters, one of the cover names used by the loyalist paramilitary group, the Ulster Defence Association. That group also claimed responsibility for a bomb explosion at a hotel in the seaside resort of Salthill in County Galway.[6] In the North, on 16 July, the Provisional IRA detonated two bombs which destroyed most of the shops in Castledawson, Co. Derry, and many families were left homeless. On 3 August, in an attack claimed by the Provisionals, six explosions wrecked the centre of Portrush, Co. Antrim. That town is one of the most popular and beautiful seaside resorts in Ireland, and this was at the height of the holiday season.

Later in August, the bombers not only damaged or destroyed property, they caused fatalities as well. On Monday, 16 August, two man were killed and seventeen people were injured when a bomb exploded outside a bar in Keady, County Armagh. On 9 October, a woman was burned to death in one of fifteen fire bomb attacks in Ballymena, County Antrim. On 14 October there was a bomb attack on a furniture store in south Belfast. Amongst four men arrested near the scene were Bobby Sands and Joe McDonnell. Both were jailed for fourteen years for the unlawful possession of a firearm found in the car in which they were arrested. Both were to die on hunger strike five years later. Towards the end of the year, on 5 December, firebombs planted by the Provisionals destroyed seventeen shops in Derry.[7]

1977 began badly. On 1 January the Provisionals threatened "to hot things up". A baby was killed and three people were injured when a 200lb bomb exploded after an inadequate warning was given in Glengormley, County Antrim. On the same day a south Belfast golf club was destroyed in an explosion and fire.[8]

There was a slight improvement as the year progressed. In the first eight months there were 97 civilian deaths, compared to 222 in the same period in the preceding year. Shootings and explosions had decreased by 33% and 52% respectively. By the end of the year the Chief Constable reported that 1977 had been the least violent year for six years.[9] Sir Kenneth Newman said "1977 will undoubtedly stand out as a year in which the police, with the support of the army, made an enormous effort to reduce violence. "[10]

The politicians were delighted and much less discreet than the Chief Constable in saying so. Mr Mason told the *Daily Express*, a London newspaper not particularly well known for its support for the Labour Government or for any sympathy towards the Irish people: "We are squeezing the terrorists like rolling up a toothpaste tube. We are squeezing them out of their safe havens. We are squeezing them away from their money supplies. We are squeezing them out of society and into prison."[11]

The Secretary of State seemed to have overlooked the fact that fourteen members of the RUC had been murdered in that year, a most dreadful rate of attrition – on average just over one killing for every month of the year. The chairman of the Northern Ireland Police Federation warned, "Words can be as lethal as bullets in the unfortunate circumstances in which we work."[12]

Such a cautious approach was completely justified, for the Provisionals changed tactics. They increased the use of cassette incendiaries to damage and destroy property. These devices – usually about four ounces of a highly inflammable mix of household chemicals, with a detonator, battery and timing mechanism, packed in a tape cassette – were placed in commercial premises.[13] For obvious reasons, paint and furniture shops were the favourite choice of target.

They also manufactured blast incendiary devices. These were produced by mixing crystallised ammonium nitrate with aluminium filings, and fixing containers of this concoction to cans of petrol.[14] The effect was enhanced by using a butcher's meat hook to hang the bomb onto the wire-mesh security grills protecting most commercial properties. The device was given a time delay of only a few minutes to prevent army bomb disposal experts from making it safe. Once detonated the bomb would produce an ever expanding fireball with the same force of a 400 lb bomb. One explosives expert told the journalist Chris Ryder: "With blast you generally get surface damage, windows blown out, that sort of thing; but with these blast incendiaries, particularly if they are planted amidst inflammable material, there is such a raging fire that you get major structural damage. I have seen instances of steel beams encased in concrete buckling."[15]

At the beginning of 1978 the Provisionals decided to plant such a device at a hotel in the heart of Unionist North Down. The La Mon House, a hotel with a noted restaurant and dance hall, is situated in the Castlereagh hills at Comber in County Down, some ten miles east of Belfast. On the evening of Friday, 17 February 1978 the premises were packed with groups of people; two of the largest groups there were attending annual prize distributions by the Northern Ireland Collie Club and the Northern Ireland Junior Motor Cycle Club.

According to two journalists, Patrick Bishop and Eamonn Mallie, three Provisionals from the Ballymurphy area of Belfast fixed a blast incendiary device to a window of the hotel. They chose the outside window sill of the Peacock Room. Inside, a group of forty members of the Irish Collie Club were attending their annual dinner and dance. The bomb was primed, and the men drove away and stopped at a call-box to telephone a warning. The phone had been vandalised. They drove on and were stopped by a patrol of the Ulster Defence Regiment. They were not detained but by the time they found a other telephone in working order and telephoned a warning to the RUC, there were only about nine minutes left before the device exploded.[16]

The warning was too late to be effective. There was a further warning, but that too was ineffective. The first warning was recorded by the G.P.O. as having been received at 8:51 p.m. and the second at 9:03 or 9:04 p.m., and the evidence was that the explosion occurred between 9 and 9:05 p.m.. There were about 500 people in the hotel at the time, in various parts of the buildings, and no indication was given in the warning messages of even the approximate location of the device. Indeed the message was both cryptic and misleading. It said "There are three bombs in La Mon and one in the car park." In fact there was only one explosive incendiary device on the premises; there was no bomb in the car park.

In the explosion, the blast shattered the interior of the premises, and a sheet of blazing petrol in the form of a massive fireball, estimated to be sixty feet in diameter and forty feet in height, was thrust into the Peacock Room, engulfing and raging it.[17]

People ran towards the exits as the lights went out. Those who were caught directly in the path of the flames were instantly incinerated. Twelve people – seven man and five women – died. They were so badly burned that it took several days to positively identify them, and only then by dental records. Twenty three people were grieviously injured. Those touched by the scalding heat had their clothes and skin scorched off. Some staggered from the building, with their clothes and flesh on fire.[18]

There was revulsion and outrage everywhere at the pitiless killings. This was increased the next day when the RUC appealed to the public for information leading to the arrest of those responsible. To assist that appeal the police issued 10, 000 posters showing one of the charred bodies from the hotel fire. The Provisionals made no attempt to deny that they were responsible for the deaths of those innocent people, nor did they make the slightest attempt to explain how such a terrible atrocity could advance any cause which they purport to espouse.

The *Republican News*, the organisation's weekly newspaper stated: "There is nothing we can offer in mitigation bar that our enquiries have established that a nine-minute warning was given to the RUC. This was proved totally inadequate given the disastrous consequences. All killings stem from British interference and from their denial of Irish sovereignty."[19]

One of the men detained immediately after the bombing was Gerry Adams, later elected Sinn Fein M.P. for West Belfast. He appeared before a Belfast court on Thursday, 2 March 1978, on a charge of membership of the IRA. He was described in court as the Belfast brigade commander of the Provisionals.[20] When he was tried for that offence in the autumn of that year, he was acquitted on 6 September, on a ruling by the Lord Chief Justice of Northern Ireland, Lord Lowry[21], that the prosecution had not proved their case against him.

At 5:35 a.m. on Monday, 25 September 1978, the RUC arrested Edward Manning Brophy, aged 38, at his home in the Turf Lodge area of Belfast. He was a former member of the British Army who had served with the Royal Ulster Rifles from 1958 until February 1961 when he was discharged on medical grounds.

Born in Belfast, Brophy was married with seven children aged from

18 to 2. After his arrest he was taken to Castlereagh Police Office for questioning. Between the time of his arrival there and Thursday, 28 September, he was interviewed by the RUC on ten occasions. The treatment he received there was to form the subject of much dispute at his subsequent trial.

Castlereagh had a total of thirty-eight cells and twenty-one interview rooms. It had been in the news for some time prior to Mr Brophy's arrest and had acquired a certain reputation. On 2 March 1977 BBC television had broadcast a programme – *Tonight* – which featured two cases of Catholics from Enniskillen, Bernard O'Connor, a schoolteacher, and Michael Lavelle, a production controller at a factory. Mr O'Connor had a horrifying story to tell about the way he had been treated by his interrogators at Castlereagh. He had been arrested at 5:30 a.m. under section 12 of the Prevention of Terrorism Act, 1974, and driven from his home in Enniskillen in County Fermanagh to the RUC headquarters at Castlereagh in East Belfast. There he was detained for five days before being released without charge.

He said: "I was made to stand on my toes with my knees in a bent position and my hands out in front of me." If he moved, he was slapped. He was kicked, punched and hurled across the room. The interrogators made him run on the spot, and do press-ups and sit-ups, and then repeat these activities whilst stripped naked. They made him stand with hiss lightly soiled underpants over his head, and pick up cigarette butts from the floor with his mouth; a tracksuit top was tied over his head blocking his nose and mouth so that he fainted.[22] He alleged that a detective said, "Choke the bastard."[23] The purpose of these activies was to obtain a confession to terrorist crime. He did not confess to any offence of any kind.

The Northern Ireland Secretary, Mr Mason, was reported in *The Guardian* on 4 March 1977 "to be very annoyed indeed" when the programme was transmitted on television. Yorkshiremen constantly proclaim to the point of boredom their capacity to speak bluntly; this may be not a privilege they are prepared to extend to others; in any event on this occasion clearly Mr Mason didn't like either the content or the message behind the programme. In his attempt to deflect public criticism he said that the interrogation "was fully justified in the light of the evidence available."[24] He seemed completely unable to comprehend that Mr O'Connor was complaining, not of the fact of his arrest and being questioned thereafter and whether that was justified, but about the coarse and brutal treatment during detention. In the event Mr O'Connor was awarded £5.000 exemplary damages and his costs in an action against the Chief Constable of the RUC on 30 June 1980.[25]

Allegations of maltreatment during interrogation, especially at Castlereagh, continued to be reported. On 12 May 1978 Brian Maguire, a twenty-seven year old electronics engineer was found hanging in a cell at Castlereagh. He had been held in custody for three days in connection with inquiries into the murder of an RUC constable.

Another man, Phelim Hamill, a zoology student at Queen's University, Belfast, had also been arrested on suspicion of being involved in that same murder, and he too had been interrogated at Castlereagh. A doctor who examined him found extensive injuries on him; he was literally covered in bruises. Amongst them were three on his neck. The doctor's report stated that Mr Hamill "detailed how, on one occasion, someone got a towel and put it around his face, making it difficult for him to breath. Water was then poured over the mouth and nose area. This was frightening and was repeated on a number of occasions." Although he was charged with the offence of murder, the only evidence against him was a verbal admission he was alleged to have made to the RUC. The charge was subsequently withdrawn and he was released.[26]

At the end of October 1977, Thames Television transmitted a programme entitled *Inhuman and Degrading Treatment*, featuring ten cases of alleged maltreatment at Castelereagh between February and October of the preceding year. Between 28 November 1977 and 6 December 1977 a team from the Human Rights organisation Amnesty International visited Northern Ireland and examined a total of seventy-eight cases of persons arrested on suspicion of involvement in terrorism and who alleged maltreatment during detention following arrest.[27] In June 1978 the Labour Government appointed Judge Harry Bennett Q.C. to chair an inquiry into Police interrogation in Northern Ireland. It was against the background of some of these cases that Edward Manning Brophy had been arrested and taken to Castlereagh where he was interviewed on ten occasions between 25 and 28 September. There were four interviews on the first day, of approximately one and three-quarter hours, three and a half hours, one and three-quarter hours and two hours, respectively. On the following day,Tuesday, he was interviewed for four hours and then for five a half hours. On Wednesday he was interviewed twice, for five hours and for one and one-quarter hours. On the final day, the Thursday, there were two interviews, of one and three-quarter hours and two hours respectively. All these times were based on the police records. Mr Brophy thought that interviews two, eight and nine were shorter than the recorded times, and interviews three, five and six were longer. Because he was deprived of his watch there was no way in which he could accurately note the times.

While at Castlereagh, the RUC maintained that Brophy freely and voluntarily made verbal and written confessions to a substantial number of crimes, some forty-eight in all. These were to form the basis of the forty-eight counts in the indictment against him when he appeared before the court. It was alleged by the RUC that all the offences were committed while Mr Brophy was acting as a member of the Provisional IRA and in furtherance of their terrorist activities in Northern Ireland; for that reason the last count in the indictment, count 49, charged him with belonging to that proscribed organisation between 15 August 1976 and 1 March 1978.

It was common ground that, without the confession evidence, the prosecution had no case against Mr Brophy, for there was no other evidence of any kind against him. The odd feature about this aspect of the case was that in order to exercise the power of arrest without warrant under the Prevention of Terrorism Act 1974, the RUC had to have reasonable grounds to suspect that Mr Brophy was or had been concerned in the commission, preparation or instigation of acts of terrorism. An honest or genuine suspicion would not be enough for the exercise of the power; the suspicion has to be a reasonable one, and that is an objective test, decided as a matter of law by the trial judge. If, as the trial Judge, Mr Justice Kelly accepted, that the entire case against Mr Brophy was based on the confession evidence provided by him between the time of his arrest on the Monday morning and the conclusion of the second interview on the Thursday, it would be interesting to know upon what grounds the arresting officer based his reasonable suspicion before he exercised the power of arrest on his arrival in Turf Lodge and before Mr Brophy had uttered an incriminating word.

The details of the offences alleged against him are set out in chronological order in some detail and with great clarity by Mr Justice Kelly.[28]

The first offences relate to a fire bombing in the Smithfield area of Belfast. Two bombs exploded almost simultaneously at 3:50 in the afternoon of 6 September 1976. The first was in a paint shop in Smithfield Square, where two men armed with a gun had placed a bomb about thirty minutes earlier. The second was in a carpet shop in the same Square, where two men, one armed with a gun, placed a bomb about the same time. The men were not identified and it was not alleged that Mr Brophy was one of them. The prosecution case was that he had acted as scout and look-out for the bombing team, and that while riding as pillion passenger on a motor cycle he led the team to the designated targets. It was alleged that he was ready to warn the team by means of the motor cycle lights and indicators of the presence of the Security Forces if they should appear. When the explosive incendary devices went off in both premises, damage in excess of £56.000 was caused.

The next series of offences were committed four days later, on 10 September 1976, when at about 4 p.m. two men, one armed with a gun, entered a car hire company in Grosvenor Road, Belfast and placed two explosive incendiary devices on the premises. Both bombs exploded and caused extensive damage to the amount of £100, 000. The building itself was reduced to a shell. The case for the prosecution in respect of this was that Mr Brophy's role was the same as in the previous series of offences, namely that he was the scout for the bombing team.

The third series of offences were alleged to have been committed on 31 December 1976, shortly after 5 p.m, when a soldier of the Royal Welsh Fusiliers on sentry duty at Fort Monagh Military location, on Glen Road, Belfast heard three shots fired over the camp. The shots came from the direction of some shops on the Turf Lodge Estate. The prosecution said that Mr Brophy fired those shots and his purpose was to lure the army out of the camp into a terrorist ambush.

Although that event took place almost twenty one months before his arrest, there was no evidence from anyone to support the charge, apart from the confession evidence. If anyone saw Mr Brophy fire the shots, that person never came forward to say so; no forensic evidence of any kind implicated him in that or any of the other offences; nor was a gun ever found in his possession. It should not have been too difficult for Mr Brophy to have been able to give an account of his movements on New Year's Eve, and for the RUC to conduct a check on any information which was given. He appears not to have done so, and of course he was entitled to stay silent without any inference of guilt being drawn in accordance with his common law rights. The identities of others who must have been involved with him in the commission of these offences, where they were, what form the ambush was to take, in which area, was not disclosed to the court by anyone.

The next series of offences were committed by someone on 12 August 1977, when at about 2 p.m. a blast bomb was thrown at an army patrol in the Nonash Gardens/ Norglon Parade area of the Turf Lodge estate. Two soldiers were injured in the incident. The prosecution alleged that Mr Brophy had been in possession of the bomb and had given it to the person who threw it. The identity of that person, and the maker(s) of the bomb, if known, was not revealed.

The prosecution then listed six series of offences, committed between November 1977 and February 1978, when blast incendiary bombs exploded in, and virtually destroyed, six business premises in Belfast. A

131

furniture store in Victoria Street was the target on 7 November 1977, when damage to the amount of £95, 000 was caused. A carpet shop on the Lisburn Road was next, on 23 November, when the loss and damage was £17,000. On 22 December, two shops were damaged on the Lisburn Road, where the total damage amounted to £256, 000. A D. I. Y. shop on the Lisburn Road was the target on 30 January 1978, and the damage caused was in the sum of £78,000. Three days after that, a motor showroom on Boucher Road was damaged to the extent of £35. 000.

In each one of these offences Mr Brophy is supposed to have taken a secondary role, in the sense that he did not actually manufacture, carry or place the incendary devices on the attacked premises. His part was said to be that of look-out and scout; from the pillion seat of a motorcycle, he led the bombing team from Turf Lodge to each one of the bombings and when they arrived unchallenged he left the scene. As the trial judge noted, by some good fortune there were no injuries at any of the scenes of explosion, except on 12 December 1977, when a reserve Constable of the RUC was hit by shrapnel and received a compound fracture of the leg.

The RUC seemed to have had a particularly detailed knowledge of Mr Brophy's degree of participation in all these offences; that he was the pillion passenger and not the driver of the motor cycle for example, and that the shots were fired at the Welsh fusiliers not for the purpose of killing one victim, but for luring others into an ambush. In spite of that knowledge admissible evidence was simply in short supply.

The prosecution even had an extremely detailed account to put before the court of Mr Brophy's involvement in the La Mon House hotel bombing. It was alleged that he had kept the bomb in the coal-shed of a maisonette in Turf Lodge, and that sometime around 7:30 to 7:45 on that Friday evening in February he had handed it over to a bombing team. That team consisted of six man in two hijacked cars.

He had, so it was alleged, handed the bomb to a man who was sitting in the back seat of one of the cars; two others were in that vehicle, the remaining three were in the scout car which was to lead the way to the La Mon House Hotel. Mr Brophy knew, according to the Crown, the exact destination of the bombing team, and that the bomb would be primed there for the purpose of causing an explosion. It was on that basis that he was charged with twelve counts of murder, one for each of the dead. The prosecution even knew, they said, that after the departure of the car Mr Brophy had visited two social clubs that evening while those terrible murders were being committed.

It is quite self-evident that if this information was based on fact and was true, then an informer, someone very close to Mr Brophy, had supplied it to the RUC. What is strange to note, however, is that apparently no other name except his was supplied by the informer (if there was one) to the police.

During the time he was in Castlereagh, Mr Brophy signed six written statements and verbally admitted to the police his complicity in these terrorist offences. He did complain to the court that he had been denied access to a solicitor throughout the time he was detained there.

As a matter of law, a person who has been arrested and detained under section 12 of the Prevention of Terrorism (Temporary Provisions) Act, 1976 has certain legal rights. One of these is to be able to communicate and to consult privately with a solicitor. This is so even if he is in custody provided that in such a case no unreasonable delay or hinderance is caused to the processes of investigation or the administration of justice by his doing so.[29] This is a right recognisedby the Judges' Rules, which, at the time of Mr Brophy's detention in Castlereagh, were in force in England and Wales as well as Northern Ireland. These Rules arose in this way.

During the 19th Century the judiciary began to formulate the approach to be adopted by police officers in the conduct of interrogation of suspects. This was because of substantial judicial suspicion of the police. Some judges took the view that there should be no questioning of a suspect, since he was not allowed to give evidence in his own defence at trial, and therefore could not explain or expand any answers he gave to questions. In one case in 1893 the judge said in his summing up to the jury: "The law does not allow the judge or the jury to put questions in open court to prisoners; and it would be monstrous if the law permitted a police officer to go, without anyone being present to see how the matter was conducted, and put a prisoner through an examination, and then produce the effects of that examination against him. Under these circumstances, a policeman should keep his mouth shut and his ears open. He is not bound to stop a prisoner in making a statement; his duty is to listen and report, but it is quite another matter that he should put questions to prisoners. A policeman is not to discourage a statement, and certainly not to encourage one. It is no business of a policeman to put questions, which may lead a prisoner to give answers on the spur of the moment, thinking perhaps he may set himself out of a difficulty by telling lies."[30] Five years after that case, in 1898, the defendant in a criminal trial became competent, but not compellable, to give evidence in his own defence at his trial. Accordingly, the reason for prohibiting police questioning of a suspect vanished. Another rule then evolved; namely that if questioning was permissible the suspect must be cautioned, that is told that he need not say anything unless he wished to do so. However, difficulties for the police persisted. In 1906 at the Birmingham Assizes, one policeman was judicially criticised for using the caution, and another for not using it.[31]

Accordingly, in 1912 a code called the Judges' Rules was issued and approved by the Judges of the King's Bench Division. There were four rules in all; another five were added in 1918. They were greatly criticised for lack of clarity and of efficacy for the protection of persons who were questioned by police officers; on the other hand it was alleged, certainly by a substantial number of police officers, that their application unduly hampered the detection and punishment of crime.

In the years following 1918 the Rules were revised and approved eventually in 1964. That version was introduced in Northern Ireland in 1976 with the approval of the Supreme Court Judges; it was stated in a Parliamentary Written Answer given on 13 October 1976 that the Secretary of State had "agreed with the Chief Constable of the RUC that these Rules should be brought into use in Northern Ireland on October 8, 1876."[32]

It was widely accepted that the Judges' Rules did not have the force of law but were made as a guide for police officers. A breach of the Rules would go to the issue of admissibility of evidence which might be obtained as a result of that breach. In addition there were some Administrative Directions on interrogation and the taking of statements, drafted by the Home Office, which were appended to the Rules. There were some judges who refused to accept that these directions had any binding force, since they were separate and independent of the Judges' Rules and had never been approved by the Supreme Court Judges. One of the Directions, No. 7 was headed: Facilities for defence: (a) A person in custody should be allowed to speak on the telephone to his solicitor or to his friends provided that no hindrance is reasonably likely to be caused to the process of investigation or the administration of justice by his doing so.

These Rules did not affect the principle that every person should be able to consult a solicitor. The words of the preamble to the Judges' Rules make it clear however that this is only a qualified and nebulous right, but its exercise is clearly governed by the discretion of a police officer. However, in addition to this principle set out in the preamble there was in existence in Northern Ireland a set of regulations issued by the Chief Constable and other most senior members of the RUC to members of the force concerning the treatment of prisoners in custody. This RUC Code contained 195 paragraphs, and some further instructions which related specifically to Castlereagh Police Office.

The RUC Code stated that a prisoner *must* [emphasis added] be allowed to see his solicitor unless:

(1) the prisoner does not wish to see the solicitor, or

(2) the visit is likely to hinder the investigation of a crime of the administration of justice or is calculated to disrupt or delay police investigations or the course of the interview or interviews, or

(3) is likely to prevent or delay further arrests The decision rests formally on the Duty Inspector, but there is provision for him to consult the detective officer in charge of the case.[33]

That is the legal position, and it worked only in theory, because in practice, as Judge Bennett accepted, solicitors were not admitted to see terrorist suspects before they were charged. The evidence in support of this was almost unanimous, from solicitors, former prisoners, other members of the public and from the RUC themselves. Judge Bennett found himself unable to decide whether the police had a true discretion whether to admit or exclude solicitors at all, but he did not pursue the point because it was always exercised so as to produce the same outcome; a suspect could not and did not consult a solicitor whilst being detained before charge. Such a consistent approach, clearly based on grounds of policy, gave rise to the inference that the discretion was not being exercised at all, or that it was not exercised fairly. Judge Bennett could find no case in Northern Ireland in which a court had ruled that a confession statement was inadmissible in evidence on the ground that access to a solicitor had been denied. Accordingly, his Committee recommended, for what it was worth, that a prisoner should have an absolute right of access to a solicitor after detention for forty-eight hours, but only if by then he has not been charged and had not already been allowed to consult his solicitor.

Mr Brophy had other allegations to make about the content and conduct of the police interviews. He denied that he had been cautioned. He further alleged that he was not allowed to see his wife,or be examined by a doctor. If he was right on this latter point the police officers would have been in breach of the RUC Code, which requires a medical examination of a prisoner to be arranged as soon as possible after his arrival at a police station, and also where the prisoner alleges that he was assaulted before, during or after arrest. Mr Brophy's principle complaint against the RUC, and the main grounds of the challenge to the admissibility of statements made during interview, was that he was subjected to torture or to inhuman or degrading treatment in order to induce him to confess to the offences alleged against him. He maintained that when he was not being physically ill-treated the police were, by threats, oppression and trickery trying to get him to admit membership of the IRA at a high level, as well as confessing to the matters with which he was subsequently charged. As the hearing progressed it became apparent that Mr Brophy was denying the content of some of the confession statements, so that he then was contending not that he had made the statements in a manner that was involuntary but that he had not made them at all.

Whether a confession is admissible in evidence is a matter of law for the trial judge to decide, in the absence of a jury. The witnesses give their evidence on a special form of oath known as the voir dire. The adjudication before the judge is called the hearing on the voir dire, or the trial within a trial. The burden of proving torture or inhuman or degrading treatment did not lie upon the accused who alleged them, but he would have to lay the foundation for such an allegation, and once raised, those issues have to be disproved by the prosecution. In the Diplock courts in Northern Ireland, questions of law and fact are decided by the trial judge alone, since these courts sit without a jury.

These courts were set up following the Report of a Commission to consider legal procedures to deal with terrorist activies in Northern Ireland, under the chairmanship of the late Lord Diplock, a world renown authority in International Law, and a member of the House of Lords. His knowledge of criminal law and the law relating to terrorism may not have been so extensive as His Lordship thought it was. The Commission recommended the abolition of jury trial in cases of scheduled offences, and in addition said[34]: "We consider that the detailed technical rules and practice as to the admissibility of inculpatory statements by the accused as they are currently applied in Northern Ireland are hampering the course of justice in the case of terrorist crimes and compelling the authorities responsible for public order and safety to resort to detention in a significant number of cases which could otherwise be dealt with both effectively and fairly by trial in a court of law."

Mr Brophy decided to give evidence on oath, as indeed he had to if the defence were to have any chance of persuading the trial judge to exclude the confession statements. From the witness box he alleged that over a period of three days, from 25 to 27 September, he was physically assaulted by being slapped on the face, caught and pulled by the hair; punched and jabbed in the stomach, struck on the back of the head and the neck; hit on the chest; his head and neck were squeezed in such a manner that he became unconscious and fell to the floor; he was pushed against the wall; his hands. and arms were bent and twisted into his armpits; his feet were stamped upon, and a heel ground on his big toe. He said that he was made to squat in uncomfortable and exhaustive postures, and to do press-ups and on occasions was kicked and knocked

136

over while doing these exercises.

He told the trial judge that he was humiliated and degraded. On no less than three occasions, he said, police officers opened his trousers, exposed his private parts and flicked his penis up and down by hand. One officer spat in his face and at one time tried to force him to drink the contents of a cup which Mr Brophy was told was urine. When he was unable to do this the liquid was thrown over him and he was made to wipe up what was spilt on the floor.

As noted above, Mr Brophy had asked to see his wife but he was not allowed to do so. At some stage over these three days he was told that his wife had been arrested and was also in custody at Castlereagh. She would be detained there and might be roughly treated, but if he confessed then he would be allowed to see her and she would be released. On two occasions, he said, he heard the sound of a woman crying and screaming outside his interview room, and he was made to believe that it was his wife.

His description of these two episodes almost certainly helped to bolster Mr Brophy's credibility in resolving the conflict between his version of events as against that of the RUC. The trial judge accepted that there was evidence that there was one woman present in Castlereagh on the 26 September, and she was being interviewed in a room next door to Mr Brophy at or about the same time as he was. Why she was screaming, or who caused her to scream, was not a matter which was canvassed before the court.

Mr Brophy did not maintain that all the interviewing officers who had made witness statements had ill-treated him; only some of them had. What he did allege with some force, and perhaps with some degree of accuracy, was that only two of his interviewers – Detective Chief Superintendent Mooney and Detective Superintendent Hyland – ever revealed their names to him, and that no less than seven officers, who were not on the record as having made witness statements, had in fact taken part in the ill-treatment. In the event, he was able to identify three of those seven officers; the other four remain unidentified.

It was the defence case at the voir dire that the ill-treatment he had suffered left Mr Brophy ill, exhausted, beaten, degraded and apprehensive about his wife, where and how she was, and aware that unless and until he confessed the unlawful conduct would continue. In such circumstances he signed four written confession statements – exhibits, 67, 68, 69 and 70 – on the evening of 26 September, and two further statements – exhibits 71 and 72 – on the following day.[35] In addition he agreed verbally to police suggestions to his complicity in terrorist crime.

Mr Brophy's evidence lasted for ten days of the forty-seven-day trial. The trial judge was not greatly impressed with him. "I think he is of poor moral character – unreliable, untrustworthy, foxy, weak, although he liked to pose . . . as a tough guy . . . and although denying in evidence that he was the officer commanding the Turf Lodge IRA, and a member of the Brigade Staff of the IRA, his face clearly showed these suggestions flattered him."[36] The judge found his evidence rambled, at times Mr Brophy was incoherent and he contradicted himself, was evasive and on occasions lied.

After Mr Brophy's evidence at the trial within a trial, the prosecution called those police officers who were on the record and made statements for the preliminary enquiry at which Mr Brophy had been returned for trial at the Crown Court. In the witness box, as the judge found, the officers appeared impassive, controlled, bland."[37] They denied all charges of ill-treatment and impropriety. They had little independent recollection of events of the interviews, and relied on their notes of interviews, their personal journals and documentary evidence from Castlereagh Police Office for the purpose of giving their evidence. Their evidence was supported by uniformed police officers from Castlereagh who were responsible for Mr Brophy's safe custody, and they saw or heard nothing improper or even irregular during the detention at the police office.

There were some factors in Mr Brophy's favour, as the trial judge found. He stood up well to a long and searching cross-examination from counsel for the prosecution and maintained a remarkable consistency in his evidence about the infliction of ill-treatment. There was some slight support from the medical evidence of some signs of ill-treatment, although a considerable amount of the physical assault he described was not corroborated by the doctors, but, said the judge, " . . . there must be some allowance made for the technique of striking without marking."[38]

The most important defence evidence related to five detectives, against whom he made a number of serious allegations. He accused two officers – Detective Constable Patterson and Sergeant Clements – of bursting into the interview room on the morning of 25 September, between 10:40 and 12:30 p.m. They had no authority to be there, as two other officers who were detailed to conduct the interview were in the room doing so. Mr Brophy alleged that Sergeant Clements assaulted him there. Neither Constable Patterson nor Sergeant Clements had made a statement about being in the interview room on that date or at that time, and both denied being there; the assault was also denied.

As the trial judge noted, if he was lying then Mr Brophy was taking an enormous risk in identifying these two officers, for there might have been strong, unchallengeable and independent evidence that they were far away from Castlereagh police office at the particular time on that day. In fact, Detective Constable Patterson was on the premises that morning, and he had no assigned duties, so it was open to him, if he so wished, to go into the interview room.

The position regarding the Sergeant was slightly different. He produced his personal journal of duties for 25 September which indicated that he had spent the morning at the Belfast City Commission and did not arrive at Castlereagh until after lunch. However, an inquiry with that court disclosed that the case in which he was involved did not go on, or even begin on that day. The officer then recalled that he had spent the morning at home, although it was admitted that he knew the first briefing of detectives about the questioning of Mr Brophy and his first interview would be held at Castlereagh that morning. Moreoever, the Sergeant knew that it was likely that he would be one of the interviewers. Of Sergeant Clements' evidence on this issue at the voir dire the trial judge said "I was not impressed."[39] Does that mean that the trial judge did not believe this witness? If it does, why not say so?

A further allegation of assault against Sergeant Clements related to the interview on the afternoon of the following day, the 26th, between the hours of 12:50 and 5 p.m. The officer denied this and said that he left the interview room at 1:45, and he was given the afternoon off fifteen minutes later. Another officer, Inspector Meeke took over the interview. Sergeant Clements' personal diary was produced and examined in court. One part showed that he was on duty until 5 o'clock, but this was crossed out and changed to 2 o'clock. The trial judge had a mild word of criticism for both officers for he found, "The evidence related by both Detective Inspector Meeke and Detective Sergeant Clements as to why and from what time Clements was given the afternoon off, was not at all convincing."[40]

The learned judge had not hesitated to castigate Mr Brophy when he came to summarise his evidence, with the references to his poor moral character. If by stating that the evidence of the Inspector and Sergeant was not convincing, the judge really meant he did not believe either of them, it seems a pity he did not say so.

There was more to come. Mr Brophy said that another detective not on the record had threatened him on the morning of 25 September sometime between 10:40 a.m. and 12:30 p.m. He further alleged that this officer had assaulted him and indecently assaulted him on the following day, in the afternoon between 12:50 and 5 o'clock. In his evidence Mr Brophy said that this detective's name was Marshall, that he had a very cultured accent when he talked about interrogation techniques, and he appeared to be an ex-British Army officer.

Accordingly, a group identification, which involves a witness seeing the disputed subject among a group of people rather than a formal identification parade, was held at the back of the courtroom in which Mr Brophy's trial was being conducted. Mr Brophy picked out a man from a group of detectives assembled there. That man gave evidence at a later stage. His name was indeed Marshall. He was a detective constable in the RUC. He was English, with what the judge called "a good accent"[41], and he had served in the British Army for eight years before he joined the RUC. He was on duty in Castlereagh on the morning of 25 September, although no specific duties were assigned to him. He had attended the briefing on the Brophy case. Constable Marshall was also present in the police office in the afternoon of that date, and had no detailed duties between 3:15 and 5 o'clock, so he had the opportunity, if he so wished, to enter the interview room.

Clearly Mr Brophy had a remarkable memory for events, personal characteristics including, but not limited to, faces, but also details which enabled him to link what was said and the way in which it was said to specific times, places and persons. The judge was impressed with the evidence in which Mr Brophy said that there was an "alleged query from Marshall (an ex-British soldier) to Brophy, himself an ex-soldier in the Royal Ulster Rifles, if he had ever done interrogation techniques in the British Army."[42] It must have been clear beyond any doubt that Marshall had not only been in the same room as Brophy, but that he had spoken to him as well.

There was another officer, again not on the record, who Mr Brophy said had entered the interview room on 25 September on two occasions without authority; the first towards the end of interview one, between 12:50 and 4:15 p.m., and during interview two, 4:15 to 6 p.m. He said that officer threatened and assaulted him. Mr Brophy did not know the officer's name, but in evidence he described the man physically and said that the officer had interviewed him previously when he was being held in Castlereagh in February 1978. Again there was a group identification at the back of the courtroom; again Mr Brophy picket out a man from a number of detectives assembled in court. His name was not disclosed, for he was a Special Branch officer, given the prefix "C". This officer had in fact interviewed Mr Brophy in Castlereagh in February as had been alleged, and "C" was indeed in Castlereagh on the day and at the times of the alleged assaults. Of all the officers Mr Brophy should choose to identify as being responsible for entering the interview room and assaulting him, he did pick out a person whose police journal showed that he was on the premises and he was free from assigned duties between 3:45 and 5 o'clock that afternoon of 25 September. He too had the opportunity therefore to enter that room if he wanted to do so.

However, the main target of Mr Brophy's attack was another detective sergeant not on record at the preliminary inquiry. That was Detective Sergeant Burnside who, Mr Brophy alleged, had been one of the main agressors at Castlereagh. This officer, he said, had assaulted him physically and indecently during interview five on 26 September, between 12:50 and 5 o'clock. The detective sergeant denied he was ever in any room with Brophy at any time, let alone that he had interviewed him. The prosecution attacked Mr Brophy's evidence on this point, saying that his description of the officer was quite inaccurate and his identification in court was only by name. The trial judge, however, found Mr Brophy's explanation of how he was able to pin-point this officer to have the ring of truth about it.

Mr Brophy had alleged that apart from two senior officers, no other member of the RUC had identified themselves by name or in any other way to him. During one interview Detective Sergeant Burnside had mentioned the ex-British soldier DC Marshall by name. Because of this he was called out of the room by Patterson, and Mr Brophy remembered the Detective Sergeant's discomfort when he returned. Mr Brophy identified Sergeant Burnside in court after he had described him. The Sergeant denied what was being alleged against him, then the officer's personal diary was called for, produced and examined. It contained the following entry: "Reported for duty at CID Office at Oaks and then to Castlereagh Police Office and assisted and supervised interview re Brophy."[43] This entry, indicating as it did that Mr Brophy's visual identification was correct, called for an explanation. These words, said Detective Sergeant Burnside, were intended to signify duties which he performed outside Brophy's interview room, e.g. ensuring that Brophy's interviewers were present, gathering information from police records of details of crimes Brophy had confessed to. They did not mean or imply that he was ever inside Brophy's interview room or that he ever questioned or interviewed him. Thus, it seemed the officer was asking the trial judge to find that it was just a remarkable and inexplicable coincidence that the person visually identified as himself by Mr.Brophy should have a written entry in his diary for that very day that Mr Brophy said he was interviewed and assaulted by the very person.

The trial judge was unable to so find. He said, "I have considerable reservations about this explanation."[44] At a later state, in referring to this and the evidence of another officer, the judge said, "I did not form a favourable impression of the credibility of Detective Constable Marshall or Detective Sergeant Burnside in the witness box."[45]

The trial judge said in terms that he had not heard all that went on at Castlereagh from the police over those four days in September. He rejected the argument put forward on behalf of the Crown that the defence allegations were all part of Brophy's subtly prepared script or that it was impossible to understand the workings of Brophy's mind. In the result he ruled that the Crown had not, as a matter of law, discharged the burden of proof to satisfy him beyond reasonable doubt that the verbal and written confession statements were not induced by torture or inhuman or degrading treatment. Accordingly he ruled that the confession evidence relating to the counts in the indictment was not admissible. He included in his rejection the statements in which Mr Brophy had verbally confirmed, on the afternoon of 28 September to two senior police officers, his earlier admissions of involvement in the La Mon House bombing.

What that ruling amounted to gave rise to a dispute between myself and the Information Officer of the RUC. Did it mean that the trial judge accepted that Mr Brophy had been ill-treated and degraded, which was my view, or was it simply that the Prosecution had failed to establish that this had not happened to him, this being the Information Officer's view of the decision?

The case of Regina -v- Brophy was reported in the Criminal Law Review, a highly respected monthly journal and commentary on the criminal law, at page 831 of the volume for 1981. There seemed to be an error in the language of the summary of the case and, accordingly, I sought to put the record straight and made reference to the House of Lords decision as it appeared in the All England Law Reports, volume 2 for 1981 at page 705. In the House Lord Fraser said this: "The respondent [Mr Brophy] challenged the admissibility of the statements, under section 8(2) of the 1978 Act, on the ground that he had been induced to make them by being subjected to torture or to inhuman or degrading treatment while in custody. The learned trial judge, after a voir dire, delivered a careful and exhaustive judgement holding that he was not satisfied that the statements had not been so obtained, and he excluded evidence of them from the substantive trial."[46]

I then offered the following comment on the trial: "This case is important for many reasons, not least of which is the date of the arrest of the accused – 25 September 1978. This was three months after the appointment of the Committee of inquiry into Police Interrogation Procedures in Northern Ireland (The Bennett Committee) on 8 June 1978, so that whilst that Committee was actually taking evidence Mr Brophy was being subjected to 'torture or to inhuman or degrading treatment while in custody' as the trial judge so found."[47]

This was the reply from the RUC in the form of a letter to the editor of the Criminal Law Review:

"In his letter at (1982) Crim. L.R. 194, Michael O'Connell of Nottingham is incorrect in his reference to an alleged error in the report of the case at (1981) Crim. L.R. 831.

What Mr O'Connell ignores is that the trial judge did not find that Brophy was subjected to torture or to inhuman or degrading treatment while in custody, but that the prosecution had failed to prove beyond reasonable doubt that Brophy's allegations were unfounded. To assert therefore, as Mr O'Connell asserts, that the trial judge found that Brophy was subjected to torture etc., while in custody is incorrect; the judge made no such finding."[48]. That letter was signed by the RUC Information Officer, Press Office.

This obviously called for a reply and explanation. This was published by the Criminal Law Review.[49] It included the following:

"At the seventh interview (on 27 September 1978) Mr Brophy made verbal admissions and a written confession of his involvement in the La Mon House Hotel bombing, in which twelve people died. Mr Justice Kelly ruled out those verbal admissions and the written confession on the ground that he could not be satisfied that they had not been induced by torture or inhuman or degrading treatment."

So far, the RUC Information Officer and I are in agreement with what the case decided. What was overlooked by him however was the evidence relating to two RUC officers.

"However, two senior police officers, Detective Superintendent Hyland and Detective Superintendent Mooney gave evidence, which the trial judge accepted as being true, that on the afternoon of the following day Mr Brophy verbally confirmed those earlier admissions in relating to the bombing. No allegation of ill-treatment was made against either of those officers, and "Brophy described their attitude as 'nice' and the interview as 'friendly'."[50]

There is no reason in law why the trial judge should not have ruled that this evidence was admissible; no allegation of ill-treatment or improper conduct was made against either of these two officers whilst Mr Brophy was at Castlereagh between 25 and 28 September. Indeed in McKearney (unreported) at the Belfast City Commission on 11 December 1978, Mr Justice Murray excluded an admission of membership of an unlawful organisation on the ground that the Crown had not proved it had not been induced by ill-treatment, but when at subsequent interviews the defendant admitted to different officers against whom no ill-treatment was alleged that he was implicated in a murder, that admission was allowed in.

Thus there must have been a compelling reason, in the light of this authority, for the trial judge to rule that he would not permit this confession evidence to be given by those two senior officers. Mr Justice Kelly said in the clearest terms: "I am not satisfied beyond reasonable doubt that the effect of the ill-treatment and impropriety has clearly been shown to have been dissipated."[51] This is conclusive proof that the judge found as a fact that Mr Brophy had been ill-treated whilst in custody in Castlereagh; it had happened and the effects had not worn off by the time he volunteered the confession to the two superintendents.

At the conclusion of his ruling, the voir dire ended and the trial proper resumed. In a jury trial they would have been absent from the court during the evidence and argument and would return to the courtroom. If appropriate the trial judge would give the jury some directions on the law, for example the judge might direct them to acquit the accused on some or all of the counts in the indictment. If the legal argument related to the admission of confession evidence then the jury would hear nothing of its existence if it was ruled inadmissible. However, if it was allowed in, at some stage the jury would hear the evidence and they would have to decide whether in fact the confession evidence was true.

Mr Justice Kelly then directed that in the absence of the confession evidence there was no remaining evidence of the first forty-eight counts in the indictment, and Mr Brophy was found not guilty of all these offences. On the 49th count however, the judge found there was a prime facie case for Mr Brophy to answer. That count alleged that Mr Edward Manning Brophy between the month of 15 August 1976 and the 1st day of January 1978 in the County of the City of Belfast, belonged to a proscribed organisation, "namely the Irish Republican Army."[52] The prosecution closed its case at the trial proper, by calling two witnesses, first a police officer, Inspector Colgan, and the court shorthand writer, Miss Beattie.

The defence had objected to this evidence being given, but the trial judge overruled the objection by holding that the statement of IRA membership was not strictly relevant to the central question on the voir dire, namely the admissibility of Mr Brophy's confession statements to the police.

The defence having submitted that there was no case for Mr Brophy to answer on this count, and that having been rejected, decided to call no evidence on behalf of the defence.

The trial judge then reviewed the evidence which Mr Brophy had given on the voir dire from the witness box, and which had been related, on the application of the prosecution, to the court at the trial proper, by

144

the shorthand writer. It was necessary to do this because Mr Brophy had exercised his important constitutional right to stay silent at the trial, as opposed to the voir dire. That evidence included the following questions and answers:

Q. 20. Before 1970 did you take any interest in politics or political affairs?

A. No.

Q. 21. Do you remember internment day?

A. Yes.

Q. 22. Were you arrested on internment day?

A. I was not arrested but my house was raided. They made a mistake and my house was raided.

Q. 23. What, if anything, happened to the house?

A. They went through all the rooms, and got all the children out of bed, the British Army, and were very abusive to my family and me.

Q. 24. After that did you join any organisation?

A. Yes, I was a member of the Irish Republican Army.

Q. 25. When did you join the Irish Republican Army?

A. In September 1971.

Q. 25. And how long did you remain a member of the IRA?

A. I remained a member of the Irish Republican Army until December 1977." [53]

In the light of this evidence, Mr Justice Kelly said: "I believe that for a trial judge in a non-jury trial not to act on the evidence freely volunteered by Brophy in all the circumstances in which it was given, would be grossly unjust."[54] Accordingly, the judge found Mr Brophy guilty of membership of the IRA and sentenced him to five years imprisonment.

Mr Brophy appealed against his conviction on this count to the Northern Ireland Court of Appeal. There the prosecution advanced the argument, which they repeated when the case eventually went to the House of Lords, that Mr Brophy had not admitted on the voir dire that all or any of his pre-trial confessions were true, but simply that he had been a member of a proscribed organisation, which was an entirely separate crime for which he had been separately charged albeit in the same indictment. Such an admission, it was further submitted, could only be relevant to the issue of admissibility of his pre-trial confessions; it would have to be shown that the police regarded him as a member of the IRA and therefore be hostile towards him and to ill-treat him.

Both the Court of Appeal and the House of Lords rejected those arguments. The House thought that if Mr Brophy could show that he had been a member of the IRA for several years, up till a date less than two months before the date of the murders charged in counts 1 to 12 in the indictment – the twelve deaths in the La Mon House Hotel bombing – then that would be, contrary to the view of the trial judge, relevant to the issue of admissibility of the confession evidence on those counts. If, as would be likely, the police knew or suspected membership of this proscribed organisation then not only would they be more hostile to him than if they did not, but also they would expect him to have received instructions in how to avoid succumbing to the normal techniques of interrogation which do not involve any physical ill-treatment.

In so holding the House was restating the two basic rights which the accused is said to have in a criminal trial,first the right to challenge the admissibility of confession evidence, and second the right to stay silent at the trial proper thereafter. Lord Fraser said that the right of the accused to give evidence on the voir dire without affecting his right to remain silent at the substantive trial was absolute. He did add the caveat however that if the accused went out of his way on the voir dire to boast of the crimes with which he is charged, or if he uses the witness box as a platform to make a political speech, it would be open to the court to hold that this evidence was not relevant to the issues. It would then be proper for the prosecution to adduce evidence of what the accused had said.

There appears in this case the unquestioned conclusion that the IRA was engaged in providing counter interrogation techniques so that arrested members of that organisation would not break under questioning from the police. If Mr Brophy was given that training it was singularly unsuccessful. To the ordinary individual moreoever the fact that a suspect volunteers information that he is a member of a proscribed organisation, not in an interview with the police, but in a court of law. in the presence of his barrister and solicitor, and the judge that hears that evidence must therefore generally exclude it, then such an approach offends against common sense. The Law Lords in Mr Brophy's case and who decided such evidence was inadmissible were Lord Diplock, Lord Fraser, Lord Russell, Lord Keith and Lord Roskill. The hearings were on 2 and 15 June 1981.

Five months later, on 13, 20 and 21 October and 19 November 1881, those same Law Lords, with the exception of Lord Fraser (whose place was taken by Lord Brandon) decided another case of public importance, that it was proper to strike out a civil case an an abuse of the process of the court, where the same issue as in the civil case had already been decided by a court of competent jurisdiction, namely a criminal court.

In this case six men had been convicted of the murder of twenty-one people by causing explosions in two public houses in Birmingham in 1974. At their trial the six attempted to show, on a voir dire, that confessions of guilt made by some of them were involuntary and inadmissible on the ground they had been ill-treated whilst in custody by the police. The trial within a trial lasted for eight days. The judge at trial said, in allowing the confession evidence in: "Certainly, according to the police evidence, no sort of violence was used and no sort of threats were addressed to any of the prisoners. On the other hand, the defendants all gave evidence, with the exception perhaps of Callaghan, of gross personal violence being used to them . . . All of them, including Callaghan, complain of the most outrageous threats as to what would happen to them or, in.some cases, their families . . . all allege that the whole of the police evidence . . . was substantially fabricated evidence . . . it is an inescapable conclusion that there is gross perjury being committed by one side or the other."

The trial judge believed the police and not the six accused. So did the jury. They convicted the six who were sent to prison for life. The Director of Public Prosecutions, however, decided to bring criminal charges against fourteen prison officers who, it was alleged, had assaulted the six men at Winson Green prison in Birmingham. Their trial lasted from 10 June to 15 July 1976. None of the prison officers gave sworn evidence in their own defence. Had they done so they could have been cross-examined on that evidence by the prosecution. They simply made an unsworn statement from the dock: "Each said 'It wasn't me'." [55] Their defence called in evidence Dr David Paul, a specialist in forensic medicine. He had examined photographs of the six convicted men which had been taken at a police station before they were remanded to the custody of Winson Green prison. Dr Paul concluded that "careful examination of the photographs and the medical evidence reveals that all the injured men sustained injuries around 24-27 November, 1974 . . . It is obvious that some injuries were sustained prior to the time of the photographs of 24 November. and some between 24 and 27 November." Thus the evidence of the doctor was adverse to the police in that he concluded that the six men had been injured whilst in police custody before the photographs were taken, but that they had also been injured whilst in the custody of the prison officers after the photographs were taken. [56]

After the acquittal of the prison officers, perhaps somewhat surprisingly in view of the evidence of their own witness which implicated someone at Winson Green prison in the violence against the convicted men, the six tried to bring civil proceedings for damage against the Chief Constables of the West Midlands and Lancashire and the Home Office. They claimed damages for injury, and suffering caused by assault and battery whilst in police and prison custody. The police asked the court to strike out the actions against them on the basis that the issue of violence and threats was decided in favour of the police at the criminal trial and that it should not be reopened in a civil action. The police also alleged that the action was an abuse of the process of the court. The Home Office, on the other hand, did not seek a stay or striking out of the civil proceedings against them; they admitted that the men were assaulted after they got to prison and sustained some injury. The only outstanding question therefore in the case against them was the amount of damages each one of the six should be awarded.

The six man wished, on their part, to adduce the fresh evidence, as it was called, of Dr Paul in relation to the injuries shown in the photographs.

Lord Denning who presided over the case in the Civil Division of the Court of Appeal, began his judgement with the statement: "This is the case of the Birmingham bombers."[57]

When the case reached the House of Lords, Lord Diplock said this: "Hunter is one of six murderers ['the Birmingham bombers'] members or supporters of the IRA, the Irish Republican army, who were responsible for planting and exploding two bombs in public houses in the centre of Birmingham on 21st November 1974 . . . "[58]

He goes on to refer to Mr Hunter "and his fellow murderers" and uses the phrase "the Birmingham bombers!" no less than thirteeen times in the course of his speech.

Some of the truth about that case is now known. On 14 March 1991, after some sixteen years in prison, the so called Birmingham bombers were freed by the Criminal Division of the Court of Appeal. Their innocence has now been established, and their confessions were not voluntary and were untrue. Three police officers face charges in connection with their part in the investigation of the two public house bombings.

The House of Lords in Mr Brophy's case had been anxious to uphold a principle of constitutional importance. In the civil action brought by the Birmingham Six, four of the Law Lords concentrated entirely on another legal issue, whether the action for damages was an abuse of the process of the court and seem to disregard the paucity of evidence against the Six. There was no identification evidence, and no identification parade had ever taken place although there must have been people in the two public houses who might have seen the men enter the premises. The confession evidence was contradictory; four of the six seemed not to know how many bombs they planted, for the numbers varied between three and seven; two man said the bombs were carried in parcels, three said in plastic bags – bombs in earlier IRA attacks in England had been concealed in plastic bags.

The forensic evidence, however, not known to the police at the time the confessions were made, was that the explosions were probably caused by two bombs, placed side by side in each of the pubs, and were probably concealed in brief cases. No witness ever came forward to say he saw the incongruous sight of any of the six men, all manual workers, carrying a brief case in the centre of Birmingham on that night of the explosions. One of the six, supposedly a member of an active service unit of the IRA. had to borrow the train fare from a Catholic nun in order to get to Belfast. That was hardly consistent with a plan to escape after the biggest mess murder in British criminal history, and equally inconsistent with an organisation which the House of Lords considers provides tuition in counter interrogation techniques for its members in the IRA. In the case of four of the Birmingham Six, if they were so tutored, the training didn't work either, for they too confessed to crimes which it is now accepted, they did not commit. Nor did it seem strange that five of the men stayed together on the train, openly playing cards on the way to Heysham, rather than splitting up and travelling separately. The sixth man, Hugh Callaghan, who must, if he was a member of the IRA, have been told of the arrest of the other five, was arrested at his home on the evening of the day after the bombings. He had more than twenty-four hours before his arrest in which to make good his escape.

The confession statements said nothing about where the bomb making materials had come from, who supplied them, where they were manufactured and where and by whom the bombs were primed. The men were not even questioned on these matters. Such material, or lack of it, in the confession statements troubled the House of Lords not in the slightest. They were not prepared to allow the fresh evidence of Dr Paul to be admitted in evidence, because they said that the dominant purpose of the action was not to seek damages against the police; it was brought to establish that the confessions were induced by police violence and with a view to putting pressure on the Home Secretary to release them from the life sentences. that they were otherwise likely to serve for many years to come.

The Home Office is no longer concerned in assessing the amount of damages to be paid for the assaults in prison custody; it is now more concerned with paying very substantial sums to the six men for the lost years in prison.

As for Mr Brophy, the postscript in his case is slightly different. The five years sentence of imprisonment he had received at Belfast Crown Court was of course set aside when his conviction of membership of the IRA, which he had admitted, was quashed. On Thursday, 7 November 1991, just over ten years after his being set free, Mr Brophy was in a newsagency shop in Corporation Street near Belfast City Centre when a masked gunman walked in and shot him several times. He was taken to hospital where his condition was described as being "seriously ill" after emergency surgery.[59]

Memories are very long in Northern Ireland.

Chapter 5

SUFFER LITTLE CHILDREN – PART I
THE KILLING OF MAJELLA O' HARE AND JOHN BOYLE

Loyalist death squads went on the rampage in two counties in Northern Ireland in January 1976. On Sunday the 4th, at Ballydougan near Gildford, on the borders of Down and Armagh, three members of the same family, Barry O'Dowd aged 24, his brother Declan aged 19, and their uncle Joseph O'Dowd were shot dead when gunmen burst into the family home. The family were Catholics.

On the evening of that day, Brian Reavey, aged 22, John Martin Reavey, aged 25, and their young brother Anthony were shot at the family home near Whitecross. All three were Catholics. Brian and John died in the house; Anthony survived and was able to tell his father that two gunmen, both dressed in khaki and wearing black masks walked into the house and opened fire, one using a sub-machine-gun. Anthony ran to the bedroom and hid under a bed. One of the gunmen followed him and fired six shots at him from close range. The gunman left, thinking his victim was dead like the others. In fact Anthony was able to crawl to a neighbour's house and summon help; an ambulance took him to Daisy Hill hospital in Newry. His youth and strength seemed to help him to survive the murderous attack, and after three weeks in the hospital he was allowed home. On 30 January, however, he collapsed and died in the house in which he had been shot.[1] He was seventeen years old.

One of the nurses at Daisy Hill hospital was Alice Cambell, aged 22. She was engaged to marry Brian Reavey; their wedding day had long been set for Saturday 14 August 1976. Instead of meeting her bridegroom on what should have been a happy day, arrangements were made for her to visit his grave. She was collected from the hospital at 9 o'clock on the morning by Seamus Reavey, the eldest son of that family. A wreath was bought and together they travelled to Whitecross to collect his father – James Reavey – and Colleen Reavey, aged 8. First, however, Alice went to the old house where Brian had been murdered, and cut some roses from the garden to place on his grave. The four then travelled by car to St. Malachy's Church at Ballymoyer near Whitecross. They arrived at about 11 o'clock.

Alice Cambell and James Reavey carried flowers into the graveyard. Seamus Reavey carried a bucket for water and a knife. As they slowly walked forward, about six soldiers, members of the Royal Marines, and a paratrooper approached them. The paratrooper said, "Seamus Reavey?" and when that was acknowledged he said, "I want a word with you when you are finished."[2]

That incident was also recorded by Brigadier Peter Morton in his memoirs – *Emergency Tour – 3 Para in South Armagh* – even though the Brigadier was not present. He relates how a patrol of five members from B Company 3 Para and six Marines from 40 Commando RM were in the area "to familiarise the Marines with the region and to meet some of the local people in this mixed area where Catholics and Protestants lived contentedly side by side. To this end the patrol commander, Second Lieutenant Nick Kirk, stopped at the entrance to the Ballymoyer cemetery so that he could introduce Seamus Reavey, who was tending a grave there with three other people, to the Marines."[3]

One might be forgiven for thinking that this was to be a friendly and civilised conversation resulting in an open and welcoming introduction to one of the local people by a member of the army. To do this would be to overlook deep-seated distaste which the Nationalist people in that area held then and hold now for the Parachute Regiment and Royal Marines, not merely for their coarse conduct and brutal tactics, but even for their very presence in that part of Northern Ireland.

For his part Seamus Reavey was not anxious to converse with the soldiers. He told Father Raymond Murray (and his statement was recorded that same day, 14 August) that he went to the graves and " . . . tidied up and the others placed some flowers. Alice placed a wreath. I stayed as long as I could, thinking the soldiers might move off, but they stayed about my car. After fifteen to twenty minutes we came back to the car. As I closed the gate the Para called me. I went to open the car to let the others in, when I heard a loud shout: 'Seamus Reavey, come up here or I'll knock the fucking block off you'."

A man who lived nearby, Hugh Kennon, heard and witnessed this conversation and remonstrated with the soldier for his use of such language in an area of peace and repose.

Seamus Reavey's statement continues: "The Para then called a member of the Marines over. He said to him: 'This is a Provo.' I said, 'You are wrong.' The Para then said, 'Meet officer . . . ' – I can't remember his name – 'who will be looking after you for the next four months.' He said, 'What are you doing up here so early in the morning?' I said, 'We were placing flowers on my brothers' graves.' He said, 'What's so special about this morning?' I said, 'One of my dead brothers was to have been married this morning to that girl in the car.' He then started to laugh and said, 'That's some fucking excuse. What are you doing up here?'"

As this conversation was going on, a number of children in a group, some seven girls and two boys, were walking along the left hand side of the road towards St. Malachy's Church. They were going to confession which started at 12 noon. The childrens' ages ranged from 16 years to 3½ years. One of them was twelve year old Majella O'Hare. Majella's father was a council worker; he saw the group of children, including his daughter, approach the Church as he cut the grass around the building. He also saw the two Reaveys in the graveyard and about six soldiers. As he watched, a container lorry which came from the Whitehouse direction was stopped and searched at a vehicle check point.

Brigadier Morton describes that part of the incident:

"As two of the soldiers talked to Seamus Reavey the patrol split into two groups with four men under Lance-Coporal Burton moving just a little down the road to the east where they set up a vehicle check point. To protect this point Burton sent his General Purpose Machine Gun (GPMG) gunner and two others a further fifty metres to the east. The road was undulating and the GPMG was facing downhill looking eastwards and in particular towards the hedges surrounding St. Malachy's Church some 200 metres away."

Morton goes on: "All three groups, those by the churchyard, at the vehicle check point and with the GPMG remembered a group of young girls and boys moving happily down the road towards the church, and some of the soldiers exchanged words with them."[4]

Again one might be forgiven for considering that friendly bantering words might be exchanged between the children and the soldiers, some of whom would not be very much older than the eldest of the children to whom they talked. The truth may be rather different.

One of the girls in the group said that she saw the soldiers lying at a gate in a field. "We did not speak but they spoke to us. He asked us were we going for Communion to visit our God. This man had very brown eyes and black hair. He was sweating a lot. We ignored them and then they said, 'You don't talk to the likes of us.'We pretended to be speaking among ourselves."[5]

The group of children continued to walk down the road towards the Church. Suddenly there was gunfire. The young children started to scream. Majella O'Hare gave a scream and fell. The sixteen year old girl saw her fall on her stomach: "Majella was wearing a nylon blouse and skirt. A hole appeared in the blouse on the right hand side of her back. She rolled over then on her back."[6] She had been shot.

Majella's father had seen the children some twenty-five to thirty yards past the soldiers when he recognised Majella in the group. He heard a bang. "I saw a child fall. Immediately I ran towards the children, about 150 yards. When I got to the point it was my own little girl. She was lying on her left hand side with her head against the brow of the hill. On my way up I noticed the child try to get up on two occasions. On the second time she went down with a bang. I went down on my hunkers and held her up in my arms and the blood pouring from her left hand side. The other children were hysterical, . . . Shortly after a Paratrooper approached and said 'What the fucking hell are you doing here?' I said I was the girl's father. And the next word he said was, 'Close your fucking mouth.' "[7]

Another child in the group gave this version: "At this time Majella's father was up holding her in his arms and he was saying things to her, and one of the soldiers who was applying a field dressing said, 'Shut up.' Jim said, 'She is my daughter,' and the soldier replied, 'I don't give two fucks who she is, take your fucking hands off her.' "[8] This statement, coming from a thirteen year old, surely has a ring of truth about it; if it is true then there can be no words sufficient to condemn the callousness and inhumanity of the soldier who spoke in such terms to James O'Hare at a time when he held his dying daughter in his arms.

At the graveyard Nurse Cambell had heard a loud bang behind her. She thought it was an explosion. Then she thought they had shot Seamus Reavey. She pushed Colleen Reavey down in the back seat of the car and lay down in the front. Seamus Reavey crawled down the roadside and opened the car door and the nurse and the child left the car and lay alongside a wall. A soldier shouted: "That's an armalite." One of the soldiers from the lower part of the road came up and said that a child had been hurt. Nurse Cambell wanted to go to help, but the soldier refused to allow her to leave the spot where they were.

Nurse Cambell states: "After five minutes the soldier took me down by the hand to where the child was lying, a little bit out from the left hand side. The soldier who came with me was shouting for bandages and he was helping me with her. The child was lying on the road. Someone had taken the father to the side. The child was lying on her back. A wound was visible on her abdomen – exit wound. I tried to deal with this. She was semi-concious and groaning. I was tilting her chin with my hand to give her more air, and she pushed my hand aside and muttered, 'Don't do that.' The soldier who was assisting me kept saying 'This is your fucking Provos for you.' "[9]

Majella had been grievously injured. She had received two bullet wounds: there were two small entry holes in her back with two larger (exit) wounds in her abdomen.[10] The parish priest from Whitecross, Father Peter Hughes, had arrived at St. Malachy's Church a few minutes before 12 noon. As he arrived there were soldiers standing around the church gate. One of them shouted at him, "Go on up the road immediately. There's a little girl shot." Father Hughes drove on up the road, and there were a soldier and Alice Cambell with the little girl. The first thing the soldier said to the priest was, "Isn't this a terrible thing, to see a little girl shot by an armalite rifle?"[11]

Soon after a helicopter arrived. James O'Hare was put in first. Nurse Cambell said: "The girl was put in head first with her legs dangling out, the wrong thing to do as it cut off her air supply. She was thrown in on her wounded side. I then got in with a lot of effort. There was very little space for me. They lifted off with the child's legs dangling out. I was kneeling with my red trousered legs out of the helicopter, holding onto a strap. With the help of the father I tried to get her head up. I thumped the soldier on the back and told him to bring the child's legs in and he did so. He said, 'It'll only take five minutes. We have a doctor standing by.' I started to give her the kiss of life in the helicopter and I told the father to start saying the Act of Contrition."[12]

It is stated that James O'Hare was carried by soldiers and put inside the helicopter; such was his grief and shock that he could not walk. But once placed inside the helicopter he was right beside his dying daughter. James O'Hare described the scene in these words: "Majella had her hand in her long hair on her left side, and I could see her moving her hand which I thought she was trying to ease herself. She was hurting. Eventually she took it up my chest near my right shoulder and she says, 'Daddy, Daddy,' in a very faint voice. On the next second she just fell between me and Nurse Cambell and to me she just died . . . I said to Nurse Cambell, 'She's dead.' Nurse Cambell said, 'No,' and gave her the kiss of life about one minute before we landed at the hospital."[13]

That hospital was Daisy Hill in Newry. Majella's mother was told her daughter had been shot and she rushed to the casualty department of the hospital. There she was placed in a room where Nurse Cambell spoke to her and told her they were doing all they could. Then Mrs O'Hare saw the parish priest, Father Hughes. He was crying. "I asked him if Majella was dead, and he said yes."[14]

The British Army, true to form, began to establish the bodyguard of lies. Majella was pronounced dead at 12:10 p.m.[15] At 12:14 in the afternoon of Saturday, 14 August 1976 the army press office at Lisburn issued a statement saying a gunman had opened fire at an army patrol and a twelve year old girl had been hit.[16] The army claimed that "At 11:15 a.m. two or three shots from an automatic weapon had been fired at a foot patrol, who had not returned fire, and a young girl had been found injured.[17]

After this first unequivocal statement, the army's explanation became more convoluted. They said they had returned fire; then resiled from that somewhat by declaring that "fire may have been returned". The final explanation came after 2 p.m. when it was believed that the soldiers had returned fire and the child was caught in the cross-fire.[18]

Brigadier Morton's version of the incident is as follows: "That Saturday morning I was briefing Clare Hollingworth (*Daily Telegraph* Defence Correspondence) on South Armagh's problems and she was accompanied by Brigadier David. The briefing over, a pleasant morning was interrupted by the news that there had been a shooting near Whitecross and in the 'crossfire' between terrorists and a B Company patrol, a young girl had been shot and seriously injured. We finished our pre-lunch drink by which time the story had changed somewhat. The girl was dead and the story of the 'crossfire' was a little less certain. We started our lunch, but halfway through a further message caused me to excuse myself and go straight out to the scene.

"When I arrived there it was far from clear why we were getting such a confused story, but slowly we got nearer to the facts. The confusion of course was reflected in the news bulletins and the story being put out by the Press Desk at Headquarters Northern Ireland, but they all stemmed from the fact that the only soldier who knew what really happened, the patrol's General Purpose Machine Gun (GPMG) gunner, was shocked and frightened because a child had been killed."[19]

What in fact had happened was that Majella O'Hare had been shot, twice, in the back, by that soldier. Questions immediately arise: did the soldiers at the scene near the church lie in their first report of the incident by saying that a terrorist, not a soldier, had shot the young girl, or did the army press office simply invent that version without prompting from anyone? Who was responsible for the second version, that of cross-firing between the army and terrorists (note the plural)?

Brigadier Morton makes an interesting observation that the "principal problem in unravelling what happened was the evidence of the patrol members, five of whom were from B Company 3 Para and six were Marines from 40 Commando RM, *conflicted*." [emphasis added].[20] What the conflict actually was is not explained by the Brigadier. Was there a division on regimental lines – the paras against the marines – and was it a conflict of substance or on a question of minor fact? Which of the conflicting versions, if either, formed the basis for the first report from the army press office? The existence of this "conflict" seems not to suggest an honest and genuine difference of opinion amongst eye-witnesses to an incident which happened very quickly and would be seen from a different position and perspective by different witnesses, but two opposing sides, with one contesting the other's version of the event.

The position of the wounds in Majella's body indicated beyond any doubt that she had been shot from the back, and the only weapon to be fired from behind her, as was eventually admitted, was the General Purpose Machine Gun. Brigadier Morton declared that: "The soldier who fired was one of his men and no matter what his personal opinion of events might be as the story unfolded I intended to back him to the hilt as he would, quite inevitably, face prosecution for his action on that morning. He had been doing his best, and had he hit a gunman rather than a young girl we would have been ecstatic."[21]

This demonstration of loyalty may be commendable, but it is not consistent with the events. The first army version was put out because it was hoped it would be believed. If it had been, no prosecution against anyone was inevitable. Because of the number of people at the scene, none of whom saw any terrorist there or nearby, the army version was not believed. Moreover, the Royal Ulster Constabulary officers at the scene insisted that the machine gun be handed over for forensic inspection. Once that had been done it would have been easy to establish that the shots that killed Majella had been fired from that weapon.

The British press on the following day (Sunday, 15 August) had this to say: "[Majella] was hit by a ricochet from a gunbattle between terrorists and paratroopers . . . An army spokesman said that a foot patrol of the Paratroop Regiment had come under fire as they neared Whitecross church." (*The Sunday Express*). "A twelve-year old was killed . . . in another shooting incident involving troops. The army said later that the girl was caught in crossfire after gunmen [note the plural] had opened up on a foot patrol." (*The Observer*)

The relevance of the comments about the armalite rifle, a weapon traditionally associated with the Provisional IRA, made to Father Hughes, and the immediate reaction of the soldiers to blame that organisation for Majella's death now becomes apparent. Brigadier Morton notes, perhaps with some regret that "as Majella lay mortally wounded in the road her father appeared from the churchyard where he had been cutting the grass in approximately the area where the GPMG gunner had seen his gunman."[22] The plural has now been reduced to the singular – now the story reduces the terrorists to a single gunman, and he for some reason was not seen by James O'Hare or any other civilian at the scene.

That reduction was not the only retreat beaten by the army. The gunner was quite adamant, he told Brigadier Morton, "that he saw a gunmen in the hedge which surrounded the RC Churchyard and on seeing this man he instantaneously cried out, raised his weapon to the shoulder, cocked it and fired. The more he reflected on the event over the next few weeks . . . the more he came to accept that the gunman did not fire at him first and that his action was so instantaneous that he could not have achieved a good sight picture, for had he done so he would surely have seen the young girls and boys."[23]

So the truth, or at least part of it, slowly began to emerge. This soldier who had killed Majella had not returned fire: he had in fact fired first, at a gunman no civilian ever saw. No spent cartridge cases were ever found by anyone in that area then or at any time. In addition, did the soldiers whose evidence was in conflict fail to see that gunman as well?

Brigadier Morton's version has to be read in the light of events described in *The Sunday Times* on 22 August 1976, eight days after Majella's death. The journalist David Blundy notes as follows:

"Majella was shot about 11:45 a.m. According to the first report of the incident issued by the Press desk at the army HQ in Lisburn, it seemed that yet another child had been the victim of terrorist violence. The report, issued at 12:14 p.m. said that a gunman had opened fire on an army patrol in Whitecross in County Armagh, and a twelve year old girl had been hit. It seemed that the army had not returned fire. This report was carried by Belfast's local commercial radio station, Downtown, in its news bulletins at 1 p.m. and 2 p.m. that day.

"But just after 2 p.m. the army's story began to change significantly. The second report said that a gunman had opened fire on the army patrol, and it was "believed" that the army may have returned fire. By 3:30 p.m., the army Press desk said it was then certain that the army had returned fire, but had failed to hit the gunman. Majella O'Hare had died in the crossfire.

"Last week one of the senior army public relations officers at Lisburn said he didn't have the faintest idea why the army had initially denied opening fire. 'We were under pressure from the Press to get a statement out,' he said. 'Perhaps it was over-enthusiasm to get a statement out quickly.' The confusion is puzzling, however, because the one fact the army patrol could have quickly and easily ascertained was whether or not one of the soldiers fired his gun.

"The next day, after the post-morten report on Majella, the Royal Ulster Constabulary issued a statement 'confirming that the fatal bullets probably came from an army weapon. Report that the army came under fire is still under investigation.' The post-mortem revealed that Majella had been hit by two bullets, both of them believed to have been fired by one of the army's general purpose machine-guns.

"But there are still serious doubts about the army's claim that the patrol was fired at by a gunman. Eye-witness reports do not confirm this claim and, unofficially, police investigating the case refer to the army's 'phantom gunman'.

"In fact, police say that the army fired at least three rounds. Majella was hit by two bullets, and these have been found to be army ones. So far they are the only bullets to have been recovered. One short burst from a general purpose machine gun would not make individual explosions, but because of the speed of fire might sound like one loud bang.

"Neither the army nor the police would comment further on the shooting last week. The army repeated the statement put out at 3:30 p.m. on the afternoon of the shooting that an army patrol came under fire from a gunman and shot back."

Assuming that Mr Blundy wrote his article on or about the day before publication and did his research into the case within a few days preceding that, it is clear that, notwithstanding Brigadier Morton's account that the soldier who shot Majella was accepting that he fired first and was not returning fire, the army was not yet ready by 22 August to admit that fact to the press. The attraction of the cross-fire version clearly was that it could always be assumed, by those who wished to do so, that the fatal bullets were fired by the terrorists and not by the army. Of course, given the fact that the victim was a twelve year old child, the soldier could hardly say he saw Majella reaching into a pocket or a bag, intending to press a button to detonate a bomb or reach for a firearm, and that left little room for manoeuvre. It may be that only the story that was eventually settled on, that of the phantom gunman was the only one ultimately available. If the two other members of the patrol who accompanied the machine gunner to the point fifty metres to the east of the vehicle check point saw the phantom gunman, then Brigadier Morton omits to mention it. Had they done so he could hardly have failed to cite their evidence as supporting that of the soldier who killed Majella.

In April 1977 that soldier was put on trial for the unlawful killing of Majella O'Hare. On 2 May 1977 he was found not guilty on the ground that the honestly held belief, even if mistaken, that he was firing at a gunman would amount to a defence in law to the charge. No one in the Nationalist community in Northern Ireland was surprised in the least at the verdict. In fact it was probably expected in the light of the decision in the case of Regina versus MacNaughton, heard by the then Lord Chief Justice of Northern Ireland, Lord Lowry in September 1974.

The accused in Mac Naughton's case was a British Army sergeant. He was in command of an eight-man foot patrol in the border area of

159

South Armagh, when he shot and wounded John Martin Walsh, on 7 April 1973. Mr Walsh, who lived in a farmhouse nearby, was wearing an overcoat and wellington boots when he encountered the foot patrol; it was alleged that he was coming from the direction of an explosion where there had been military casualties. (The distance between that place and the point where he was detained by the soldiers is not stated in the law report.) He had in his possesion a piece of folded plastic. Mr Walsh said he had been feeding the cattle; the plastic sheet had been a bag in which animal footstuff could be stored. He had seen the plastic bag as he was walking home and he picked it up because it would be dangerous if cattle were tempted to chew at it.

There were two conflicting versions of what happened next. According to Mr Walsh he was challenged by the patrol then subjected to violence and threats and forced to lie down. Various threats were repeated and his life was threatened. One soldier, Sergeant MacNaushton, advised him to try to make a run for it and escape. When Walsh would not do so he was eventually ordered by the Sergeant to get over a fence to the flank of the patrol. When Walsh did so the Sergeant shot him just after he got over the fence. There was talk, according to Walsh, of finishing him off and an attempt made to smother him.

Sergeant MacNaughton denied this, saying that Mr Walsh had tried to escape over the fence, and that after calling on him three times to halt, he failed to do so, and the Sergeant then shot him with the self-loading rifle he was carrying. That account was supported in broad outline by other members of the army patrol. The Lord Chief Justice considered that there seemed not to have been much chance for the soldiers to collaborate in a false account of what happened, and their version was consistent with the case which was made by Sergeant MacNaughton a few hours after the incident in his statement to the military police. Whether he simply handed the military police a written statement prepared by himself or with others is not known. What is known is that, unlike any ordinary civilian in Northern Ireland, he was not subjected to the investigative process including interrogation to test the truth and accuracy of his account, by the RUC.

The trial judge rejected Mr Walsh's version of events. He thought it "more likely that he broke away thinking, that once over the fence, he might make good his escape." This was risky and no doubt extremely foolish, said Lord Lowry, but he may have considered that the alternative was certain arrest and accusation of serious crime. Why Mr Walsh should have ever let that thought cross his mind defies comprehension, since after he recovered from his injuries he was never charged or, as far as is known, ever questioned about any terrorist offence. He had not the slightest reason to fear arrest or accusation and to flee from the patrol. He had not the remotest chance of escaping from eight heavily armed soldiers. Mr Walsh knew the countryside; would he have chosen to run at a spot where he was faced with a formidable obstruction of a fence which would slow if not stop his progress away from the patrol? Would it not have been easier to choose a more convenient place and to elect to run downhill into the cover of trees or undergrowth if he really wished to make good his attempt at escape?

As for the talk of finishing him off, the tendency may be to reject that out of hand; the security forces in Northern Ireland would find that type of conduct repellent and would reject it. In February 1985, however, Martin McCauley gave evidence to Belfast Crown Court. He stated that he was shot and wounded by the RUC (together with Michael Justin Tighte who died) at a hayshed in County Armagh in November 1982. A gun was held against his head by a policeman who spoke of finishing him off. What Mr McCauley did not know, and the policeman didn't know either, was that the entire events at the hayshed, the voices, the shots and the events afterwards, had been recorded on tape by a police and army technical unit. The attempts by John Stalker, the former Deputy Chief Constable of Greater Manchester Police, to obtain that tape have been well documented.

Stalker never did obtain it. If Mr McCauley had been lying about his evidence of the threat to finish him off, the very side that would have benefited most by producing the tape, namely the Security Forces in Northern Ireland, did not do so. In fact, rather than produce the tape to Mr Stalker, he was maligned and then removed from the inquiry he was conducting.

In the event it may be that the Lord Chief Justice could not accept Mr Walsh's evidence on the threats to finish him off, and that being so found it easier to reject his evidence on other, more material, points as well. He acquitted Sergeat MacNaughton of attempted murder and causing grievous bodily harm on the ground that there had been a lawful arrest . The accused was entitled to use reasonable force to prevent an escape. Sergeant MacNaughton's evidence, which was more cogent and consistent than Mr Walsh's, raised a triable issue that the force used to prevent the escape was reasonable in the circumstances. The burden of proving beyond reasonable doubt that the force used was unreasonable lay on the prosecution, and they had failed to discharge this legal burden.

In the light of that decision the Nationalist people of Northen Ireland never expect a conviction against a member of the security forces charged with murder or wounding.

Majella O'Hare had been the fiftieth innocent victim to die by the guns of the British Army in the space of four years.[24] Apart from the most terrible tragedy for her and her family and friends, there was one political casualty in the case as well. Mr Seamus Mallon, a moderate and committed member of the Social Democratic and Labour Party and member of the Westminster Parliament for the area, had accepted the truth of the initial statements of the army and publicly blamed the IRA for Majella's death. When some of the truth eventually emerged, he complained about the army having issued false statements to the police, to the media and to himself. That complaint did not stem the flow of lies or change the army's practices and procedures in the north of Ireland then or at any time thereafter.

There may be those who consider that the death of this young girl in such tragic circumstances was an isolated incident so far as the Securiity Forces were concerned. The facts prove otherwise. Amongst the list of children under the age of 15 who have died in the current round of the troubles in Northern Ireland are the following:

Patrick Rooney, aged 9 years, shot dead in a bedroom in the Divis Flats in Belfast on September 14, 1969 by a member of the RUC;

Desmond Healey, aged 14 years, shot dead by the army in Anderstown, Belfast on 9 August 1971 (Frank McGuinness, aged 15, was also shot dead by the army in West Belfast on the same day when internment without trial was introduced into Northern Ireland.);

Annette McGavigan, aged 14, shot dead in Derry on 6 September 1971 by the army; the allegation was that she, like Majella O'Hare, was hit in "cross-fire";

Francis Rowntree, aged 11 years, shot in the head with a rubber bullet fired at him at point blank range by the army in the Divis Flats area of Belfast on 23 April 1972;

Kevin Heatley, aged 12, shot in the head by the army in Newry on 28 February 1973 (This case is mentioned in outline in Chapter 1 of this book.);

Stephen Geddis, aged 10, hit in the head with a plastic bullet fired by a soldier of the Royal Anglian Regiment in West Belfast on 28 August 1975. Stephen died two days later. He had just returned home to Ireland after a three week holiday in the United States, sponsored by the National Society for the Prevention of Cruelty to Children;

Brian Stewart, aged 13, hit in the face by a plastic bullet fired by a soldier of the the Kings' Own Scottish Borderers in the Turf Lodge Area of West Belfast on 4 October 1976. Brian died six days later;

Paul Whitters, aged 15, shot with a plastic bullet fired at fairly close range by a constable of the RUC on 10 April 1981, in Derry. Paul died ten days later;

Julie Livingstons, aged 14, hit on the head by a plastic bullet fired by a soldier in an army saladin armoured car in the Lenadoon area of West Belfast on 12 May 1981;

Carol Ann Kelly, aged 12, shot with a plastic bullet by an army patrol on May 19, 1971 in West Belfast. Carol died three days later;

Stephen McConomy, aged 11 years, shot in the City of Derry with a plastic bullet fired at fairly close range by the army on 19 April 1982.

On Monday, 4 July 1983, the Northern Catholic Bishops issued a statement entitled "Ban Plastic Bullets" and made reference to the findings following the inquest iinto Stephen McConomy's death that he was shot from a range of seventeen feet.

There were no prosecutions in any of the foregoing cases, except the two mentioned in the text, namely those involving the deaths of Kevin Heatley and Majella O'Hare. However, when two soldiers of the SAS shot and killed sixteen year old John Boyle on 11 July 1978, a prosecution did follow. These are the circumstances:

John had been a pupil at our Lady of Lourdes School, Ballymoney in County Antrim. He was the second youngest of eight children, seven boys and a girl. The family had a farm near Dunloy, a mixed Catholic and Protestant area in the north of the County. On the afternoon of Monday, 10 July 1978 John had been haymaking with his brother Hugh on the farm. At about 4 o'clock he decided to walk across a narrow lane to a disused graveyard to look for some ancestral names on the gravestones. Beneath a headstone that had fallen forward John found a number of items of use to a terrorist.

However, what he actually found depends on what account of the case one reads. Father Raymond Murray says[25] that John found " . . . an arms cache in a plastic bag . . . The cache included an armalite rifle, a revolver, an incendiary bomb, a face mask, combat jacket and black beret." According to Desmond Hammil[26] he found " . . . a polythene package which contained an armalite." Tony Geraghty's history of the SAS contends[27] John found " . . . a blue plastic sack hidden under one of the gravestones . . . It contained a detonator cap, cordex fuse, what appeared to be gelignite bound with black tape and, in a separate fertilizer bag, what appeared to be a rifle. The cache also contained a revolver." In their book *Ambush – The War Between the SAS and the IRA*, three *Sunday Times* journalists – James Adams, Robin Morgan and Anthony Bambridge – narrate that John found " . . . a plastic fertilizer bag" and list the contents similar to those listed by Father Murray.[28]

Whatever was found, John did the sensible thing and told his older brother Hugh. Together they told their father Cornelius Boyle. He in turn telephoned the RUC station at Ballymoney to tell them of the graveyard find. According to Tony Geraghty the detective constable to whom Cornelius Boyle spoke "said he would have the matter attended to. Later that day, this constable and three other RUC man checked the bag."[29] In the light of subsequent events, one wonders why, if they did not remove the firearms, at the very least, they ensured that neither the rifle nor the revolver could be fired, and remove any ammunition there or nearby.

The *Sunday Times* journalists write[30] that "The police passed the information to an army captain who was acting as liaison officer with the RUC from his base at Ebrington Barracks, Londonderry. It was decided that a four man team from the SAS would move into the graveyard, under cover of darkness, to keep the arms under surveillance. As is usual in these cases, the army captain was briefed by the RUC, and he in turn passed all relevant information to the SAS." This account may give rise to the inference that there was no direct contact between the RUC and the SAS because the information was relayed from one to the other by means of the army captain, and that in the process there was a danger of something being said and not fully explained or explored or misunderstood, or else some material detail might have been omitted in the process.

That inference would not be correct, for as the then Lord Chief Justice of Northern Ireland, Lord Lowry noted at the subsequent trial[31] " . . . at about midnight a briefing was held at Ballymoney Police Station at which members of the Special Air Service (SAS) stationed at Ballykelly were present. First there was a conference upstairs in the police station at which the police gave information to the SAS, including a captain whom I shall call Soldier F. It was thought that the cache might have been left in the graveyard with a view to collecting it and using it for offensive purposes during the Twelfth of July demonstrations. On this assumption there was a good chance that a terrorist might return to the graveyard in the immediate future, and accordingly it was arranged that a patrol of four men, consisting of Soldiers A, B, D and E and under the command of Soldier A, would go to the graveyard and keep watch with a view to effecting his arrest.

"The patrol had assembled in a downstairs room at the Police Station and, on conclusion of the conference upstairs, was briefed by Soldier F and one of the police, a detective constable who knew where the cache was and was also able to brief the patrol on the surrounding geographical features and roads and tell them something about the inhabitants of the neighbouring countryside. He also showed an army driver where the entrance to the graveyard was."

Thus it is abundantly clear that in fact the RUC officer had spoken directly to the SAS soldiers, and there was thus no possibility of error in the conveying of information from him to them by means of a third party. That fact does not prevent Messrs Adams, Morgan and Bambridge from making a false point. They say,[32] "First, the RUC said that the arms had been found by a boy or young man. *By the time that information reached the SAS patrol, the description had been translated to 'found by a child'* " [emphasis added]. In other words, in the course of repetition of the original description a mistake had been made. However, that could not have happened because the information was conveyed not through any conduit but directly from the detective constable to the four soldiers who went to the graveyard.

Desmond Hamill records that "Sergeant Bohan, who was to lead the SAS patrol, had already been to the graveyard with the detective constable . . . "[33] Nonetheless there was no time apparently to check whether the armalite or the revolver were loaded. A deadly weapon might have been available for use to anyone who picked it up there, and a visit by the RUC and the army had not made that weapon safe for whoever might challenge the collector of the weapons at the cache. Father Raymond Murray poses this question on this point: "How could security forces who plan a stake-out possibly leave their own personnel in danger by leaving loaded weapons as bait and allow the person or persons coming to retrieve them to take such loaded weapons in their hands?" His comment is that, to the public, this is incredible.

Such a viewpoint fails to take into account the reason the SAS were staking out the graveyard and not the RUC. Whatever may have been said to the contrary, this was not an arrest operation. The SAS simply did not want to know whether the weapons were loaded or not. If they had checked and did know that the armalite and revolver were unloaded they could not have justified either in law or in fact their decision to open fire on John Boyle. Such conduct would have been unlawful. The test in law of whether reasonable force has been used in self-defence is an objective one. The tribunal must be satisfied that the accused was reasonable in considering it necessary to use force to defend himself against the victim

In applying this test, account should be taken of all the circumstances in which the accused was placed, including in particular the nature and degree of force used on each side, the relative strength on each side, the seriousness of the evil to be prevented (or of the offence for which an arrest is being made) and the possibility of preventing it by other means.

Thus if the SAS soldiers at the graveyard knew John Boyle effectively posed no threat against them, because any firearm in the cache was unloaded, to shoot him dead would not be lawful self-defence.

The four-man SAS patrol was driven to the graveyard at about 2:30 a.m. They took up positions. Soldiers D and E were concealed in an observation post in a disused farm building on the road opposite the path to the graveyard. Their main task was to observe anyone approaching the cemetery and to keep in contact with their two colleagues by pocket phone. Sergeant Bohan and Corporal Temperley were concealed in a hide between a hedge and a stone wall about twelve yards from the cache. They sat back to back, so that one was facing the approach to the gravestone and the other was looking directly at it. It was the army's case that they did not expect any member of the Boyle family to return to the cache. The detective constable told the soldiers that he had warned his informant to keep away from the graveyard and he would repeat this warning. This version was given to the court by the army liason officer. The detective constable, on the other hand, said that at the midnight meeting he had warned the army officers (whose names he was never given) on at least three occasions during the briefing that the information had come from a family with children between the ages of ten and twenty-four, and advised them to be careful in case any returned to the scene out of curiosity.

The detective constable was on duty until 2:30 a.m. on 11 July. At 9:40 a.m. he did telephone the Boyle household and asked that no member of the family should go to the graveyard. John and his brother Hugh had left the house ten minutes before the phone call.

Around 10 a.m. John Boyle went to the graveyard. He drove from the field in which he had been haymaking to the entrance of the graveyard in a tractor. He could hardly have drawn more attention to his presence such was the noise that accompanied his approach. Soldiers D and E apparently did nothing to inform Bohan and Temperley of John's approach; in the circumstances a warning was hardly necessary. Apparently they saw nothing of what happened next, because it was alleged their view was obstructed by the wheels of the tractor.

John opened the gate and walked into the graveyard, passing within nine feet of the two concealed SAS men. According to them he walked straight to the arme cache, knelt down, pulled out a bag and pulled an armalite rifle (the butt of which had been protruding) out of the bag. He then, according to Bohan, held the rifle in his right and left hand, with the left hand on the stock, and turned round in a left-handed turn to face Sergeant Bohan and Corporal Temperley, bringing the armalite rifle to bear on them.[34] They both fired their rifles and shot John Boyle

166

in the head, neck and trunk.

According to the post-mortem report of the assistant state pathologist Dr J.R. Press, a bullet had entered the right hand side of the back of the head and fragmented. Some fragments lodged within the skull, while the remainder passed forwards lacerating the brain before making their exit on the upper left eyelid. Two bullets had entered the back of the right upper chest where they fragmented, and some fragments passed fowards and upwards, lacerating the right lung, the oesophagus, the pharynx and the right common carotid artery before lodging in the muscles on the right side of the neck; other fragments passed downwards and forwards, fracturing the fifth right rib and lacerating the right lung, the stomach and the liver before lodging beneath the skin on the right side of the chest.[35] In the pathologist's view, John Boyle had been shot from the back.

Hugh Boyle heard the shots and ran from the field into the graveyard. The soldiers detained him and made him lie face down for two and a half hours. During that time he was threatened several times that he would be shot if he looked around.[36] His father told the *Newsletter* newspaper: "Knowing my two boys were working down there I went to see what was happening. I was aware that people were around somewhere so I stopped short of the field and soldiers surrounded me. They were in uniform with blackened faces and there was no visible transport. They ordered me to lie face downwards and they kept me that way for about an hour." He heard one soldier in the background say "We have got the bastard – he's lying over there."[37] He and his son Hugh were handed over to the RUC.

Almost at once the army propaganda machine went into over-drive; it needed to in order to justify and explain the brutal killing of an innocent sixteen year old. Not unexpectedly, there was a mixture of truth and lies in the information that was put out to the media by the army press office.

The first statement said " . . . at approximately 10:22 this morning near Dunloy a uniformed military patrol *challenged three men.* [emphasis added] One man was shot; two men are assisting police enquiries. Weapons and explosives have been recovered."[38]

To their credit the RUC also issued a statement. It contained the entire truth: "An incident occurred at an old graveyard at Dunloy when a young man was shot dead and two arrested. Both have since been released. The police are satisfied that the three men were not connected with terrorism."[39]

The army issued a further statement. Again it raises the question: just who provided the detail set out in the statement? Was it the soldiers directly involved or others at the scene? Or did the press office simply get some basic information and put out a mixture of simple fact and acceptable fiction to paint a picture of the army in the best possible light?

In this statement the army said: "On Monday July 11, a two-man patrol operating in the area of Dunloy graveyard heard a tractor approaching the graveyard. It stopped and shortly afterwards a man ran into the graveyard, went to a gravestone and reached under it. At this point the man saw the two soldiers and he straightened up pointing an armalite rifle at them. The soldiers fired five rounds at the armed man who was killed. The armalite was subsequently found with its magazine fitted and a round in the breech ready to fire. In addition, a blast incendiary bomb, a revolver, a mask, a combat jacket and a beret were found under the gravestone. A man leaving the scene on the tractor was arrested by the army, and a third man who arrived shortly afterwards in a car was also detained. Both were handed over to the police."[40]

The so called patrol consisted in fact of four men, not two. The four lay in ambush, and were not moving on patrol around the countryside. John Boyle walked into the graveyard, he did not run. He was hit by three shots, and if five were fired then two must have missed him completely. The biggest lie however, straight from the standard textbook of the Joseph Goebbel's school of Nazi propaganda, was that the armalite was subsequently found with its magazine fitted and there was a round in the breech ready to fire. In fact the gun was unloaded. Whoever constructed that gigantic lie, whether a soldier or a civilian press officer, has much to answer for.

There wasn't a man leaving the scene on a tractor; the inference being of course that the tractor involved was the same one that had approached the graveyard; Hugh Boyle had been working on a tractor also hay making, and he was approaching the graveyard, not leaving it when he was detained, and it was his father who had arrived in the car.

The army shifted ground again when it was admitted that, although it was stated initially that a challenge was given, a detailed investigation found this was incorrect. "It was impracticable for the soldiers to issue a warning before firing as the man was ten yards away from them pointing a rifle in their direction."[41]

The RUC began an investigation. There must have been a sense of outrage within that force at the killing of a young, innocent lad who, with his family, had been responsible enough to report the finding of the cache in the graveyard to the RUC the day before. That outrage would not have been eased by the propaganda statements put out by the army. The investigating officers did not formally interview the SAS soldiers.

Instead they were handed written statements by a major in the army's legal service.[42]

Sergeant Bohan made two written statements, one of which contradicts the other on a point of some importance. In the first he said: "Believing that our lives were in imminent danger I aimed and fired." In his judgement, the trial judge, Lord Lowry considered that "One possible inference from the first statement is that A took deliberate aim, not being in a situation of emergency."[43]

This is difficult to follow. Bohan said in clear unequivocal terms he aimed his rifle and fired it – two deliberate, concious, purposeful and separate movements. How can aiming a rifle be anything other than deliberate? Can such a thing be done accidently? Someone had realised the significance of this admission which points beyond any doubt to the fact that Bohan had the opportunity to aim and fire his rifle, rather than a swift reaction to the rifle which in the words of the army's statement was held by " . . . the man . . . ten yards from them pointing in *their direction*" [emphasis added].

In Bohan's second statement to the RUC this was put right. In it he said: "Believing our lives to be in danger I fired."[44] No longer did he fire aimed shots. Lord Lowry observed, without further comment: "Soldiers A and B handed the draft of statements to the police which they had prepared with help from a legal officer . . . "[45] One wonders what form that help took. Why was it not thought right to allow each of these two soldiers to write in their own time and in their own way their own version of the events starting at the beginning and going on until the end? Were these not two experienced soldiers? In his judgment Lord Lowry refers to soldier A as Corporal Allan Michael Bohan, when all the other literature about the case refers to him as a sergeant. Lord Lowry refers to Ronald Joseph Temperley, Soldier B, as a trooper, whereas everyone else who has written about the case refers to him as a corporal. Whatever their rank, however long their years of service, they were experienced enough to be entrusted with the stake-out in the graveyard.

However, did the help from the legal officer, which the judge referred to, amount to tailoring the evidence, and cutting, changing and editing that evidence? After all, in the last analysis, is there only one version of the truth, but were the army anxious to disclose or conceal that truth? The first statements were handed to the RUC on the afternoon of the shooting, 11 July, and "further and much more elaborate statements" on 7 August. These statements "foreshadowed the defence of self-defence" which soldier A advanced in his evidence at the trial.

When John Boyle was shot two rifles were clearly used. The RUC did not get their serial numbers. Lord Lowry noted "No information was put before me (until Soldier A himself gave evidence) as to the serial numbers of rifles issued to A and B; as against that, rifles which included *the one from which one of the bullets* was fired were given to the forensic experts by the military staff at Ballykelly" [emphasis added].[46]

What does this mean? Why was there a failure or refusal to give the RUC a simple piece of information, namely the serial numbers of the rifles fired by Bohan and Temperley? Why did the military staff at Ballykelly give the forensic experts a number of rifles (that clearly means more than two for if it was two why not say so) and included in that number was *one* which was fired in the graveyard?

When the Lord Chief Justice dealt with the wounds to John Boyle's body he noted: "One bullet entered the head of the deceased. This would have been enough to kill him instantly. Two other bullets entered his body. To judge by the forensic science report, one of these was fired by a rifle the serial number of which differed from that of the rifle claimed in evidence by soldier A to have been his rifle."[47] That seems to suggest that one of the two bullets in the body clearly was not fired by Soldier A, but the other bullet was. However, Lord Lowry goes on to contradict that by stating, "It may reasonably certainly be inferred from the close and parallel position of the two body wounds that the bullets which caused them came from Soldier B's rifle and that Soldier A hit the deceased in the head."[48]

Any difficulty or ambiguity that arose here would never have arisen if the army had properly disclosed the evidence about the two rifles used to fire the fatal shots at John Boyle.

As John lay dead, "Soldier A sent a pocket phone message to Soldiers D and E (who had been concealed outside the graveyard) saying, 'Contact. Get QRF,' meaning the Quick Reaction Force. He then went forward and conducted a negative search of the body for weapons and documents and went down the avenue ('by fire and movement,' he said) with B to the main road."[49] The two then left the scene.

At the trial the prosecution had an amazing allegation to make about what had happened shortly after the killing. Leading Counsel for the Crown, instructed by the Director of Public Prosecutions for Northern Ireland, was Mr Michael Nicholson Q.C., a very distinguished and experienced advocate and now a High Court Judge in Northern Ireland. The way in which it was raised is summarised by the Lord Chief Justice. "Before proceeding to a conclusion, I must advert to what may be styled the alleged cover-up, as put foward on behalf of the Crown. And here it is necessary to be careful, since proof merges with assertion and the army as such are not represented in these proceedings or charged with

170

anything. It was suggested that the scene was set by the army before the police arrived, in that the tombstone was tilted up and the contents of the cache scattered to give the impression of a terrorist caught at his work."[50]

On what evidence did Counsel for the Crown base that suggestion? Was it true? And if it was, then this was the clearest evidence of perverting the course of justice by the British Army. Since Sergeant Bohan admitted searching the body – and tipping out the contents of the bag – standing or crouching in the immediate vicinity of the gravestone and the arms cache, no suggestion can now ever be made that the reason the arms cache was not examined the previous night, in order to check whether the guns were loaded, was through fear of a booby-trap.

More sinister still, however, was the point noted by Lord Lowry that, "Despite a careful search by the police only one spent case was found, although no fewer than three rounds were fired and one possible inference – or speculation – is that someone destroyed evidence."[51]

The army's original press statement refers to the firing of five, not three rounds. If the person who removed spent cases had done so accidently or without realising their evidential significance, then there seemed no reason why he should not have come forward to say so. The fact of the matter may be that, in the course of concealing the truth about what happened in the graveyard, someone not only interfered with the evidence by scattering the contents of the cache, but also removed vital evidence from the scene. To have done that would have required an instaneous decision on the spot. It wasn't until later that the army discovered that the lad who was dead was the one who initially found the cache. If it was honestly, reasonably and genuinely believed at the outset that a terrorist had been shot, why was it ever necessary to tamper with, and remove, vital pieces of evidence from the graveyard?

Sergeant Bohan gave sworn evidence in his own defence from the witness box. The two statements he had made formed part of the prosecution case against him and were adduced in evidence by the prosecution. In the second statement, dated 7 August 1978, Bohan said that a detective constable had taken him to the graveyard with another soldier and had briefed him about the area. The detective had also assured him that the family who found the bundle under the gravestone would not be back to the site of the find. "I believed we would be up against armed terrorists. Our mission was to capture the terrorists. To apprehend a terrorist would be of great value for long-term intelligence." He said that when he saw the boy at the gravestone on the morning of 11 July, he thought the boy was a terrorist whose photograph he had seen and who was believed to be an expert in explosives.

171

These matters, which formed a fundamental part of his case, were put by the defence to the RUC detective in cross-examination. He denied on oath that he had suggested the name of a man wanted by the police as a possible collector of the bomb and weapons in the graveyard. He also denied mentioning any particular person to the army officers, whose names he did not know, who were at the first briefing at the police station.[52]

The Sunday Times journalists see no difficulty on this point. They recite the army line as though it was the clear, unvarnished, unchallenged truth: "In their final briefing before they left for the stake-out, the SAS men were told that a wanted IRA terrorist, Eugene O'Neill, was in the area and it was suspected the arms might have been left for him."[53] Desmond Hamill's version reflects the conflict between the army and the RUC. "There was no doubt, though, about police anger over the affair; anger at both another killing by soldiers in a stake-out, and at the apparent immunity of the army. The atmosphere of the courtroom changed noticeably so that the case became almost a trial not so much of murder but of the policy that had put the soldiers with their blackened faces and high velocity weapons there in the first place. The mutual suspicion of the police and the army came through clearly. The detective constable bristled with indignation when it was suggested that he had told the army the name of his informant or given personal information about other Catholic families. Time and time again his answers started with the phrase 'I did not tell the army . . . "[54]

Such mutual distrust and suspicion says much about the situation in Northern Ireland at that time. If the detective had mentioned the name of Eugene O'Neill why should he deny that in evidence on oath? The army, for its part, was determined to reinforce its case that the soldiers in the graveyard were told to expect the arrival of a terrorist, one who was specifically named and dangerous, and that was whom they thought confronted them.

Sergeant Bohan's statement continued: "I did not challenge because of the possibility of other terrorists supporting him. He started to remove the rifle from the bag, and turned, bringing it to bear on us. We fired and he fell."[55] Tony Geraghty adds to that sentence: "I fired not more than twice and probably once."[56] Thus it is apparent that the army press office had got the five shots fired from: one or two fired by Bohan, three fired by Temperley.

Corporal Temperley also made written statements to the RUC, but he did not give evidence in his own defence on oath at the trial. He was quite entitled to do this, and the court could not and did not draw any inference of guilt from this failure to give evidence.

The legal position in Northern Ireland has now changed, since the Criminal Evidence (Northern Ireland) Order 1988 came into law on 15 December 1988. That Order provides that the court, in determining whether the accused is guilty of the offence charged, may draw such inferences from the accused's silence as appear proper. On the basis of such inference, the silence may be treated as, or as capable amounting to, corroboration of any evidence against the accused which is material. For the purpose of the Order silence is: (1) a failure to mention particular facts when questioned or charged; (2) a refusal to be sworn in court, or having been sworn, to answer questions without good cause; or (3) a failure or refusal to account for objects, marks on person, clothing etc.; and (4) a failure or refusal to account for presence at a particular place.

If that Order had been in force in 1979 one can only speculate about whether Corporal Temperley's in-court silence would have been treated as evidence against him.

In his statement he said he saw the young man standing with the weapon at his right side at hip level. "Sergeant Bohan stood up, and I thought he was going to make a challenge. There was a noise like the rustling of clothing or branches. The man turned round and the rifle came up, pointing towards the observation post. Sergeant Bohan fired, then I fired three shots at 'single fire'." Templerley also alleged in his statement that at the briefing with the police they were told that the cache had been discovered by a ten year old child.[57] When this was put, as it had to be, in cross-examination to the detective constable, he denied it. It must have been clear to the court that on this issue, as on several others, one side or the other was lying. Why in fact the detective constable should ever have told the army that a ten year old child had found the cache is not understood. That did not happen; he knew it had not happened, and there was no need for him to say it had. This statement is entirely self-serving by the army. If a ten year old child had found the cache, then since John Boyle clearly looked older than ten, he could not have been that person, and if he was not, then he was a terrorist.

The matter did not end there. Leading Counsel for the defence was Mr Michael Lavery Q.C., a senior and experienced advocate who is one of the most formidable cross-examiners in the criminal courts in these Islands. According to the summing-up of the trial judge, when the detective constable was giving evidence, it was put to him first that he had told the army that a ten year old child had found the cache and second that a ten year old girl had found it. In putting these matters Counsel was following the convention required by the criminal courts of putting his case to the witnesses for the other side: if Soldier A proposed to say in his defence evidence that that RUC officer had told him the cache was found by a ten year old girl, then when that officer gave his evidence the convention required that this be put to the witness so the witness could accept it or deny it. Failure to put a material point to a witness may result in that witness having to be recalled, so that the point can be properly put. Alternatively, if a defence witness mentions in his evidence something which was not put to an opposing witness, it might be suggested that because it was never put in cross-examination it has just been invented and fabricated by that witness.

Mr Michael Lavery is much too exact, methodical and capable to have made a mistake on this point. He must have had specific instructions to put to the prosecution witness the allegation that the detective constable had told the soldiers that the cache had been found by a ten year old girl.

In the event the trial judge made no comment about the fact that when Sergeant Bohan gave his evidence he appeared to refer only to the *child* and not a girl; the witness was never pressed for a reason why it was suggested in cross-examination the finder was a girl. In the event, however, Lord Lowry said that on this point he found Bohan's evidence to be untrue.[58] Given the straight conflict of credibility between the detective constable and sergeant, the judge believed the constable's version on this point.

The sergeant could have been in a further difficulty. As noted already, Temperley said in his written statement that "Sergeant Bohan stood up . . ." In that form, this was not evidence against the sergeant, because it was not on oath and was probably not made in his presence. Therefore, he did not have the opportunity, at the time it was made, to challenge and deny it. If Temperley had gone into the witness box at the trial, and if he had repeated this point, then it would be evidence against Sergeant Bohan. The real relevance of whether he stood up or not related to his defence. He was so well concealed in the hide that John Boyle passed within three yards of him and failed to note his presence. He said did not issue a challenge "because of the possibility of other terrorists supporting him." Yet Soldiers D and E, who were in contact by pocket phone, would have warned him of the presence of others had there been anyone else approaching the graveyard. In standing up, when he could have challenged from the concealed position, did he not present himself as an easier and more accessible target for others and especially for the so called terrorist in the graveyard, who had been allowed to pick up a rifle?

In cross-examination Sergeant Bohan was unable to remember

whether he had fired at John from a sitting position or a standing position. That might be regarded by some as a rather convenient partial loss of memory. Moreoever, it is hardly likely that Temperley would have said in his statement that "Sergeant Bohan stood up . . ." unless that had actually happened. Nor was Bohan able to remember whether he fired from the hip or the shoulder; nor could he say what of part of John Boyle's body he had fired at.

All this may be contrasted with the original version he put forward in his first written statement that "believing that our lives were in imminent danger I aimed and fired." That "aiming" had been abandoned by the time the second written statement was made, and the reason for doing so was now apparent at the trial. The changed version of the event suited the defence very well.

Prosecuting Counsel made substantial inroads on Bohan's credibility as a witness. So much so that in his judgment Lord Lowry said of the sergeant: "I found him to be, on the whole, an untrustworthy witness, easer to make unmeritorious points . . ."[59]

Only three people knew the exact truth of what had happened in the graveyard: John Boyle, who was dead; Corporal Temperley, who did not say what he knew on oath in evidence, so his version was never subject to the searching test of cross-examination; and Sergeant Bohan, who was untrustworthy. In it at least one specific point relating to the finder of the cache he was expressly found by the trial judge to be lying.

Lord Lowry found Bohan to be lying on another issue as well. The judge said: "I should explain that no responsible person has said a word either expressly or by implication against the standing and respectability of the Boyle family . . . Soldier A [Bohan], however, in the course of his evidence seemed to say that the deceased not only appeared to aim his rifle at A and B but was actually doing so. Considering that the weapon was not loaded, this statement may be regarded as self-justificatory and, in the context of the Boyle family's reputation, untrue."[60]

Sergeant Bohan also maintained in evidence that there was a "plan to capture whoever came to the cache but was vague and unsatisfactory when questioned as to the details of the plan."[61] It is difficult to avoid the conclusion that unless the witness was willing and able to give details of the supposed plan to capture, which surely would have been straightforward and easy enough to do, then no such plan ever existed.

Sergeant Bohan admitted that he left cover and ran to the body of the deceased after shooting him despite his fear that there might have been other terrorists nearby. He further admitted that he removed the plastic bag from its position, and accepted that photographs taken by the scenes-of-crime officers gave the impression that John Boyle had just emptied the cache when he had been shot. "The truth was that he lifted the plastic bag at the boy's feet and emptied the contents out."[62]

In the light of all this it would not have been surprising if both soldiers had been convicted of murder. The judge, however, acquitted them both. His decision was greatly influenced by the medical evidence in the case.

The post-mortem on John Boyle was carried by the Assistant State Pathologist Dr J.R. Press. His evidence "was a clear indication," said Lord Lowry, "that the deceased was shot in the back and the defence of self-defence foreshadowed in the statements of the two accused and to be put forward in the evidence of Soldier A could not possibly stand up." [63] That report must have caused great difficulties for the Director of Public Prosecutions for Northern Ireland in deciding whether to bring a prosecution in the first instance against both soldiers. To have shot John Boyle in the back would not have been justified in law as the use of reasonable force in self-defence.

The prosecuting authorities may have hesitated in view of the decision in the House of Lords in the case of The Attorney General's Reference under section 48A ofthe Criminal Appeal Act 1968 (No.1 of 1975) decided on 7 July 1976. That case arose out of a killing of a civilian by a member of the British Army in County Tyrone on 7 August 1974.

The deceased was Patrick McElhone, a young farmer. Sometime during the day of 7 August, Patrick was questioned by an army patrol whilst he was working on a tractor in a field on the family farm. Later in the day, when he had gone to the farmhouse for his tea, the soldiers came to the house and ordered him outside. He was taken into a field by one of the soldiers, Private Jones. He was shot by that person at a range of less than twenty yards with one shot from a self-loading rifle. Neither Patrick McElhone nor any member of his family had any connection with any paramilitary organisation or activity.[64]

Private Jones was charged with murder. He appeared before Mr Justice MacDermott at Belfast City Commission. The learned judge acquitted him and the prosecution appealed first to the Court of Criminal Appeal in Northern Ireland, and when that appeal failed, it went to the House of Lords.

The reference to the House contained thirteen sub-paragraphs setting out the facts of the case. They were as follows:

"(1) The accused, who was a soldier on duty, killed the deceased, who was a young man, with one shot from his S.L.R. when the deceased was less than twenty yards from him in a field in a country area in daylight. The field was close to the farmhouse where the deceased lived with his parents and formed part of the farm.

"(2) The shot was a quick snapshot at the body of the deceased after the accused had shouted 'halt' and the deceased had immediately run off. The shot was not preceded by a warning shot.

"(3) The deceased had not been under arrest at the time when the accused shouted 'halt'.

"(4) At the time of firing the shot, the accused was a member of an army patrol of sixteen men which was on foot and which had been engaged in searching the area and seeking information about persons suspected of terrorist activities.

("5) The said area was one in which troops had been attacked and killed by the IRA; it was an area in which soldiers faced a real threat to their lives and where the element of surprise attack by the IRA was a real threat. The said patrol had been briefed to expect attack and be wary of being led into an ambush. The patrol was in an area which the members of the patrol were entitled to regard as containing people who might be actively hostile.

"(6) There had been no terrorist activity in the said area on the day on which the accused shot the deceased or during the days preceding the day of the shooting, but this did not mean that there was not a real threat of attack to the said army patrol, and the threat was increased by the patrol having spent a number of hours in the said area.

"(7)Before firing the shot the accused and other members of the said army patrol had been searching the out-building of the said farmhouse, and the said patrol had been briefed that the said farm, and two other farms in the said area, were places where terrorists might be hiding.

"(8) The deceased was unarmed and appeared to the accused to be unarmed.

"(9) The deceased was alone and was not one of a number of persons acting in a group.

"(10) The accused was wearing full military equipment and a pack.

"(11) When the deceased ran off after the accused's shot of 'halt', individual pursuit by the accused was not a reasonable possibility. The accused was 70 yards from the other members of the patrol and the chase could have led anywhere and over open ground, and the briefing about the risk of being led into an ambush was in the mind of the accused.

"(12) The deceased was an entirely innocent person who was in no way involved in terrorist activity.

"(13) When the accused fired he honestly and reasonably believed that he was dealing with a member of the Provisional IRA who was seeking to run away, but he had no belief at all as to whether the deceased had been involved in acts of terrorism or was likely to be involved in any immediate acts of terrorism. This being the state of mind of the accused when he fired, he did so because he thought it was his duty so to do and that firing was the reasonable and proper way to discharge his duty in the circumstances."

Lord Diplock gave the Opinion of the House of Lords in the case. He thought the thirteen sub-paragraphs were "a veritable hotchpotch of statements of fact of various kinds and include expression of opinion. Some are simply statements of what the accused himself had done and observed at or before the shooting. Some are statements of what had happened in the absence of the accused."[65]

Whatever he may have thought of the way in which the case was drafted for referral to the House, Lord Diplock was not prepared to interfere with the trial judge's findings of fact. In his view, the case was not one of self-defence, for "the deceased was in fact, and appeared to the accused to be, unarmed. He was not attacking the accused; he was running away. So if the act of the accused in shooting the deceased was lawful it must have been on the ground that it was done in performance of his duty to prevent crime or in the exercise of his right to stop and question the deceased under section 16 or to arrest him under section 12 of the Northern Ireland (Emergency Provisions) Act 1973. "[66]

Lord Diplock identified the issues which the tribunal of fact would have to consider. In setting these out he referred again and again to the tribunal as "the jury" whereas in fact Private Jones had been tried by a judge alone, sitting without a jury, ironically in the so-called "Diplock" courts.[67]

His Lordship said, " . . . the jury would have first to decide what were the facts that did exist and were known to the accused to do so and what were mistakenly believed by the accused to be facts."

"The jury would also have to consider how the circumstances in which the accused had to make his decision whether or not to use force, and the shortness of the time available to him for reflection might affect the judgment of a reasonable man. In the facts that are to be assumed for the purpose of the reference there is material on which a jury might take the view that the accused had reasonable grounds for apprehension of imminent danger to himself and other members of the patrol if the deceased were allowed to get away and join fellow members of the Provisional IRA who might be lurking in the neighbourhood, and that the time available to the accused to make up his mind what to do was so short that even a reasonable man could only act intuitively . . .

"In the other scale of the balance it would be open to the jury to take the view that it would not be unreasonable to assess the kind of harm to be averted by preventing the deceased's escape was even graver – the killing or wounding of members of the patrol by terrorists in ambush, and the effect of this success by members of the Provisional IRA in encouraging the continuance of the armed insurrection and all the misery and destruction of life and property that terrorist activity in Northern Ireland has entailed."[68]

This decision formulates the proposition that if a soldier tells the court that he honestly and reasonably believed a person to be a member of the Provisional IRA, even though that belief is mistaken, that the court must accept that as being true. If a soldier kills that person in the belief that if that person is not killed he may escape and continue his terrorist activities, then his conduct is justified and not unlawful.

In the light of that decision it was hardly surprising that the prosecuting authorities showed a marked reluctance to prosecute Sergeant Bohan and Corporal Temperley. In the event of prosecution they need not have raised the issue of self-defence at all, nor the allegation that John Boyle brought a gun to bear on them. All that was needed was a statement that they honestly believed Boyle to be a terrorist, and they shot him because he sought to escape, and they thereby prevented him from continuing any contribution he might have been making to the armed insurrection in Northern Ireland.

The House of Lords decision in the McElhone case has evoked the critical comment: "We believe that Lord Diplock and his fellow House of Lords judges have effectively discouraged the prosecuting authorities from bringing members of the security forces to trial and simultaneously encouraged the belief that members of the security forces are above the law or subject to different laws from those governing both the Nationalist and Unionist communities in Northern Ireland."[69]

There was another version of the events of 7 August when Patrick McElhone died. On the prosecution version he had attempted to run away from a heavily armed sixteen-man patrol in broad daylight. He was unarmed. He had no connection with terrorism. He had not the slightest reason to fear arrest and detention. Why did he fail to halt, if he did run, when called on to do so?

How far did he expect to go, and what did he intend to do and where did he intend to go? Would this entirely innocent man have run away and stayed away from his home for ever? At least in his case there was no gate obstructing his escape from the scene, as there had been in the case of the equally innocent Martin Walsh.

According to Patrick's brother Michael, however, the true facts of the case were these: his mother saw soldiers beating Patrick after he had been taken from the house, and his father went out to ask them why they were doing that. One soldier then took Patrick into the middle of a meadow and ran back towards the roadway, where he turned and fired, killing Patrick. The father ran towards the soldiers, who hit him in the stomach with a rifle butt.

Michael McElhone told Kader Asmal's inquiry that Private Jones made two statements. In the first he claimed that the shooting had been accidental. Then he made the second statement claiming that Patrick had run away from him and that he believed him to be a member of the Provisional IRA.[70] If this is true, one wonders whether the second statement foreshadowed the defence which was to be put forward, and was clearly prepared in the latter case with the help of a legal officer.

The effect of Patrick's death on his family was catastrophic. The British Government paid the family the sum of £3000 in respect of his death. It was made clear that this was an ex-gratia payment and no liability was admitted. Patrick's mother died one month after that payment was received; his father died shortly after that. Michael's only surviving brother required psychiatric treatment as a result of the traumatic circumstances in which Patrick died.[71]

From the very outset there was much public disquiet at the killing of John Boyle. As early as 19 July 1978 – eight days after John was killed – the matter was raised in the House of Commons. On that day Mr Gerard Fitt of the SDLP asked the Secretary of State for Northern Ireland:

"(1) whether the Royal Ulster Constabulary will be permitted to interview the soldiers involved in the killing of John Boyle'on llth July in Northern Ireland;

"(2) whether the Royal Ulster Constabulary will be able to question the use of the yellow card instructions during the course of the inquiry into the death; . . .

"(3) whether the Royal Ulster Constabulary inquiry into the death of John Boyle will be able to question the instructions given to the soldiers involved in this incident."[72]

The written answer to these questions was short and not entirely accurate. Mr Roy Mason, the Northern Ireland Secretary, replied: "The conduct of the investigation into the circumstances surrounding the death of John Boyle is a matter for the Chief Constable. The police may of course question anyone whom they believe can assist them about matters which they consider relevant to their investigation."[73]

In fact, as the RUC found, they were presented with written statements by the SAS soldiers involved, and there was no proper interrogation as there would have been in a case involving civilian suspects. Mr Fitt further asked when Mr Mason expected the report of the inquiry, and whether the Secretary of State would facilitate arrangements for the holding of an inquest into John Boyle's death. Mr Mason replied that "It is not possible at this stage to forecast when police inquiries will be completed" and "The decision on the timing of the inquest into the death of John Boyle is solely a mattter for the coroner." [74]

On 3 August 1978 Mr Gerard Fitt tried again. He put down a question in the House of Commons asking the Secretary of State for Northern Ireland "whether he is now in a position to announce the findings of the police investigation into the death of John Boyle" and asked if the Secretary of State would make a statement. Mr Mason, in a written reply, said, "I have nothing to add to the answer that I gave to a Question from the Hon. Member on 19th July."[75]

No progress seemed to be made in the case until Thursday, 1 February 1979. On that day two Irish newspapers, the *Newsletter* and the *Irish Times* published details from the post-mortem report that had been given to the Press Association. The *Newsletter's* front page headline was "SAS accused in death report". Then in the text it said, "A secret report leaked last night suggested that SAS marksmen gunned down an innocent schoolboy and that evidence was faked to justify the shooting. The army had claimed the boy, sixteeen year old John Boyle of Dunloy, Co. Antrim, was shot dead after he aimed an armalite rifle at the soldiers. But a report prepared by the RUC reveals the boy was shot in the back and police forensic experts could find no trace of his fingerprints on the rifle supplied by the army."

The Irish Times report under the headline "Commons query on killing by SAS" on the same day mentioned the same point:

"The file is also understood to state that John Boyle's fingerprints were not found on any of the guns in the arms cache, which his father Cornelius Boyle had reported to the police the previous day."

For some reason which is not now apparent, no mention is made in Lord Chief Justice's judgement about the fact that if the defence case was true and John Boyle had picked up the armalite, why his fingerprints were not found upon it on forensic examination.

On 5 February 1979, four days later, the Rev. Ian Paisley asked the Attorney General – Mr Sam Silkin Q.C. – in the House of Commons if "the Northern Ireland Director of Public Prosecutions sent to him the papers in the case of Mr John Boyle who was shot in the back and killed by the army on 11 July 1978," and asked him if he would make a statement about the matter.

In a written reply Mr Silkin said: "There is no legal requirement on the Director of Public Prosecutions for Northern Ireland to send to me papers in connection with possible prosecutions. He discharges his functions of directing whether or not a prosecution should take place independently. He is however required to discharge all his functions under my superintendence and subject to any directions which I may give and he is responsible to me for the due performance of his functions.

"On 19 October 1978, the Director informed me of the then known facts of the case relative to the death ot John Boyle, considering it to be one of importance and sensitivity which justified his consulting me. We agreed that further inquiries were desirable and these were completed by the end of 1978. On 9 January 1979, the Director and counsel attended me in London for further discussions. Following those discussions the Director issued a direction in this case, directing that certain soldiers be prosecuted."[76]

Whether it was the leaking of the police report to the Press Association which hastened the decision making process is not known, but once the information from Dr Press's post-mortem was in the public domain a prosecution was almost bound to follow.

In opening the case at the trial, counsel for the Crown placed much reliance on the Assistant State Pathologist's opinion that John Boyle was shot from the back. The defence, however, has detailed information from a distinguished British pathologist – Professor J.M.C. Cameron. His findings enabled Mr Michael Lavery Q.C. to "cross-examine the witness [Dr Press] in such an effective manner and with such a wealth of convincing anatomical and scientific detail as to cast the gravest doubt on the reliability of his principal conclusion. Put shortly, counsel achieved a position in which the witness admitted that the wound at the back of the head was for several reasons characteristic of an exit rather than an entrance wound, whereas the wound at the left eyelid was oval, regular in shape and at least equally consistent with its being an entrance wound as an exit wound. "[77]

When it was found that there had been number of errors in some important areas such as the basic measurements of John's body, it rapidly became apparent that " . . . the case was now a great deal more open on the self-defence issue, instead of being rather tightly sewn up against the accused, as the Crown might have expected from the outset." [78]

At the close of the case for the prosecution, Mr Michael Lavery made a legal submission to the trial judge that the defence had no case to answer and,accordingly Lord Lowry should direct an acquittal of both accused without them being called on to give evidence in their own defence. Lord Lowry rejected this submission on the "ground that prime facie evidence had been given that the accused shot the deceased dead with intent to kill or seriously injury him (and either is sufficient mental element to prove a charge of murder where death follows) and that the statements of the accused explaining and justifying their actions were in that respect self-serving and that it was still for the defence to raise a defence of justification which, once raised, the Crown would have to rebut so as to satisfy me beyond reasonable doubt that it was unsustainable."[79]

This was a courageous stance to adopt at this point of the trial, because the defence might have called no evidence at all and stood over its submission. And it was a stance that not every court would have adopted because, while the prosecution must offer sufficient evidence to establish a prime facie case as to each element of the offence charged, no burden lies on them to deal with any further issues unlead these are expressly raised by the defence. If therefore the accused wishes to rely, on some issue or explanation which does not amount to an affirmative defence, he bears an evidential burden of raising the issue by evidence sufficient to justify a finding in his favour on the issue involved. This evidential burden means nothing more than laying a proper foundation for the issue; the issue in this case being that of self-defence.

The accused were not required to prove it, but they had to lay the proper foundation for it to be made a live issue in the case. It might be argued that here both Sergeant Bohan and Corporal Temperley had laid the foundation for self-defence in the written statements they had made before the trial began. If Lord Lowry's ruling was followed in every case, then where an accused raises self-defence in any crime, such as homicide or assault, he would have to go into the witness box and give evidence of it. This is very near to saying that unless he does so, the defence will fall on that issue and a verdict of "guilty" must inevitabily follow.

As already noted, only one of the two accused, Sergeant Bohan gave sworn evidence in his own defence. What he was evidence on his own behalf, and also for and against Corporal Temperley – in this case any evidence which was unfavourable to his co-accused was evidence against him.

At the conclusion of the evidence, and following the closing speeches from counsel for the prosecution and the defence, Lord Lowry gave his decision. In reaching it he considered a number of important points. He considered that John Boyle was probably shot from the front through the head by Bohan and, as he twisted and fell, twice through the back by oblique fire from Temperley. His Lordship thought that John may have had a rifle in his right hand held near his body (which would be consistent with the inner arm brusing) and left hand and had turned left-handed from the grave to face both soldiers. It should be noted that in his post-mortem report, Dr Press stated that "bruising and abrasions on the inner side of the right arm were probably due to the arm having been in contact with the right side of the chest when the bullet fragments lodged there."[80]

Thus at the beginning of the case the prosecution evidence indicated that, because the inner right arm was injured in that fashion, John Boyle could not possibility have been holding the gun under that arm. Yet at the end of the case the trial judge was prepared to accept that he may have done so.

However the judge accepted the fact that the rifle was not loaded and therefore Bohan and Temperley were never in actual danger. If John did get the rifle into his hands, both soldiers must have seen him kneel or husker down at the grave, take out the plastic bag, extract the rifle and stand up with it in his hands, and while all this was going on, "strangely enough," comments Lord Lowry "they must have done nothing . . ."[81] There was no challenge, no contact with the other two soldiers outside the graveyard, simply nothing. if there really was a plan to capture, then was this not the ideal time to put that plan into effect? If the soldiers thought that John Boyle was a terrorist, one wonders why they let him get the rifle (if he did) into his hands, because for all they knew, it might have been loaded. Indeed, someone was prepared to say to the press that the rifle was loaded and there was a bullet in the breech. The *Sunday Times* journalists, in *Ambush*[82], consider that it would have been impractical to find out whether the weapon was loaded "for the SAS could not risk breaking cover to inspect the cache for fear their presence might be detected." That point completely overlooks the fact that Bohan went to the graveyard in the darkest hours of the early morning, some time between 12 midnight and 3:00 a.m., whereas the alleged terrorist arrived to pick up the cache in the brightness of that July morning at about 10 a.m.

Lord Lowry appeared to have accepted the fact that Bohan knew John Boyle was alone: Bohan's behaviour after the shooting supported that inference – so does any evidence that he stood up to fire the rifle. There was still the question that the Boyle family had been warned to stay away, and therefore only a terrorist would have approached the cache in the graveyard. Lord Lawry found as a fact that John Boyle did not attack or conciously menace Bohan and Temperley, but they may well have believed their lives were in danger[83]. John could only have led them to believe that if he picked up the rifle, something which he apparently had not done the day before when he was alone and unobserved in the graveyard, and if he did as Bohan suggested, why were John's fingerprints not found on any part of that weapon?

As Lord Lowry noted, if Bohan had inspected the rifle at any time, he would have found out that in its actual unloaded state it posed no threat. He said that " . . . the army, and Sergeant Bohan and his patrol gravely mishandled the operation because they shot an innocent boy who, whether he was holding the gun or not, had no capacity to harm them . . . Nothing would have been easier with better planning than to capture the deceased alive, always assuming that to be the primary object."[84]

One wonders whether there was evidence before Lord Lowry of what Tony Geraghy wrote in his book *Who Dares Wins*[85]: "But it was clearly a matter of fine judgment, and perhaps split-second timing, if any terrorist were to be caught in the act, as the law required, yet simultaneously unable to threaten any soldier who had allowed him to arm himself. This may explain why, at the briefing, a 'killing' as alternative to capture was mentioned during the planning of the operation." Was the Lord Chief Justice told that a "killing" was discussed, and would this explain why Sergeant Bohan was so "vague and unsatisfactory" when questioned as to the details of the plan to capture?

This ambush was conducted in accordance with the SAS's Standing Operation Procedures, which have evolved, according to Geraghty[86], "from hard experience in Ireland." According to Geraghty, whose book was described by the magazine *The Listener* as "An excellent and timely semi-official history (Its accuracy can be judged by the fact that the Regiment itself has bought 2000 copies.)" Bohan was following Standing Operating Procedures "in moving the body, searching it, and then moving forward to clear his area. Stupidly, he agreed, he had emptied the arms cache on the same basis, and once the Quick Reaction Force had arrived, he again followed the procedure in returning to his base before the Police appeared on the scene. Asked whether it was part of the Standing Operating Procedures not to give his name to the police when they came to interview him, Bohan replied 'I believe that is part of an agreement between the army and the police but I am not absolutely sure.' "

Bohan and Temperley returned to regimental duty with the SAS after the trial. According to the journalist Mark Urban "colleagues say the men were changed by the experience and felt deep regret at the teenager's death."[87] That must signify a change of heart on the part of Sergeant's Bohan, for when he was asked at the trial, "How did he feel when he discovered that John Boyle was not a terrorist? . . . [He replied] that his actions indicated to me he was a terrorist . . . Nothing else . . . I was told that the person who had been shot was not a terrorist but I didn't accept it . . . I cannot regard any person who points a weapon at me as being a completely innocent person."[88] These are words of justification for his conduct, and show not the slightest remorse or regret for what he had done.

One wonders if Sergeant Bohan and Corporal Temperley ever considered the risk that the true terrorist might have armed himself before entering the graveyard, rather than wait until he laid his hands on concealed weapons which may or may not have been there at the time he called to collect them? If Bohan really told the truth when he said that he thought John Boyle was "someone whose picture I had seen previously," what was the explanation of his failure to challenge and arrest him before he ever reached the arms cache?

One fact is certain: amongst all the untruths and dissembling of information, especially by the army press officers, the whole truth about the death of John Boyle has yet to be established.

Chapter 6

SUFFER LITTLE CHILDREN – PART II
THE CASE OF STEPHEN PAUL MCCAUL

Section 11 of the Northern Ireland (Emergency Provisions) Act 1978 enables a constable to arrest without warrant any person whom he suspects of being a terrorist. The power is exercisable on subjective suspicion only, and there is no requirement, as there normally is in the ordinary criminal law, that the arresting officer should have reasonable suspicion to form a gound of arrest. A terrorist is defined in section 31 of the Act as " . . . a person who is or has been concerned in the commission or attempted commission of any act of terrorism or in directing, organising or training persons for the purpose of terrorism." That is defined in the same section as meaning "the use of violence for political ends and includes any use of violence for the purpose of putting the public or any section of the public in fear."

On 7 March 1979 at 10:55 a.m. Stephen Paul McCaul was arrested under section 11 of that Act at his home on the Twinbrook estate in Belfast. He was taken to Castlereagh police office, since the then current Orders of the Royal Ulster Constabulary stipulated that anyone arrested under section 11 must be taken to Castlereagh.[1] There he was subjected to a number of interviews and, as a result of written confession statements that he was alleged to have made, he appeared before the Belfast City Commission on 5 and 6 December 1979. He pleaded not guilty to an indictment charging ten offences: hijacking a bus on two occasions; arson of one of the buses; carrying firearms with intent to commit an indictable offence, namely robbery on one occasion and hijacking on another, or to resist arrest or to prevent the arrest of another; and two counts of possession of firearms and ammunition under such circumstances as to give rise to a reasonable suspicion that he did not have the same in his possession for a lawful object; and two dwelling house burglaries. He was convicted of all offences and received a custodial sentence of three years.

Even a cursory examination of the indictment setting out the ten charges may give the impartial observed a deep feeling of troublesome unease. The first count in the indictment and the third count charged Stephen Paul McCaul with hijacking, contrary to the Criminal Jurisdiction Act 1975. In count 3 the particulars of the offence are as follows:

"Stephen Paul McCaul on the 21st day of January 1979, in the County of Antrim, by force or threat thereof or by any other means of intimidation, unlawfully seized control of a motor vehicle, namely a bus, registration number COI 1462."

So that charge sets out a specific date and identified the registration number of a specific vehicle. The particulars of the offence in count 1, however, are different. They are:

"Stephen Paul McCaul on a date unknown between the 1st day of December 1978 and the 31st day of January 1979, in the County of Antrim, by force or by threat thereof or by any other means of intimidation, unlawfully seized control of a motor vehicle, namely a bus."

Here no specific date is alleged and no registration number of the vehicle is given. The offence is said to have taken place on a unknown day amongst sixty-two days, and the vehicle alleged to have been involved has not been identified in any way save for the general description of "bus". It follows from this that no evidence was given to the trial court by any witness that any particular vehicle was involved, or any particular day was specified to the court. The reason for this is simple: the count was drafted and the offence laid against the accused because he had confessed to committing that offence. Even with the confession in their hands, the prosecution were unable to identify the occasion when the offence was said to have been committed.

In fact the totality of the prosecution case was founded on the confession statements of the accused. Without that evidence against him, he would not have been convicted.

The accused was interviewed in room BF 9 at Castlereagh Police Office by two officers of the RUC. Both were members of the divisional CID from the area where it was suspected the offences charged had been committed. As Judge Bennett noted, CID officers in Northern Ireland, like their colleagues in England, receive no formal training in the techniques of interviewing. Their detective training overall consists of a two week course whilst an aide to CID on law and practical subjects relating to detective work; if he receives a permanent appointment to the CID he attends a further two week course. Later, that officer will normally attend a ten week detective course at a police training centre in England.[2] It is likely therefore that the RUC officers who interviewed Stephen Paul McCaul had received the majority of their formal training in England.

The first interview started at 2:45 p.m. on the day of the arrest, 7 March. At the outset at least one of the officers knew the age of the accused. That officer completed three separate forms[3], setting out his

188

name, his age, his occupation, where he was born, a description of him, and the offences.

Stephen Paul McCaul was on his own, with no solicitor, family member, friend or adviser with him, when he faced the two officers. Judge Bennett notes: "The essential feature of interrogation procedure is that questioning of the suspect by police officers takes place in private, the officers and the suspect being alone together. This was expressed by the Supreme Court of the United States in the Miranda judgement in the following terms: 'The principal psychological factor contributing to a successful interrogation is privacy, being alone with the person under interrogation.' "[4]

Stephen was 15 years old. As the RUC knew and noted on one of the three forms completed before the first interview began, Stephen was not merely a schoolboy, but he attended St. Aloysius Special School.[5] Doctor Dermott Nugent, a consultant psychiatrist, gave evidence on oath to the trial court that Stephen had the mental age of seven.

That first interview lasted until 4:15 p.m. There was a second interview that day, starting at 7:30 p.m. and concluding at 10:15 p.m. So the total time spent in the interview room on the day of arrest was four and one quarter hours.

The third interview was at 11 a.m. on the following day. It lasted until 12:55 p.m. The fourth interview started at 2:15 p.m. and concluded at 4:30 p.m. The fifth interview started at 7:50 p.m. and lasted until 9:35 p.m. when one of the two interviewing officers was replaced by another. The interviewing continued until 12:10 a.m.

The total amount of time that Stephen Paul McCaul spent with two RUC officers in the interview room at Castlereagh Police Office on 8 March was some eight and one half hours. Four hours and twenty minutes of that time had been without interruption either for refreshments or toilet facilities. He had been in custody since 10:45 a.m. the previous day.

Within ten minutes of the beginning of the fifth interview, Stephen Paul McCaul began to make the first of three written statements under caution – exhibit 1. It was written down by one of the detective officers conducting the interview. It began at 8 p.m. and ended at 9:05 p.m.

Five minutes later at 9:10 p.m. the second statement – exhibit 2 – came into existence. Like the first, it was written by the police officer. It ended at 10:20 p.m.

At 10:30 p.m. exhibit 3, the third statement started. It was the shortest of the three and ended at 10:52 p.m. Yet, despite the obtaining of three confession statements, the interview continued until ten minutes after midnight.

The three statements were written by the police because Stephen Paul McCaul could not write. All three had to be read over to him because he was unable to read.

The first confession statement began as follows: "I Stephen Paul McCaul wish to make a statement. I want someone to write down what I say. I have been told that I need not say anything unless I wish to do so and I understand that anything I say may be given in evidence."

These words, the words of the caution as they are known, also appear at the head of the second and third statements, exhibits 2 and 3. Those headings do not follow the wording of Rule IV of the Judges' Rules 1964 set out in Home Office Circular No 31/1964 or in Rule IV of the Judges Rules set out in Home Office Circular No. 89/1978. The words " . . . and I understand that anything I say may be given in evidence" do not appear in Rule IV – instead the actual wording is . . . whatever I say may be given in evidence."

No doubt the reason for the change, which was not explained by the RUC officer to the court, since the point was never raised by anyone, was that it became important to establish that the 15 year old schoolboy with a mental age of seven understood what he was saying. In the hundreds of statements made under caution which I have examined over the years, I have never encountered a change in the wording of the caution as it was changed here.

The body of the statement is as follows:

"About two months ago I asked K.D. if I could hijack and burn a bus. K said I could do it but he was not giving me permission to do it and told me that if I done it it was off my own bat. I asked him if I could use one of the cubs and he said I could ask one of my own. I went down and saw J. K. at his home about 7:30 p.m. and asked him if he would do it with me and he agreed. J. went upstairs and got a toy gun that was bigger than a 45 Colt and a mask. I asked Joe if he had any petrol and he said that he had a can of petrol at the back of his house. We went to his back garden and poured some of the petrol into two milk bottles. We then hid a bottle each up our coats and walked to the bus stop up at the top of the Twinbrook Road. We hid the two bottles of petrol in the hedge and waited on a bus coming I already had a hood on me. Somebody was waiting at the bus stop for the bus. When the bus came along and stopped I jumped on and ordered everybody off. J. was standing at the doors in case the driver tried to close them. It was a single decker bus and there were only five or six people on it. Everybody got off and I put the gun into the driver's side and ordered him to drive the bus straight across the Stewartstown Road. When he had done this I told him to take all his belongings and get off. When this was happening J. was getting

190

the petrol from the hedge. As the driver was getting off the bus I saw the army coming along in two jeeps and J. and I ran. As I was running I pulled off my hood and threw it over a fence. I then threw J. his gun back and we split up. I ran on home and stayed in the house about 10 minutes. I then went back out and watched what was happening at the bus. I hi-jacked this bus about 8 p.m. – 9 p.m. on a Friday night I think. Not long after I done this I was at a disco in Twinbrook on a Saturday night. I was approached by C.T. and N.M., they asked me to hijack and burn a bus. C.T. did all the talking and he wanted me to do the job with N. We went out to look for the 10 o'clock bus but it was too late and we missed it. We went back into the disco and saw C.T. and told him. C. said that we were to do it the next night instead. I made arrangements to meet N. at my front the following night at 7:30 p.m. but I am not sure of the time. The next night I met N. at my front and as I met him we saw the bus coming so we ran across towards it. As we were running towards the bus both of us were pulling on masks, we both put up the hoods of our snorkel jackets and zipped them right up. I lifted a toy gun from the garden of my house when I came out at first. When we got to the bus there was a couple of people at the bus stop, I ran on past them and shouted "Everybody off the bus." A woman, who was on the bus, said something to me but I didn't quite catch what she said. I told her that if she didn't get off I would shove this into her and made a movement with the gun. This woman then got off the bus. When this was happening M. was away getting the petrol. I think he already had the petrol stashed near the bus stop. When everybody was off I ordered the driver to put the bus across the road. This bus was a single decker as well. When he had the bus across the road I told him to take all his belongings and get off. N. then came over and gave me the petrol which was in two milk bottles. I sprinkled it all over the inside of the bus and set a match to it. The petrol went on fire very quickly. N. was standing at the doors of the bus when I saw lighting the petrol. When I was getting off the bus I pulled my hood out and threw it on the bus. We both then ran off. We split up and I ran home, and threw the gun into my front garden. I then went into the house and changed. I came out after I had changed and went and watched the bus burning. While I was watching the bus burning C.T. came up to me and said that we had done a good job."

The statement then ends with the declaration "Stephen Paul McCaul being unable to read the above statement, I, Detective Constable F.D.S. of Dunmurry Police Station read it over to him before he signed it." That declaration is signed by the officer who obtained the statement.

That statement formed the basis of counts 1 to 5 in the indictment.

No exact date is given anywhere in the narrative, but clearly the hijacking and burning of the bus was sufficiently particularised to enable the RUC to identify the date and the vehicle involved. It would appear therefore that in the absence of any other evidence the prosecution had to rely on the statement to draft the first count of hijacking in the indictment; if any bus driver complained about the hijacking between the dates stated – 1 December 1978 and 31 January 1973 – then his evidence about that appears to have been witheld. Such a statement, including any detail about the time, place as well as the date, the number of hijackers involved, would all have help to give independent support to the confession statement – if it was true.

The officer who wrote down the statement was asked by prosecuting counsel at the trial: "Now what was his attitude while he was making that statement?" He answered: "He seemed happy enough to make the statement. There was no pressure put on him or anything. He did not seem unduly worried at what he had done." The questions and answers continued:

"Q. Was there any threat made to him to induce him to make that statement?

"A. There was no threat made to him, your honour.

"Q. How was the statement actually taken?

"A. Well, I wrote out the heading and then the caution. I read the caution over to him and I invited him to sign it, which he did.

"Q. Yes, you have told us that.

"A. And then I took the body of the statement down at his dictation.

"Q. So that the writing is yours, is that right?

"A. The writing is mine.

"Q. And whose are the words?

"A. The words are his, your honour.

"Q. Was that a voluntary statement that he made?

"A. It was, your honour, yes."[6]

Bearing in mind that this statement was alleged to have been dictated on 8 March 1979 and was describing a number of events, going back on the dates in the indictment until possibly December 1978, Stephen Paul McCaul demonstrated not marely strong powers of observation – he noted for example that there were only five or six people on the first single decker bus that was hijacked – but he has detailed recollection of those events, and he was not inhibited in any way in giving a detailed description of what actually happened. This was all the more remarkable considering his illiteracy and his mental age of seven.

Psychologists believe that memory is a complex network of interacting systems which operate in a reconstructive and subjective fashion. They conceptualise memory functions as a three-stage process:

(a)encoding – when new information is required and coded for retention;

(b) storage – when the coded information is retained;

(c)retrieval – when the stored information is accessed and brought to consciousness, usually by recognition or recall.[7]

The technique of interviewing is of considerable importance, not least when dealing with children, who may be compliable and suggestible to leading questions. The Judges' Rules stated "Whenever a police officer writes the statement, he shall take down the exact words spoken by the persons making the statement, without putting any questions other than such as may be needed to make the statement coherent, intelligible and relevant to the material matters; he shall not prompt him."[8]

The court was told in plain terms that in this case the words of the statement exhibit 1 were those of the accused Stephen Paul McCaul.

Much depended, in this case, on what was said and by whom in the course of the interviews that preceded the taking of the first statement. If the questions were put in a form which the memory test was free recall, then there would be less grounds of unease. In this form the person is asked to recount everything he remembers without prompting, for example by saying "Describe everything that happened, what you saw and what was said."

Another test is to ask general questions such as, "Was anyone with you or were you alone?" or specific questions, "Who found the can for the petrol and where did the petrol come from?" or, most undesirable of all, leading questions suggesting the answer and stating as proved an unproved fact, such as "You were carrying a toy gun at the time, weren't you?

In this case much depended on what information the RUC officers had in their possession at the time of the interviews at Castlereagh, and how much, if any, of that information they imparted to the accused. The officer who conducted the interviews and took the three statements under caution was Detective Constable Shearer. The following exchange took place between that officer and counsel for the defence.

"Q. You told us earlier that you were sent in to interview him, is that right? How did it come about that you went in to interview him. Were you directed to do that?

"A. Well, a number of us were sent to Castlereagh to interview that morning and that is where I ended up with McCaul, your honour.

"Q.Well, was there a rota or how did it come that you went in to interview that particular person?

"A. There was no rota as such. It was just not that.

"Q. Well, how did you know to go in and interview him in particular?

"A. Well, I knew that there was people to be interviewed so somebody had to interview somebody.

"Q. Well, did you just elect to interview McCaul then?

"A. Yes, I suppose that that would be true, your honour."[9]

Thus it is clear from this that the officer had no specific instructions before he arrived at Castlereagh Holding Office to interview Stephen Paul McCaul. It was, so the officer seemed to have suggested to the court, that someone had to interview Stephen, and the task was given to him when he elected to conduct the interview. Any doubts about this would be resolved by the fact that this officer told the court that "Well, I think that we were all aware when we went to Castlereagh that morning that there were people to be interviewed, but it was not decided exactly, you know ,that I was to go and see McCaul and somebody was to go and see somebody else."

Counsel for the defence then mistakenly suggested that a second RUC officer, DC Gribben, was concerned in the first interview. DC Shearer corrected counsel, quite rightly, telling him that the other officer who was present was in fact DC Nesbitt. DC Gribben did not appear at the first interview at 2:45 p.m. on 7 March, but was present at the second at 7:30 in the evening of that day.

That officer told the trial judge in answer to these questions from defence counsel, the following:

"Q.DC Gribben, DC Shearer said that he was not in charge of the interviews; when you were in the interviews were you on an equal footing with DC Shearer?

"A.That is correct, your honour, yes.

"Q. And the file relating to the various crimes that you were investigating that was available to you and was known to you in the same way as it was to him?

"A.I was instructed at Dunmurry that morning, your honour, on the morning of the 7th March 1979, your honour, by my detective, inspector to go to Castlereagh and interview McCaul.

"Q.That is where your direction came from?

"A.Exactly, your honour.

"Q.From the detective inspector at Dunmurry.

"A.That is correct, yes, your honour.

"Q.And where did you get your file or your briefing?

"A.I was briefed at Dunmurry RUC Station, your honour.

"Q. And that included the antecedents of the person that you were to interview?

"A. I cannot exactly remember as to that. I remember that it was to do with what he questioned him about; that was the hijacking and burning of buses and burglary, your honour. I cannot remember the detail as to it.

Q. The Judge. In any event you were told to go and interview McCaul?

A. I was.

Q. Specifically?

A. I was, your honour, yes."[10]

The most important point in this part of the evidence, and indeed the purpose of the questions, seemed to have been overlooked. The very officer who had specific instructions issued at Dunmurry to interview Stephen at Castlereagh did not do so at the first interview, but that was done by an officer, DC Shearer, who had no specific instructions to interview anybody. Why that happened in that way was never pursued by anyone either at the trial or at the subsequent appeal.

Of equal importance was the format of the questions put to Stephen Paul McCaul. On 8 March at 11 a.m. DC Gribben without any other officer, or any other person being present, interviewed Stephen. He told the trial judge: "I have written in my notes, your honour, that McCaul was already aware of my identity and the nature of my inquiries and I reminded him that he was still under caution." He was asked by the judge "Well, what does the phrase 'the nature of your inquiries' mean?" He answered, "What we were questioning him about in the previous interview, your honour." When asked what that was, the officer replied: "Burglaries and the hijacking and burning of buses."

Prosecuting counsel then asked: "What happened after?" The constable answered: "After that McCaul was put over his story that he had previously given in the previous interviews, your honour. I asked him to read the notes made to date and McCaul . . .

"Q. Now which notes are those?

"A. Those are the notes of the previous interviews.

"Q. You say plural, 'interviews'

"A. Yes, your honour. I am sorry, interviews.

"Q. Well, there had been two interviews; which was it?

"A. The previous interviews. Interview.

"Q. Is that the one that you had been present at?

"A. That is correct, your honour.

"Q. And what happened? Did he say anything to you?

"A. McCaul replied that he cannot read, your honour.

"Q. Did you ask him anything about that?

"A. I asked McCaul why he could not read and he told me that he couldnot go to school very much and did not learn.

"Q. And what happened then?

"A. At that time it was 11:25 a.m., your honour and DC Shearer came into the room."[11]

The very officer directed to interview Stephen at Castlereagh had not done so until the second interview on the evening of the day of arrest. The officer who conducted the first interview, DC Shearer, knew from the outset not merely that Stephen could not read or write but also that he was a pupil at a special school. Yet, for some reason which defies comprehension, he failed to tell DC Gribben when he joined him at the second interview, and that officer did not know, when " . . . McCaul was, put over his story that he had previously given in the previous interviews . . . " he did not appreciate that he was dealing with a person who was, at the very least, educationally retarded. This point was never raised at the trial. It should have been. Especially in the light of the evidence about what was said when DC Shearer went into Room BF 9 at 11:25 a.m. on 8 March. According to that officer, in reply to a question from the trial judge: "He was asked about something?" he replied, "Yes, he was asked if he had broken into any other houses."

Prosecuting counsel asked:

"Q. Yes, and what did he say to that?

"A. He told us that he had already told us about some and that he would tell us about some others.

"Q. [The Judge] I am sorry. Would you say that again?

"A. He said that he had told us about some and he would tell us about others.

"Q. And what was said?

"A. He stated that one day himself and three others and he named all three were on the road leading to Stewart's Supermarket and that he went up and rapped the door."[12]

This version has to be compared and contrasted with the evidence of DC Gribben on the same point.

"Q. Well, was he asked about anything relevant to this case, the subject matter of these charges?

"A. We asked McCaul to tell us how many houses he had broken into. McCaul then told us that he had already told us about two houses, and he wants to tell us about three more."[13]

This is a classic example of a leading question: It was put to Stephen as a proved fact that he had broken into houses, the only question was how many. In the Shearer version it was different: Stephen was asked if he had broken into any other houses – in other words no proved fact there as yet. And the reply is different in form and substance, for Shearer said that "he had already told us about some and that he would tell us about others." No mention of the numbers involved in that version of what was supposed to be the same reply.

It does seem exceedingly odd that once the evidence established that Constable Gribben discovered that Stephen could not read, he did not ask, and Constable Shearer did not volunteer any information at any stage about his intellectual capacity. Instead he went on to take a further two written confession statements from him.

The second statement – exhibit two – was written by Constable Shearer, but he told the trial judge that the words in the body of the statement were McCaul's. The statement began with the declaration in its altered form:

"About six to eight weeks ago I was walking about the estate when I met R.M. and his brother Mickey. M. told me that they were going to do a house and asked me if I was coming with them. I said yes. We walked out to the Cutts and turned left down the Cutts towards the main Lisburn Road. We walked down the Cutts for about 50 to 60 yards and went into a cul de sac on the right. There were about four to six houses in this street. I went to the third house which is facing the entrance to the street and knocked on the door. This was about 5:30 to 6:00 p.m. in the evening. Nobody answered the door. R and M were already at the back of the house and I went round the back and told them that nobody had answered. R then smashed a window of the bedroom and we all went into the house by this window. The three of us started to search round in the house. I was searching the bedroom and found dirty films in a case. I told R what I had found and he said put them in the kitchen. I was using matches to see things. I went into another room like a study and started to search it. I opened this cupboard and saw two shotguns and a .202 rifle. The shotguns were broken down and there was a silencer fitted to the.202 rifle. I lifted the guns out of the cupboard and told R, he said to put them on the table to we look at them. He then asked if there was any bullets and I told him I didn't know. R looked in the cupboard and found bullets in a jacket. He put the bullets into a bag with the silencer. We gathered up all the stuff in the kitchen. We got some silver, dirty films, watch, portable TV, two shotguns and about 12 bullets for the shotgun. We started to leave the house by the back door, we walked down the street towards the Cutts. As we were walking a car came along and we dropped the shotguns, dirty films, the portable TV and the silver. We hid behind a hedge until the car was away and R told me to go and get the shotguns. I went and got the shotguns and we left the rest of the stuff lying. We went back over the fields to the Estate and hid the shotguns under a shed in a back garden. We split and I went home for my tea. About half an hour later I met M.M. and a mate of his. Mickey suggested robbing a shop with one of the shotguns but his mate didn't want to get involved so he went home. Me and Mickey went down and called for R.M. I forgot to say that when we were hiding the guns R. suggested that we meet up in half an hour and rob the Twinbrook shop. The three of us went back to where the shotguns were hidden and R told me to get one of the shotguns out. I put the butt down my trousers and Mickey put the barrel up his coat. We all went down towards the shops and stopped at the back of the flats to put the shotgun together. Somebody looked out a window and saw us so we moved into the flats. We were trying to put the gun up when a policeman walked in and saw us. The policeman walked towards us and Robert threw the gun down and we all ran out the back door. The policemen shouted after us but we kept on running. We split up and I ran round to the shop and bought bubbles. When I got the shotgun out from under the shed I lifted two bullets as well. I kept the bullets in my pocket. I was making my way back home when I met P.S. I told him about the shotgun and asked him if he was coming up to look at it. I went up and got it out and showed it to P. I loaded it and fired both bullets in the air. I came back to the shed where it was hidden and loaded it again. I fired these two bullets into the air as well. P was down the street a bit keeping 'Dick'. was going to put the shotgun back and had pushed it under the shed. After I had put it back a man looked out of the window and seen me. I tried to get it out but it was too far under. I ran off and went home. Later that night I went to the Donegal Disco and met N.M. and C.T. I told them that I knew where a shotgun was in the Estate and that if they wanted it, if they came up I would give it to them. They said alright and we went up to set it. I looked under the shed but it wasn't there. I had bullets for the shotgun and the silencer for the .202 hidden close to the shed so I gave them those instead. N. took them and put them in his coat pocket. I was going to R.M.'s house when I was pulled by four fellows who took me away in a taxi and questioned me about the shotgun."

That statement was read over to Stephen and he signed it.

It had taken and hour and ten minutes to compile. Again this fifteen year old displayed remarkable powers of observation, recollection and graphic description. The language is sound and grammatical. Would a person with his incapacity after presumably one visit to a house be able to describe walking down the Cutts for about 50 or 60 yards and actually say they "went into a cul-de-sac on the right?" Would he have known what a cul-de-sac was? Would he have known and been able to recollect the exact detail that they went to the third house which is facing the entrance to the street?

This house burglary was undoubtedly committed by someone on 18 January 1979. Of the twelve items of property set out in the particulars of the offence as stolen, Stephen mentioned about seven of them, more than half in exhibit 2, quite a remarkable feat of memory. He mentioned two items: dirty films – and how he knew what they were is something of a mystery, for any label showing the unlikely title "dirty films" could not have been read by him – and a watch which are not included in the charge, presumably because the house owner did not allege that was property stolen in the burglary. It may be significant that not one single item was traced to Stephen Paul McCaul in any way, either forensically or found in his possession. It would be of considerable interest to know why the policeman mentioned in exhibit 2 seemed not to have made a statement – and if he did he did not give it in evidence – about walking into the flats and disturbing three youths, shouting at them causing them to run off. Did he then find the shotgun which R. threw down? That independent evidence would have helped to establish the reliability of the contents of exhibit 2.

The second statement with its wealth of detail was completed at 10:20 in the evening. It had taken one hour and ten minutes to compile. After a ten minute lapse in time, then if the police were right, Stephen Paul McCaul began to dictate, freely, voluntarily and without prompting of any kind, a third statement, exhibit 3. On any view of the case he displayed remarkable stamina in the hours during which he was busily dictating statements to the police.

Exhibit 3 was the third and last of the voluntary statements made under caution. It was the shortest of the three. It contained a convenient confession to the last two counts, nine and ten, in the indictment, and fitted the chronological order of events. In the statement Stephen admitted comitting a dwelling house burglary on 26 January 1979 and the possession of a firearm and ammunition on the same date.

After the caution at the head of the statement, still indicating that he understood that anything he said might be given in evidence, Stephen began the statement by setting the approximate time of the offences – exactly as he had done in exhibits 1 and 2 – showing what some may regard as a remarkable and consistent ability to start the statement in a rational and sensible way. Not only was he helpful with setting the approximate dates, but in each of the statements he gives an approximate time.

199

"About the middle of January 1979, myself, P.S. V.W. and D.C. were walking down the road that leads to Stewarts at Derriaghy, this was about lunchtime. I suggested that we do a house and P. and me went to the door of a house on the right of this road. I knocked the door and there was no answer. V. and D. went up the road to keep 'Dick'. P. and I went round the back of the house. I broke the bottom window of the kitchen door with a tile. We took the rest of the glass out and climbed in. I searched upstairs and looked in a cupboard. I saw a carpet and a box behind it. I pulled the carpet out of the way and lifted out the box and opened it. I found a shotgun and a box of bullets in the box. I closed the box and took it downstairs. Pat was searching around downstairs, he told me he had found two pens. I had a look around downstairs and found some American dollars which I took. We climbed out the same window we came in by. We went over the back fence and hid the shotgun. We then went and called V. and D. We took the shotgun out of the box and hid it on us and went to the fields nears the Cutts and hid the shotgun and bullets in a rabbit hole. We split up. About half an hour later I was walking up past the shops at Twinbrook and was met by C.T. and A.R. They threatened me and asked for the shotgun. I took them to where it was hidden, and gave it to them. They took the shotgun and bullets and split."

That statement was dictated in twenty-two minutes. There is considerable detail in it including the point of entry into the house, the means of entry and the exit from it. Of the items mentioned in the particulars of the offence in the indictment, Stephen lists the shotgun, bullets, two of the three pens and the American dollars. Strange to say, although he admitted finding and taking them, nothing is said about what happened to the dollars. None of the property stolen in the burglary was traced to Stephen Paul McCaul. Whether a prosecution was brought against those named in his statements is not known; certainly no one was jointly charged with these offences in the indictment which he faced alone.

The defence attempted to persuade the trial judge to exclude these three confession statements in the exercise of his common law judicial discretion. The main plank of the defence submission rested on the clearest breaches of the Home Office Administrative Directions attached to the Judges' Rules. The Common Law has long recognised that children and the mentally handicapped are likely to be vunerable and at risk in certain circumstances. They may, without knowing or wishing to do so, be particularly prone to provide information which is unreliable, misleading or self-incriminating. In this case the RUC were dealing with a young person who was mentally handicapped.

Administrative Direction 4 states that "As far as practicable children and young persons under the age of 17 years (whether suspected of crime or not) should only be interviewed in the presence of a parent or guardian, or in their absence, some person who is not a police officer and is of the same sex as the child . . ."

Administrative Direction 4(a) states: "If it appears to a police officer that a person (whether a witness or a suspect) whom he intends to interview has a mental handicap which raises a doubt as to whether the person can understand the questions put to him, or which makes the person likely to be especially open to suggestion, the officer should take particular care in putting questions and accepting the reliability of answers. As far as practicable, and where recognised as such by the police, a mentally handicapped adult (whether suspected of crime or not) should be interviewed only in the presence of a parent or other person in whose care, custody or control he is, or of some person who is not a police officer (for example a social worker).

"(b) So far as mentally handicapped children and young persons are concerned, the conditions of interview and arrest by the police are governed by Administrative Direction 4 above.

"(c) Any document arising from an interview with a mentally handicapped person of any age should be signed not only by the person who made the statement, but also by the parent or guardian or other person who was present during the interview. Since the reliability of any admission by a mentally handicapped person may even then be challenged, care will still be necessary to verify the facts admitted and to obtain corroboration where possible."

As stated above, at least one of the RUC officers knew that Stephen was a pupil at a special school. All the officers knew he was 15 years old, and was therefore in law a young person; mentally he was only a child of seven. No parent or independent person was ever present at any interview, or signed any of the confession statements.

Defence counsel asked Constable Shearer for an explanation.

"Q. Well, who else could have taken the decision that this person was to be interviewed in the absence of a parent or some other lay person?

"A. Your honour, I cannot remember the circumstances but I think someone was contacted in relation to this at the time, but who I do not know.

"Q. Well, are you saying that you contacted someone else?

"A. No, I didn't. I think somebody else contacted them, your honour, with reference to McCaul's age. Who that was I don't honestly know."[14]

Thus it was clear from the evidence that someone had made a conscious and informed decision that no other person, independent of the RUC was to be present at the interviews. When counsel put to Constable Shearer that both parents repeatedly telephoned Castlereagh and were told at all times that they could not have access to Stephen and could not see him, and eventually were told they could see him at his first court appearance, Constable Shearer replied "I did not even know that the parents had phoned up, your honour."[15]

The turning point of the cross-examination should have been when the following exchange took place:

"Q. Can I take it that the tenor of the interviews were that you told him that you were inquiring into this burglary, for instance, where the two shot guns were taken and you told him the address and so forth and so on?

"A. That is correct, your honour.

"Q. And then you put it to him 'were you not involved in it'?

"A. That would be correct, your honour, yes.

"Q. And similarly, with the hijacking you told him that you were inquiring into the hijacking of the bus at the corner of the Twinbrook and Stewartstown Roads and that again you were putting it to him that he was involved in that?

"A. Yes, that is correct, your honour, yes."[16]

In other words, the officer was doing something that clearly should never have been done, supplying detailed information to the suspect and simply getting his agreement to his participation in the wrongdoing.

"Q. Did you not find that he succumbed readily to suggestion?

"A. Not really, your honour, no.

"Q. Or that he was prone to exaggeration?

"A. "I don't know, your honour."

"Or invention?"

"A. *Possibly invention.*" [emphasis added]

"Q. Over and above the two crimes that you were investigating did he volunteer other incidents that you knew nothing about?

"A. He did, your honour, yes."[17]

It is possible to discover from the transcript which two crimes this officer was investigating and which counsel put to him; they were the hijacking in the Stewartstown Road of a bus and also a burglary in which shot guns were taken. Constable Gribben made it clear to the court that the crimes under investigation from the outset of the second interview, at which he was present, were burglaries and hijackings; in other words more than two offences.

Unfortunately the question about invention was never followed up, but it may be that that is the explanation of the offence in count 1 where no particulars of the offence of hijacking are set out. It is possible, if not probable, that this incident was invented by Stephen Paul McCaul, and he was convicted of a crime that had not been committed by anyone.

Yet this seems to be the hijacking which the officers were investigating, not the second one set out in count 3 in the indictment. It does seem extraordinary that they may have been investigating an offence for which they had no exact date, no registration of the bus, and nothing about its ownership. On the other hand, in count 3 the police knew the exact date, 21 January 1979, the registration number COI 1426, and that it belonged to Ulsterbus Limited, for that is set out in count 4.

When the cross-examination had finished the trial judge asked Constable Shearer: "Now it has been put to you that you suggested things to him. How did these suggestions go?" The officer answered: "Well, we asked him about certain things and we asked him was he there or did he take part in it and he would have either said yes or no. Like we never pressured him into admitting anything, your honour."

In some courts that would have been the end of the case against the accused and the confession statements would have been ruled out. Clearly the interviews took the form of leading suggestible questions to the fifteen year old, he answered either yes or no to the questions; that was recorded in the police officers' notebooks, then read back to Stephen and eventually, by some amazing feat of almost total recall he dictated three confession statements in rapid succession, encapsulating the content of the interviews of the two days he was in custody.

Constable Gribben told defence counsel that "I took it that it had been tried to contact these people (a parent or social worker) by my superiors."[18] He went on to say that "Well, as far as I am concerned, your honour, I was under the impression that my superiors had tried all ways to get the parents there."[19] He denied, as did Constable Shearer, any knowledge of the numerous telephone calls said to have been made by Stephen's parents to Castlereagh. Even though his parents knew of the fact of his arrest, common sense dictates that they would have made inquiries about him at a police station when he did not return home on the first day. The parents' telephone number appears at the top of the statements, exhibits 1, 2 and 3. No witness for the prosecution ever gave evidence that contact had been made with the parents and they had refused to attend at the police station.

Stephen Paul McCaul did not give evidence either at the voir dire on the admissibility of the three statements or at the trial proper. The defence probably considered that there was the clearest evidence of breaches of the Administrative Directions. They did not need to establish any bad faith on the part of the police officers, merely that there had been a breach. Clearly the safeguards against a reliable confession were not in place; equally clearly on the prosecution's own version leading questions suggesting the answers were put to Stephen. However, the trial judge did not have the opportunity of judging Stephen's mental capacity, for Stephen did not speak at all at the trial.

The statements themselves contain a wealth of detail. Would he have been able, apart from the other points canvassed about exhibit 2, to describe a room in the house as follows: "I went into another room *like a study* [emphasis added] and started to search it." Would a fifteen year old pupil at a special school with a mental age of seven have known what a study was, and what it looked like?

Stephen Paul McCaul was convicted and sentenced to be detained for three years. His appeal against conviction was dismissed by the Court of Appeal. That Court, however, reduced the sentence from three years to eighteen months detention.[20] No disquiet was expressed by any of the Judges about the length of time Stephen had spent at the police station, all alone save for the RUC officers, and expressed not the slightest surprise at his amazing recollection and powers of description and beautifully constructed grammatical English. The courts regarded those statements as containing the absolute truth. Not everyone shares that view.

THE QUEEN v.   STEPHEN PAUL McCAUL   674/79

Court of Trial: BELFAST CROWN COURT

Date: 17 OCTOBER 1979   /

CHARGE S

Stephen Paul McCaul   is   charged with the following offence: s

FIRST COUNT

STATEMENT OF OFFENCE

Hijacking, contrary to section 2(1) of the Criminal Jurisdiction Act, 1975.

PARTICULARS OF OFFENCE

Stephen Paul McCaul on a date unknown between the 1st day of December 1978 and the 31st day of January 1979, in the County of Antrim, by force or threat thereof or by any other form of intimidation, unlawfully seized control of a motor vehicle, namely a bus.

SECOND COUNT

STATEMENT OF OFFENCE

Carrying a firearm with intent, contrary to section 16(1) of the Firearms Act
(Northern Ireland) 1969.

PARTICULARS OF OFFENCE

Stephen Paul McCaul on a date unknown between the 1st day of December 1978 and
the 31st day of January 1979, in the County of Antrim, had with him one firearm
or imitation firearm with intent to commit an indictable offence, namely hijacking,
or to resist arrest or to prevent the arrest of another.

THE QUEEN v.   STEPHEN PAUL McCAUL

THIRD COUNT

STATEMENT OF OFFENCE

Hijacking, contrary to section 2(1) of the Criminal Jurisdiction Act, 1975.

PARTICULARS OF OFFENCE

Stephen Paul McCaul on the 21st day of January 1979, in the County of Antrim,
by force or threat thereof or by any other form of intimidation, unlawfully
seized control of a motor vehicle, namely a bus, registration number COI 1426.

FOURTH COUNT

STATEMENT OF OFFENCE

Arson, contrary to Article 3(1) and (3) of the Criminal Damage (Northern Ireland)
Order, 1977.

PARTICULARS OF OFFENCE

Stephen Paul McCaul on the 21st day of January 1979, in the County of Antrim,
without lawful excuse, destroyed by fire a bus, registration number COI 1426,
belonging to Ulsterbus Limited, intending to destroy or damage the said bus
or being reckless as to whether the said bus would be destroyed or damaged.

FIFTH COUNT

STATEMENT OF OFFENCE

Carrying a firearm with intent, contrary to section 16(1) of the Firearms Act
(Northern Ireland) 1969.

PARTICULARS OF OFFENCE

Stephen Paul McCaul on the 21st day of January 1979, in the County of Antrim,
had with him one firearm or imitation firearm with intent to commit an indictable offence, namely hijacking, or to resist arrest or to prevent the arrest of
another.

THE QUEEN v.   STEPHEN PAUL McCAUL

SIXTH COUNT

STATEMENT OF OFFENCE

BURGLARY, contrary to section 9(1)(b) of the Theft Act (Northern Ireland) 1969.

PARTICULARS OF OFFENCE

Stephen Paul McCaul on the 18th day of January 1979, in the County of Antrim,
having entered as a trespasser a dwelling house situated at
                          stole therein two double-barrelled shotguns with cases,
a quantity of shotgun ammunition, a silencer for a .22 rifle, a quantity of silver
cutlery and silver utensils, an enamelled flower vase, a portable television set,
an antique glass, a transistor radio, a towel and a suitcase, to a total value of
£1,600 or thereabouts, belonging to N.   P.   H.

SEVENTH COUNT

STATEMENT OF OFFENCE

Possession of firearms and ammunition, contrary to section 19A of the Firearms
Act (Northern Ireland) 1969 as amended by the Firearms (Amendment) Act (Northern
Ireland) 1971.

PARTICULARS OF OFFENCE

Stephen Paul McCaul on the 18th day of January 1979, in the County of Antrim,
had in his possession two double-barrelled shotguns, one silencer for a .22 rifle
and a quantity of shotgun ammunition, under such circumstances as to give rise to
a reasonable suspicion that he did not have the same in his possession for a
lawful object.

EIGHTH COUNT

STATEMENT OF OFFENCE

Carrying a firearm with intent, contrary to section 16(1) of the Firearms Act
(Northern Ireland) 1969.

PARTICULARS OF OFFENCE

Stephen Paul McCaul on the 18th day of January 1979   in the County
of Antrim, had with him one firearm or imitation firearm with intent to commit an
indictable offence, namely robbery, or to resist arrest or to prevent the arrest
of another.

D081537.5m.9/76.D.gp.191

THE QUEEN v.   STEPHEN PAUL McCAUL

NINTH COUNT

STATEMENT OF OFFENCE

BURGLARY, contrary to section 9(1)(b) of the Theft Act (Northern Ireland) 1969.

PARTICULARS OF OFFENCE

Stephen Paul McCaul on the 26th day of January 1979, in the County of Antrim, having entered as a trespasser a dwelling house situated at stole therein a double-barrelled shotgun, a quantity of shotgun ammunition, a ring, three pens and thirty American dollars to a total value of £600 or thereabouts, belonging to J.   R.

TENTH COUNT

STATEMENT OF OFFENCE

Possession of a firearm and ammunition, contrary to section 19A of the Firearms Act (Northern Ireland) 1969 as amended by the Firearms (Amendment) Act (Northern Ireland) 1971.

PARTICULARS OF OFFENCE

Stephen Paul McCaul on the 26th day of January 1979, in the County of Antrim, had in his possession one shotgun and a quantity of shotgun ammunition, under such circumstances as to give rise to a reasonable suspicion that he did not have the same in his possession for a lawful object.

COUNT

STATEMENT OF OFFENCE

PARTICULARS OF OFFENCE

D081537.5m.9/76.D.gp.191

Chapter 7

DEATH IN THE DARKNESS
THE KILLING OF SEAMUS GREW AND RODERICK CARROLL

Maureen Grew lived at a house in Mullacreevie Park, a small estate on the outskirts of the city of Armagh, together with her husband Seamus and their eight year old son Michael. Seamus Grew had been released from prison on 8 April 1982 following a sentence of fourteen years imprisonment (of which he served seven) for paramilitary activities. His father had bought him a Hillman Hunter motor car which he used to drive to market, selling flowers and plants both locally and in the towns of Omagh and Enniskillen.

According to his wife, Seamus Grew was constantly and consistently stopped and questioned at road blocks, sometimes twice a day, by members of the Royal Ulster Constabulary and also by soldiers of the Ulster Defence Regiment. In June 1982 he was arrested and detained and questioned for three days at Gough Barracks in Armagh. He was released without charge.

On the evening of Wednesday, 22 September 1982, Maureen Grew was sitting drinking coffee in the kitchen at the back of the house with a friend, Teresa. Seamus Grew was sitting on a couch in another room, watching his young son playing on the floor. At about 10:20 there was a loud knock on the front door. Seamus called out "Who's there?" A voice replied, "Brian."

Seamus Grew opened the door. He was confronted by a man wearing a mask over his face and holding a machine gun. He tried to slam the door but the masked man prevented him from doing so by placing his foot on the door.

Seamus Grew ran back into the sitting room on the right hand side of the front door and lay behind the door, holding it with his feet so that the weight of his body prevented the door being opened fully, and at the same time he was able to cover the body of his young son with that of his own. The masked man got into the house and tried to force open the sitting room door with his foot. He fired one shot into the sitting-room. He missed his intended target, and the bullet lodged in the wall of that room. The gunman fired another single shot down towards the kitchen where Maureen Grew and Teresa were sheltering under the table. Neither was hit.

There was a pause and then a third shot was fired, not by the gunman inside the house but by a second man who was outside armed with a pistol. That shot through a window also missed. Maureen Grew thought that the first two shots had killed her husband and then her son Michael had been shot. She ran out of the house through the back room. Her husband and son followed. By some miracle all four people in the house had escaped injury.

Officers of the Royal Ulster Constabulary arrived about an hour later. It was known that three men were involved in the shooting and attempted murder, two gunman and a person driving the car. The police took statements and obtained forensic evidence of the shooting. They questioned those in the house and neighbours nearby, all to no avail.

The following Wednesday, 29 September, Seamus Grew was again arrested (under the emergency legislation then in force) when driving his car in Armagh city. He was detained in Gough Barracks for three days and then released without charge. According to his wife he was told on two occasions whilst in Gough that "He would be in his box before Christmas." [1] He was, so he told his wife, physically assaulted whilst in custody, and his shoulder and jaw were injured. He made a formal complaint about his ill-treatment and went twice to the RUC to make statements, in support of his complaint and allegations of ill-treatment.

Police investigations into those two complaints were never completed. Such inquiries as the RUC made into the attempted murders of Seamus and Maureen Grew and their son might easily have been speedily concluded had they gone to Drummagh Barracks in Armagh, for at least one of the three men involved was serving there, as a soldier in the Ulster Defence Regiment. He was Geoffrey Edwards, aged 26. He was arrested in December 1983 and he told the police he wanted to get the matter sorted out because it had been preying on his mind. He had served in the Regiment for seven years and had seen at least fifteen of his friends and associates murdered by terrorists and many more mutilated and injured. He believed that not enough was being done to combat violence and as a result he was moved to do something about it. [2]

Private Edwards's contribution towards a solution of the problems of violence in Northern Ireland was not limited to the attempted murder of Seamus Grew, his wife and son in their own home in September 1982. Between May 1982 until his arrest in December 1983 he and others had indulged in a catalogue of murder and mayhem.

One of his victims had been Peter Corrigan, aged 47, who had been shot dead in the street in the city of Armagh on 25 October 1982, whilst walking with his sixteen year old son Martin. Mr Corrigan's only alleged crime was to be a member of Sinn Fein, a legal political organisation in

209

Northern Ireland and elsewhere.

If any evidence or explantion of the continuing cycle of repetitive violence in Northern Ireland is ever needed, it is to be found in this case. Martin Corrigan had seen his father gunned down in the street of the city where he lived, shot dead by a fellow Irishman who wore the uniform of the British Army. No crime was ever alleged, let alone proved against the dead man, yet he had been selected for assassination by another person whose sworn responsibility was to uphold the law of the land.

Martin Corrigan himself had only another eight years to live, for on Wednesday, 18 April 1990 he was shot dead by members of an army foot patrol when he was seen with a number of others in the grounds of the home of a part-time member of the RUC. In a telephone call to the BBC in Belfast, the Irish People's Liberation Organisation, a republican splinter group, said that he was a member of that organistion and had been killed "on active service".[3] He was 24 years old and is survived by two young sons.

Amongst the other victims of Private Edwards were two pedestrians at whom he had fired from a passing motor car. Both were Catholics. He admitted a total of eighteen offences in addition to the murder of Peter Corrigan; he was also involved in the booby-trapped car bomb in March 1983 which exploded and injured two man and a six year old child. When he was questioned about the identity of his accomplices he refused to give names or specify the location of weapons, "because it was more than his life was worth."[4]

The terrorist campaign against members of the security forces continued unabated in the late summer and autumn of 1982. It is now clear that one of those suspected of paramilitary activities was Seamus Grew. He had long been noted in military and police intelligence files as a suspected member of an illegal organisation. As long ago as 29 March 1974 there was an attempt by three men to kidnap him from the house in Monaghan town in the Irish Republic where he was living in comparative safety away from the harrassment to which he was so frequently subjected while living in the North.

According to Fred Holroyd, a former British Army captain who worked as a military intelligence officer with MI6 in Northern Ireland, the kidnap plot was hatched by army officers stationed at 3 Infantry Brigade Headquarters.[5] The army were not themselves prepared to do the dirty work involved of crossing the border into the sovereign terrority of a friendly neighbouring state and so recruited three men to carry out the kidnapping: James O'Hara, aged 34, the ringleader and former boxer; William McCullough, aged 36, a former regular soldier in the British Army; and John Flynn, aged 22. Mr Holroyd says that the briefings were careful and took place at two different locations: "An NCO from Portadown briefed them on the operation, and provided maps and photographs of the area around Grew's house near the town of Monaghan. He also gave them a sketch plan showing where the victims (another man, Patrick McLoughlin, was to be included in the kidnapping) should be dumped across the border. The fee, once again, was set at £500."[6]

The plan went disasterously wrong. The neighbours near Seamus Grew's house saw William McCullough and John Flynn acting in a suspicious manner and called members of the Garda Siochana who promptly arrested both men. According to Fred Holroyd, "O'Hara, positive that the police knew all about the kidnap and had simply made a mistake, then walked in bold as brass to demand the release of his colleagues. He too was arrested."[7]

All three man appeared before the Special Criminal Court in Green Street, Dublin the following June and were each sentenced to five years imprisonment for conspiracy to assault Seamus Grew. James O'Hara, the ringleader of the operation told the investigating officers of the Garda Siochana, who questioned him in a number of interviews, that the British Army had set the whole job up. That allegation was either disbelieved or disregarded as a mitigating factor by the Special Criminal Court and also by the Court of Criminal Appeal to which all three convicted men appealed against sentence. For an appeal which was clearly regarded as being utterly devoid of merit the sentence of all three was increased from five years to seven years imprisonment. If James O'Hara was telling the truth about the involvement of the British Army, however, then here was the clearest evidence of collusion between the security forces and loyalist terrorists, prepared together to commit criminal offences.

Included in the ninety-seven violent deaths that occurred during 1982 was that of a former member of the UDR, William McIlveen, who was killed in a car bomb in August in County Armagh. In October another member of the UDR, Frederick Williamson, was shot dead in his car. On 16 November two Reserve Constables – Ronald Irwin and Samuel Corkery – were shot dead at the security barrier in Markethill, County Armagh.

Only two days before that, on a Friday, Seamus Grew and Roderick Carroll were stopped at a UDR checkpoint on the Keady Road outside Armagh City. A taxi driver who witnessed the incident rushed to the Parochial House in Abbey Street to contact Father Raymond Murray and ask him to attend the scene to ensure the safety of the two men detained there; it was feared that they would be shot. Unfortunately Father Murray was not in the house at the time but one of the curates spoke to the taxi driver, and subsequently that priest drove hurriedly to the UDR checkpoint at the O'Hare's crossroads at Farmacaffley on the Keady Road.

On arrival the priest found that a car had stopped on the left hand side of the road just behind a UDR landrover. He approached the nearest soldier and asked to speak to the commanding officer. That soldier motioned to another uniformed man who, before the priest could tell him why he was there, said that if he had a complaint to make he should make it to the RUC. There was in fact a grey RUC landrover parked in the entry to the small road to the left of the crossroads, and the priest made as if to go towards it. The UDR man ordered the priest to stay in his car and he went over to the police landrover. He spoke to the police officers and returned asking the priest his business.

The priest told the UDR officer that he had been called to the scene because there was a fear for the lives of two young men there in the car. Two or three times Roderick Carroll called out to the priest as he talked, "Don't go away, Father, they're going to shoot us." The soldier insisted that there was no danger for the two men. The priest asked permission to stay at the scene until the army had completed their investigations and this was allowed if he remained in his car. He was asked for his driving license and it was taken away to be checked.

The priest waited for about fifteen to twenty minutes. During that time the RUC landrover drove away from the scene. Roderick Carroll left his car and approached the priest asking him not to leave. He was ordered to return to his car by the UDR. The priest told him to be calm and return to the car, which he did. The officer to whom the priest had previously spoken then ordered him to leave the checkpoint area.

A request that he be allowed to stay at the scene was refused. The priest then asked that he be allowed to park some distance from the checkpoint, but still in view of it, but this was also refused. The officer said he could not allow the activities of his men to be under surveillance. The priest was allowed to speak to Seamus Grew and Roderick Carroll before leaving; he spoke to them as they sat in the car and he stood by its door. Mr Carroll told him again that they had been threatened by the UDR men who said they would shoot them and that they had already been detained for about two hours. It was clear to the priest that both were frightened. He later noted in a statement to Father Murray, "Roddy was in a state of panic. I feared that they were under such pressure that they might foolishly try to break away from the checkpoint and so I urged them to be cool and not do anything rash. I told them that now that I had been on the scene whatever grounds they had for fear were now not there as my witnessing of their predicament would make them safe. At this point the UDR officer told me I must leave. I pointed to their frightened state and he assured me that no harm would come to them, to this he gave me his word. I asked for his name or rank or any title by which I could identify him; this he refused to give." The priest then left the Keady road and returned to the Parochial House. The next time a priest from that address was to see Seamus Grew and Roderick Carroll together in a car was to be twenty-four days later. Both had been shot dead at close range, in the car, by a member of the security forces.

Late on that Friday evening, 14 November, however, both Mr Carroll and Mr Grew were taken from the scene and detained for three days at Gough Barracks. Whilst held there before being released without charge, the house at 93, Callanbridge, Armagh where Roderick Carroll lived with his mother and other members of his family was raided and searched by the RUC. Nothing incriminating was found.

Roderick Carroll was 22 years old. He had been born in Daisy Hill Hospital, Newry. He received part of his education at the Christian Brothers' School in Armagh. Amongst the jobs he had had was one working in a fruit retail outlet. His mother, Mrs Teresa Carroll, has related[8] that from about the time he was seventeen Roderick was constantly harassed by the security forces. He was a member of a highly political family, well known in the Armagh area. His brother Adrian was shot dead in Armagh city eleven months later, in November 1983. A soldier, Private Neil Latimer, of the Ulster Defence Regiment is serving life imprisonment for that murder.

Mrs Carroll recalled that in 1980 he was stopped by the army at the post office in Armagh city. He gave all his details that he was required to give, but refused to give his date of birth. There was no legal obligation on him to provide that information and he was justified in law in declining to do so. Such an approach would not of course have commanded itself to the British Army. Roderick Carroll was taken to the RUC station where it was confirmed by the police officers there that he did not have to give his date of birth to the army.

The soldiers left the station before he did. The same soldiers saw him shortly afterwards in Scotch Street in the city and stopped him and again asked for his date of birth. He again refused to give it. An argument and then a fight followed. Mr Carroll was arrested, charged with assaulting a soldier, convicted and fined. The defence of provocation – he had indeed been provoked by the misuse of any powers the army thought they had – was not available to him on the charge of assault.

Mrs Teresa Carroll has stated that her son had been lifted under the emergency legislation then in force on three occasions when he was held for three days, and on two occasions held for seven days, and eventually released without charge. Between early February and mid-October 1982 he had been held on remand in Crumlin Road jail in Belfast. On 13 October 1982 the charges against him were dropped.[9]

Shortly after what proved to be his last detention at Gough Barracks, Roderick Carroll made a written complaint on 20 November 1982 to the Complaints & Discipline Branch of the Royal Ulster Constabulary. The basis of that complaint was that he had been threatened that he would be killed by the security forces. He didn't tell his mother the minute details of what happened to him whilst he was held in Gough Barracks between 14 and 17 November, but he did talk "about being threatened with death. 'They always kept saying,' he said, 'they would shoot him but he said: as long as they keep telling me I don't believe them'."[10] The complaint was made on 20 November.

On 23 December 1982 a letter was sent from the RUC acknowledging receipt of the complaint made by Mr Roderick Carroll. By that latter date, Mr Carroll was dead, having been shot on December 12, by a member of the very same security forces about whom he had complained about their threats to kill him.

Roderick Carroll's grandfather Thomas O'Connor had died on Friday, 10 December 1982. The funeral was to take place on the morning of Sunday, 12 December after Mass in Magherafelt, County Derry. Members of the Carroll family, including Roderick and his sister Irene arrived there about 10:30 a.m.

Following the internment at Desmartin, Irene and Roderick Carroll and Seamus Grew left the graveyard at about 1:45 p.m. and drove in Seamus Grew's yellow Allegro car back to Armagh. They arrived at Callanbridge Park around 2:30 p.m.

Immediately the car arrived in front of the Carroll family home it was surrounded by soldiers of the UDR. All three left the car and ran into the house; from there they watched about eight soldiers around the car. One of them was seen by Irene to take a book out of his pocket, look at his watch and write something in the book. Another soldier looked at the car's number plate. Seamus Grew telephoned his wife at about 3 p.m. asking her to keep his dinner warm and told her that the UDR had the house surrounded and he didn't want to go out while they were there because they would probably hold him for an hour or two.[11]

Seamus Grew arrived home about half an hour after making that telephone call from the Carroll house. He left his home to collect his eight year old son from his mother-in-law's and brought him back to the house. He left home again sometime between 5:20 and 6 p.m. telling his wife that he was to take one of the Carroll girls back home to Monaghan and that he hoped to be home about 9:30 p.m. at the latest.[12]

THE ROYAL ULSTER CONSTABULARY
COMPLAINTS & DISCIPLINE BRANCH
Ormiston House Hawthornden Road Belfast N Ireland BT4 3JW

Telephone : Belfast 672272 650222

Please reply to The Chief Constable

MR. R. CARROLL,
93, Callanbridge PK,
ARMAGH:
BT 60

Your reference:

Our reference: A47/1613/82

Date: 23.12.82.

Dear Sir/Madam

I acknowledge receipt of the complaint dated: 20.11.82.

made/by you/On behalf of/on your behalf by: . . . .

. . . .

The subject of which will receive attention.

Yours faithfully

Chief Inspector
for Chief Constable

215

Roderick Carroll and his sister Irene got into Seamus Grew's car, collected a young person called Joseph from his grandmother's house, and left Armagh at about 6:10 p.m. On leaving Callanbridge Park there was no sign of any soldiers of the UDR or any police officers of the RUC. On the journey to Monaghan through Clontibret, thus avoiding a checkpoint at Middleton, there was one stop at a supermarket. Irene went in, the two men and Joseph stayed in the car. They arrived at Irene's home at about 6:45. She asked them in but they declined the invitation. Seamus Grew and Roderick Carroll left in the car.

Although they had seen no member of the army or police, they were themselves under constant surveillance by an Inspector of the Special Branch of the RUC and other members of the security forces.

The top secret sections of the Royal Ulster Constabulary are grouped into five offices. One of the groups is Echo Four – E4. One of E4's special tasks is close surveillance of individuals who are targeted for special observation. A particular section within the group has prime responsibility for such operations; this section is a Technical Support Unit, Echo Four Alpha, E4A. It consists of serving RUC officers under the command of a Special Branch Inspector. Members of this group operate almost always in civilian clothes.

E4A operates closely with two Special Support Units – at times referred to as Headquarters Mobile Support Units – to whom it provided intelligence gleaned in the course of its own operations. These SSU's operate in unmarked vehicles, known as "Q" cars; there are about forty-eight members in total in the two groups. All are police officers but many are former members of the British Army who had served in Northern Ireland and elsewhere. All are specially selected for the units and are trained by the SAS. They are armed with non-standard RUC weapons.

It was members of E4A and the SSU which followed and confronted Seamus Grew and Roderick Carroll at Mullacreevie Park on the outskirts of the city as they returned home to Armagh at about 8:30 on the night of Sunday, 12 December. Constable John Robinson, shot both of them dead from close range. The circumstances in which he did so have been the subject of controversy ever since that date.

However, the pattern of events is familiar: first the incident. Then the immediate issuing of a false statement by the security forces, calculated to deceive the general public. Then a police investigation, carried out with a number of constraints on whom and when and where witnesses are to be interviewed, coupled with a total lack of enthusiasm for the establishment of the truth so that justice could be done. Finally a trial, where vital evidence is concealed from the

216

prosecution and the court.

Some facts are easily established. According to Doctor James Press, the Assistant State Pathologist for Northern Ireland, his postmortem report on Seamus Grew discloses that he had been struck by seven bullets most of which could have come from behind and to his left.

The cause of death was gunshot wounds to the head and trunk. A bullet had entered the left side of the back of the head and had passed through to the right fracturing the skull and lacerating the brain before making its exit on the right side of the scalp. Three bullets had struck the trunk. One had entered the left side of the back of the chest and had passed to the right fracturing the fifth left rib and had lacerated the left lung, the aorta and the right lung before fracturing the fifth right rib and making its exit on the right side of the chest. A second bullet had entered the centre of the back and had passed forwards to the right fracturing the sixth right rib, lacerating the right lung and fracturing the fourth right rib before making its exit in the region of the armpit. It had then entered the inner side of the right arm and had passed through the muscles to lodge beneath the skin on the outer side of the arm. The third bullet which had entered the back passed upwards to the right for about three inches and lodged in the muscles close to the spine. The combined effect of these injuries would have caused his rapid death.

A bullet had also transversed the right forearm and another had passed through the left hand whilst a further bullet had grazed the left buttock. These injuries, however, were not serious and would not have accelerated death.

The injuries were of a type caused by bullets of low velocity. The bullets from the body were 9 mm. parabellum.[13]

In the case of Roderick Carroll the pathologist found that the cause of death was gunshot wounds of the head and trunk. He had been struck by at least seven, and possibly nine, bullets most of which appeared to have come from behind and to his right. Two bullets had struck the head. One had passed superficially upwards and to the left through the scalp, whilst the other had entered the right side of the back of the scalp and had passed forwards to the left lacerating the brain and brain stem before lodging in the left side of the base of the skull. Four bullets had struck the trunk. One had grazed the centre of the back whilst the others had entered the right side of the back. One had passed forwards, lacerating the right lung before passing through the upper end of the breast bone and making its exit on the centre of the front of the chest. Another had passed forwards fracturing four ribs before lodging beneath the skin on the front of the chest whilst a further bullet had passed forwards lacerating the liver before making its exit on the front of the chest. A bullet had also traversed the right forearm and another had grazed the palm of the right hand. A further bullet had also passed from left to right through the soft tissues on the front of the left groin.

The injuries to the head and chest would have caused his rapid death. The injuries were of a type caused by bullets of low velocity. The appearance of some of the entrance wounds would indicate that the bullets had struck some object such as a car door before striking this man. Examination of the bullets from the body revealed that they were 9 mm. parabellum.[14]

The statement issued by the RUC press office within hours of the shootings recounted that officers in uniform were manning a road block at Girvans Bridge, five miles from the city centre. Suddenly a car broke through, knocking down a policeman; the car was identified as being owned by a known terrorist. The police at the roadblock radioed for help and another police car which was in the general area gave chase. The police car forced the terrorist car to a halt in Mullacreevie Park. The terrorist car then reversed at speed; officers were revealed in its headlights, shouting for the driver to stop, and believing they were about to be fired upon, they opened fire themselves and killed Seamus Grew and Roderick Carroll.

Crucial parts of that press statements were later shown to be untrue. The speed at which it was issued, the fundamental falsity of its approach gives rise to the suspicion that the whole episode had been planned with meticulous precision, for unless the police officers were ready to go along with that false story the whole purpose of issuing it would have been defeated.

It was not until a week after the shootings that officers of the CID interviewed Constable John Robinson. A week may be a long time in politics; it is of inestimable length in the conduct of a police inquiry. When this interview and others were collated in a file, a high ranking police office (John Stalker) from outside Northern Ireland described this file – and other files: "We had expected a particularly high level of inquiry in view of the nature of the killings, but this was shamefully absent. The files were little more than a collection of statements, apparently prepared for a coroner's inquiry. They bore no resemblance to my idea of a murder prosecution file."[15]

Constable Robinson's account of the killings was taken in question and answer form and then reduced to a written statement.[16] He said that he had reported for duty at his base in Belfast on the morning of Sunday, 12 December. He further said that he was always the observer in the Cortina car, that Constable "D" was the driver. That statement was also false, because Constable Robinson left Gough Barracks driving

218

the Cortina himself. He described the colour of the car as silver; in fact it was red/beige in colour. He further said that they had patrolled generally in the area during 12 December driving past Seamus Grow's house. That was similarly false: there was no patrolling and he had not driven past the house. He also said that he had heard on the radio that Grew's car had gone through a vehicle check point injuring a policeman. This was in accordance with the false statement issued by the RUC press office within hours of the shootings that the terrorist car had gone through the road block injuring a police officer and another police car in the general area set off in pursuit. In fact no such message was transmitted on the radio, no vehicle check point had been set up, and thus there was not one to go through, and no policeman had been injured in the way described. The explanation for these outright lies given at a later stage was that Constable Robinson and other members of his unit were told by senior police officers to give this story so as to conceal the fact that they were participating in a planned operation based on sourced information and acting in concert with army surveillance teams.[17] Why the last fact had to be concealed defies comprehension.

Constable Robinson described to the investigating police officers at this first interview how he had intercepted Mr Grew's Allegro car as it indicated to turn right into the entrance to the Mullacreevie Park housing estate. He decided to stop the car at that point because he understood it to be a strong republican area and also because there must have been a good reason for driving throught the vehicle check point earlier. In other words those travelling in the Allegro had something or someone to hide; however, the Allegro had not driven through a checkpoint, and Constable Robinson knew very well that this was so and, accordingly, this could not have been a valid reason in his mind for stopping the car.

The Constable said that he drew level with the Allegro and waved his police cap out of the window to cause it to stop. He recognised Seamus Grew as the driver. The Allegro stopped and Constable Robinson left the car he was in and went to the passenger side of the Allegro. The explantion for approaching the Allegro in this way and not confronting the driver was that he did not wish to be caught in the headlights of the other car. This may be contrasted with the initial statement issued by the RUC where the explantion and justification for opening fire was that the officers were presented as a target in the glare of the headlights. The Allegro started to rev and Constable Robinson called on the occupants to halt. The front passenger door was flung open and then shut. As the door shut the officer heard, he said, a loud bang. He believed he had been shot at. He immediately opened fire with his Smith and Wesson revolver. He said he believed he had been shot at and his life was in danger. He fired fifteen shots, empting the magazine, into the passenger door. All save one entered the interior of the car, killing Roderick Carroll.

Constable Robinson then told the CID in his statement that he reloaded his revolver, then ran around to the other side of the car – but this time around the front so being lit up in the car's headlights in full view of a man whom he believed to be dangerous – and fired four shots at the driver's door. "I knew the driver was Grew. I knew his capabilities and I still thought someone had arms in the car and they could still be used against us." [18] He had fired at a distance of about ten feet; he approached the driver's door and opened it with his left hand and the man he knew as Grew fell out onto the road.

That statement caused a number of difficulties. The pathologist's report made it clear that although some of the bullets that hit Roderick Carroll had marks consistent with penetrating the door, those that hit Seamus Grew did not. His body was found "on the road lying parallel to and about 18 inches from the car with his head towards the rear of the car." Yet Constable Robinson was here maintaining that after reloading his gun he had fired at the driver's closed door. In addition, a forensic scientist discovered, on examination of Mr Grew's Parka jacket, two upper back-entry holes around which were particles of unburnt propellant. That scientist was convinced that these particles came from ammunition fired by Constable Robinson, when the muzzle of the pistol was within 30 to 36 inches of Mr Grew's back.

The scientific evidence leads to two possible conclusions. First that the driver's door must have been open when the four shots were fired and second that Constable Robinson must have been within three feet of the victim when he fired the two shots that hit the upper back.[19]

The Constable was interviewed on two further occasions and given the opportunity to explain his previous statement. About the first interview, he said, on 9 March 1983, that it would seem that his observations at the time were not right. When he opened fire on the passenger side that door was definitely closed and when he ran to the other side he must have related the closed door to the passenger side and not the driver's. The whole thing happened in a matter of seconds and needed a split second decision. He added that he believed that his life was in danger, but that some of the shots might have been fired at a closer range that he originally believed. It was possible that he opened the driver's door as he fired his last shot and the body fell out and not after he had finishing firing his pistol, as he previously thought.

The final interview took place on 20 July 1983. This involved one of the most bewildering aspects of this case. Two senior RUC officers, a deputy chief constable and a detective chief superintendent, told Constable Robinson that any constraints imposed upon him by the Official Secrets Acts were lifted. He had "previously been reminded of the constraints imposed upon him by the Official Secrets Acts,"[20] presumably by those officers who were concocting the false story for the purpose of concealing the truth. As a matter of law, those Acts make it an offence to communicate secret information to unauthorised persons, and it is beyond any argument that the provision of information to a police officer conducting a murder inquiry is not within either the spirit or the letter of the Official Secrets Acts, since that officer is authorised to receive any such information.

Even after being told that there were no constraints upon him, no doubt in an effort to establish the truth, Constable Robinson continued to maintain that the road block at Girvens Bridge had actually existed, because he was told to keep it in his account – but not of course by the two senior RUC officers who saw him on that day. Its importance to Constable Robinson's case was self-evident. He said he had the breaking through the road block in mind when he opened fire – because someone or something must have a very good reason for going through the vehicle check point earlier.

A substantial number of people living in Mullacreevie Park had heard the sounds of the shootings. One elderly man went to the door of his house. He saw a man with a rifle. "He bent his knees and fired about twenty shots into the driver's side of the car that had stopped near a lamp-post on Mullacreevie Park Road not very far in from the Killylea Road. The guy with the rifle had a peaked cap. I figured he had a uniform. He fired from about ten foot away. There was another fella back from him. He seemed to have a hand gun, seemed to have a big jumper on him. He walked up to the car and put a few shots into it after the man had fired with the rifle. The two men kept moving up and down. The headlights were on the car but I saw no door opened. There was a car stationary at the bottom of the park, on the Killylea Road, at the left corner as I looked down; it was facing towards Caledon. The another car came to the corner from the Caledon direction and parked at the right corner of the junction as I looked down. About six man got out of it with torches and weapons, policemen. They came and went around both sides of the car, flashing the torches into it. When I was looking down I though I saw a body at the side of the car, although I didn't see anybody coming out of the car . . . When there was more light shown around the car I though I saw what was a body with a white shirt

221

lying at the side."[21]

That eye witness account describing the man with the rifle was quite exact, for there was such a person involved in the incident: Constable "D". He had fired five shots at the driver's side of the car from .223 Ruger Rifle. None of those shots hit either of the two occupants. Two shots penetrated the offside rear window and exited through the rear window; one had struck low on the door and had entered the door pillar; one struck the edge of the roof above the rear passenger's window and one struck the bottom edge of the car near to the offside wheel.[22] The circumstances in which Constable "D" fired those shots, whether before, during or after the pistols shots fired by Constable Robinson were not described by him in any public forum. Why he failed to do so can only be a matter of speculation. It is a fact that the last moments of Seamus Grew and Roderick Carroll were witnessed not only by the man who killed them both, but also by another eye-witness who could have supported his version of events but did not do so.

The killings happened about 8:30 on that Sunday evening. The Administrator of St. Patrick's Parish at that time was the Very Reverend Patrick McDonnell. He received a telephone call telling him that there had been a shooting at Mullacreevie and that a priest would be needed. He drove to the estate and spoke to a police officer who walked with him to the car.

Father McDonnell asked him who it was. He replied, "I think it's Seamie Grew. It's his car." The priest went to the passenger door. It was open and he saw a body slumped face down and part kneeling, with the head resting on the driver's seat. "I went round to the driver's side and got into the car that way as it was easier. It was only then that I noticed the body lying on the road. It was lying in a pool of blood face up. The blood seemed to be coming from the back of his neck or head. There was more blood on his lips. There were no marks on the face or front that I could see. The policeman shone the torch on the face and said, 'That's Grew alright.' I looked into the car at the body in the car. It looked so small and crumpled up that I said, 'My God, it's Michael'. I thought it was Seamus Grew's little son because I couldn't see the face. The policeman said, 'No, its Roddy Carroll.' The face was lying down in a pool of blood. All you could see was part of the forehead and there was no way of knowing who it was without lifting up the head and getting a look at the face. There was enough light around to see into the car and see the colour of the blood. I still didn't see the face of Roddy but the policeman knew it was Roddy Carroll. I anointed the two men and said prayers."[23]

It may well be that shortly after the shooting and before the arrival at the scene of Father McDonnell the police officers had established the identities of the two dead men. But there is another explanation: officers of the RUC knew before the killings who the two men in the car actually were, for throughout that Sunday the yellow Allegro driven by Seamus Grew had been under the surveillance of a Special Branch Inspector. He was actually at the scene of the shooting, although he fired no shots. Substantial efforts were made to conceal the fact of his surveillance, and his presence at the scene, and amongst the lies told by Constable Robinson at the first CID interview on 19 December 1982 was one by omission. He never mentioned the existence of the Special Branch Inspector at all – it was that officer who had driven him and Constable "D" after Constable Robinson left his red/beige Cortina car and got into a silver coloured Peugot and followed the Allegro to Mullacreevie Park. It was only after Constable Robinson was charged with the murder of Seamus Grew that some, but not all, of the truth began to emerge.

Following the police inquiries, such as they were, into the killings, Constable John Robinson was charged with murder and he appeared before Mr Justice MacDermott, sitting alone without a jury, in Belfast Crown Court. The officer pleaded not guilty. The trial lasted for seven days and concluded on 3 April 1984. The evidence from the defence, and particularly from the defendant himself, was on some material points directly contradictory to the first RUC press office release and the first statement, exhibit 42, which Constable Robinson had made to the investigating CID officers.

The Court was told that eleven members of the- Special Support Unit were sent from Belfast to Gough Barracks in Armagh on Saturday, 11 December, not the Sunday as the Constable had previously told the police. They had not carried out any vehicle checks either that day or the Sunday and they had not driven past Seamus Grew's house. In fact they stayed at Gough Barracks on Saturday night and did not leave until 8 p.m. on Sunday evening. By that time the yellow Allegro driven by Seamus Grew was within thirty minutes drive of his home.

In his written reserved judgement, Mr Justice MacDermott noted that "The members of the unit had been sent to Armagh as the police authorities believed, as a result of information from their intelligence sources, that a man called McGlinchey was coming over the border from the Republic of Ireland on either the Saturday or Sunday. McGlinchey was a man believed to be deeply involved in terrorist activity whom the police wanted to apprehend in connection with the fatal shooting of a postmistress and a man who the police believed to be coming north to kill members of the security forces. It was also the police belief that McGlinchey would enter Northern Ireland in an Allegro driven by the deceased Grew, who also was known to be a leading member of the Irish National Liberation Army, a man who had a few months previously been released from prison after receiving a 14 year sentence, a known terrorist and a man who had attacked members of the police. Both were men likely to be armed and who would have no qualms about seeking to resist arrest".[24]

There are a number of comments which may be made in respect of this part of the judgement. First, one wonders whether the learned judge was told of the number of times that Seamus Grew had been arrested and detained in Gough Barracks since his release from prison in April 1982. On no occasion then had he resisted arrest or was found to be armed. Did he know, for example, that soldiers of the UDR had been outside the Carroll house in Callanbridge Road that very Sunday afternoon, looking at and noting the registration number of his Allegro whilst Mr Grew was inside the house? If it was indeed true, and the learned judge stated it as a fact, that Mr Grew was a leading member of the Irish National Liberation Army, then why was he not charged with the offence of belonging to a proscribed organsiation, an offence which on conviction on indictment carries a sentence of ten years imprisonment?[25] That organisation, which claimed responsibility for the murder of the Conservative member of Parliament, Airey Neave, had been proscribed in July 1979 and that proscription was still in force both at the time of the killings and the trial.[26]

In fact there was no such evidence of membership of the INLA in existence, and the statement by the learned judge was based either on speculation or gossip or both. Indeed the lack of such evidence is impliedly admitted in the subsequent paragraph of the judgement. After stating that "the accused and his colleagues were fully briefed and I am satisfied that from his previous knowledge of the reputations of both Grew and McGlinchey and from his briefings the accused was well aware that his task was likely to involve contact with at least if not two of the most dangerous terrorists who were known to the police," the judge added, "The task given to the accused and his colleagues was the capture of McGlinchey. To do this Grew's car was to be stopped. If McGlinchey were in it he was to be arrested. If he were not in it the car was to be searched and if nothing suspicious were found the occupants, including Grew, were to be allowed to proceed."[27]

Thus it was admitted and accepted that there was no evidence against Seamus Grew that he was a member of a proscribed organisation, because in the absence of McGlinchey and an abortive search he was to be released then and there. Why he was described as "a most dangerous terrorist" but to be released forthwith without charge if

McGlinchey was not in the car defies comprehension. He was living at home with his wife and young son. Private Geoffrey Edwards knew exactly where to find him when he tried to assassinate him on 22 September 1982. Although Mr Grew was thought by the learned judge to have no qualms about resisting arrest, he was unable on that date to defend himself, his wife and child and his home; no firearm was in his possession at that time either. Nor had he resisted arrest on any occasion when detained by the RUC or the army in the months following his release from prison.

Two further points seem not to have troubled the learned trial judge in the slightest. Why would one of the most dangerous terrorists known to the police allow himself to be conveyed in a car easily recognisable and clearly known to the security forces as being owned by another most dangerous terrorist? It was common knowledge throughout Northern Ireland that ever since 1974 the security forces used a computerised vehicle number plate system, using the code-name Operation Vengeful. The main-frame computer was based at the headquarters of the British Army in Lisburn near Belfast, but Vengeful terminals, many of them postioned at checkpoints on the border with the Irish Republic, could be used to obtain information on a car in about thirty seconds.

Moreoever, was it really considered likely that Seamus Grew would not only use his own vehicle to drive McGlinchey across the border into Northern Ireland, but would then take him to his own home, at which address a loyalist death squad had tried to kill Mr Grew less than three months earlier? Surely a safe house and a unrecognisable car would have been available to McGlinchey and his accomplices in any part of Northern Ireland?

In summing up the evidence, Mr Justice MacDermott recited the version that had been given to him before him at the trial: "The accused [Constable Robinson] left Gought Barracks driving a Cortina police car. It contained two other constables and the three vehicles proceeded towards Keady. The army was also participating in this operation."[28]

There is very little mention of the existence of army personnel that I can find in any of the literature on this case, and their activities that Sunday night are not disclosed anywhere. Who the soldiers were, how many of them there were, and for what purpose they were involved is completely unknown. So far, the head count of other personnel involved in the operation in addition to those soldiers seems to be nine constables of the Special Support Unit and one Special Branch Inspector, whose existence had been carefully concealed from the investigating police officers at the outset of their inquiry into the killings.

The learned judge continued: "Unfortunately two civilian vehicles

225

driven by army personnel were in collision with each other a few miles outside Armagh, and the Cortina driven by the accused in turn struck the rear of the second army vehicle. This had the effect of putting the accused's Cortina out of action and reducing the screen of vehicles which was hoping to stop Grew's car. Whilst the traffic incident was being sorted out a silver Peugeot came up from the Keady direction and stopped. It was being driven by an Inspector "L" who was a member of the Special Branch and was alone in the car."

The trial judge had been misled by this evidence into thinking that Inspector "L" had just appeared on the scene by chance. He had not. In fact that Inspector had been following the yellow Allegro during its journey into the Irish Republic and back again across the border into Northern Ireland.

When John Stalker, the former Deputy Chief Constable of the Greater Manchester Police who had headed an investigation into this and other cases of killings in Country Armagh, wrote his autobiography he said this: "In an accidental collision between an undercover army car and a police car a policeman had hurt his leg. We found that during the resulting confusion the suspects' Allegro car had driven past the accident undetected, followed by an RUC Special Branch Inspector who had been on their trail in the Province and in the Republic of Ireland. He saw the shambles on the side of the road, realised that Grew and Carroll had driven past unseen, and panicked. He picked up an armed RUC officer – Constable Robinson – and pursued the car containing Grew and Carroll. On the outskirts of the staunchly Catholic Mullacreevie Park housing estate in Armagh, the undercover police car pulled ahead of the suspects' car and Constable Robinson got out. He emptied his revolver into Grew and Carroll, reloaded and fired more shots. Both men died instantly. The Special Branch Inspector, who had had the opportunity to see everything and knew the truth, drove off, and his evidence was kept secret from the CID investigating the deaths and from the Director of Public Prosecutions and the courts. Records were altered to hide the use of undercover cars in that part of Northern Ireland."[29]

Apart from the factual error that *two* Constables got into the Special Branch car, not one as Mr Stalker described, this statement raises an issue of fundamental importance in this case. Did Inspector "L" know that the two men in the car were Roderick Carroll and Seamus Grew and that McGlinchey was not, and never had been, in that car on the fateful Sunday? Mr Stalker had no doubt about this point, for he said: "The complex operation, the surveillance, the unauthorised journeys by police officers into the Irish Republic, and finally the shootings were all part of a plan to detain McGlinchey. He had not, however, been seen by any policemen that day despite the long periods of surveillance, and it was never established – certainly not by me – that Seamus Grew and Roddy Carroll had been in his company."[30]

This statement begs the question: did Mr Stalker get this information from Inspector "L"? If he did, there must be a follow up question: did the Inspector tell Constable Robinson that the man in the car with Seamus Grew was Roderick Carroll and not McGlinchey? If he did not, why not?

Certainly the trial judge displayed no interest in what evidence the Special Branch Inspector might have been able to provide to the court – had he been called. Surprising as it may seem, not one but two eye-witnesses to a double killing were not called either by the prosecution or the defence at Constable Robinson's trial for murder. As has been noted already, Constable "D" who fired the .223 Ruger rifle at the Allegro was not called; nor was Inspector "D".

Mr Justice MacDermott's comment on this point amounts to an understatement: "Other police in several vehicles were on tho scene within a matter of minutes and some of those who arrived gave evidence but, for I am sure, entirely proper reasons, I did not have the benefit of hearing either Constable "D" or Inspector "L"."[31] Thus the trial judge was content to hear the evidence of police officers who had not witnessed the shootings, while two who did told him nothing, and he saw nothing extraordinary in that. Bearing in mind what Mr John Stalker discovered about the surveillance, it is now clear that if the Special Branch Inspector had gone into the witness box and given evidence he would have had the choice of committing perjury or disclosing the entire truth. This might involve not merely what he knew, and what he told Constable Robinson as they drove towards Mullacreevie Park following the yellow Allegro but also since Mr Stalker talked of "RUC officers" – meaning more than one "making journeys into the Republic of Ireland . . . and "Records were altered to hide the use of undercover cars in that part of Northern Ireland" it might have been possible to discover how many cars were involved as well It is most unlikely that only one car driven by Inspector "L" would have been adequate for constant and continual surveillance, especially on some of the quiet country roads in that part of Northern Ireland. Moreoever if he had been detected by the two men in the other car, he would have been outnumbered, and for obvious reasons he had no radio in the silver Peugeot and would have been unable to summon assistance if detected or attacked.

When Constable Robinson gave evidence it soon became apparent that the false cover story that he had related to the CID in the first interview, on 19 December, was not of his making. He had been ordered to tell that story "so as to conceal the fact that they were participating in a planned operation based on source information."[32] After all, the Constable had been placed in great difficulty by the speedy and false statement issued by the press office of the RUC within hours of the shooting. One wonders whether he would have been allowed to tell the truth if he had wanted to do so at the outset.

In examination in chief, in reply to questions from his own counsel, Michael Lavery Q.C., "Were you aware that you would be interviewed by the CID?" Constable Robinson replied, "I was indeed, my Lord, yes." As the transcript shows, the questions and answers went like this:

"Q. And were you given instructions as to how you should deal with this interview?

"A. We were indeed, my Lord.

"Q. And what officers were involved, without giving their names? You could give their ranks.

"A. Superintendent, Chief Inspector and others present, my Lord.

And at a later stage:

"Q. Was there any discussion as to what you should tell the CID?

"A. There was indeed, my Lord.

"Q. And what was agreed, if I may call it that?

"A. *They produced a story*, my Lord. [emphasis added]

"Q. What was the story?

"A. Basically, my Lord, it removed the accident and replaced it with a vehicle check point.

"Q. What was the object of doing that then?

"A. That was to get rid of army involvement, my Lord. The accident was all sorted out and there was no source involvement at all.

"Q. So this was to appear as a chance encounter rather than a planned encounter?

"A. That's correct, my Lord."

When pressed by counsel for the Prosecution, Mr Anthony Cambell Q.C., on the details of the story and when it was first concocted and by whom, Constable Robinson stated the supposed road block was first mentioned on his return to Gough Barracks, and then again the next day, when on his return to his base at Lisnasharragh in Belfast a Chief Superintendent told him he could not mention some of the true details because of the Official Secrets Acts.

Constable Robinson, as a former soldier in the British Army, was obviously accustomed to obeying orders given to him by senior officers. A police officer must use his discretion in the exercise of his legal powers and is not in the same position as a soldier, but Robinson, because of his background and training, might have been more of the latter than the former. In addition, being stationed in Belfast meant that he, unlike other members of the security forces in the Armagh area, would not have known Roderick Carroll by sight. Unless he was told the identity of the passenger in the yellow Allegro he could well have believed that it was McGlincey, whom he expected to be there, and not anyone else. He would be a forceful, compelling and convincing witness as to that fact if he honestly and reasonably believed it to be true, notwithstanding that other unscrupulous men who placed him in that situation knew full well that it was not.

The security forces in Northern Ireland had on 12 December 1982 every reason to carry out a retaliatory attack on those they believed to be members of the Irish National Liberation Army, even though such an attack would have been unlawful, for around that time units of that organisation had become increasingly active in South Armagh, South Down, Tyrone, Derry and Belfast. On 6 December 1982 a bomb, allegedly planted by members of INLA, exploded in the disco of the Dropping Well public house in Ballykelly, County Derry. Seventeen people, including eleven British Army soldier, died in the explosion, and sixty-six people were injured. The clamour for a revenge attack within the security forces, especially those who witnessed the sight of the dead and heard the sounds of the dying must have been immense, and the urge to put to death someone, anyone, connected with the killers must have been almost overpowering.

Such sentiments, which must be resisted in a scenario where the security forces act in defence of law and order as they maintain they do in Northern Ireland, have sometimes surfaced not merely amongst politicians, but also in the courts. Earlier that year, in January 1982, three men were convicted of attempting to murder Bernadette McAliskey, who as Bernadette Devlin was a high profile Nationalist politician who had sat in the House of Commons. The three had burst into her home at about 8:15 on the morning of 16 January 1981 and shot her eight times and her husband four times in front of their three young children. Both survived the attack and Mrs McAliskey was present in court when the attempted murderers were sentenced. The gang leader was Andrew Watson, aged 25 years, a former member of the Ulster Defence Regiment. He was sent to prison for life.

According to Mrs McAliskey, during the homily on passing sentence, the trial judge said that he understood why the attempt had been made on her life. If that was said, then an explantion should have been given why a person who advocates the use of the democratic process to achieve political change should be a target for assassination, and when she is, then it is understandable why she is, since on the face of it the remark seems almost to condone the use of violence as a means of suppressing political protest. It would have been better for the reputation of an already discredited legal system in Northern Ireland if that comment had not been made. The judge who made it in that case was Mr Justice MacDermott.

When Counsel for the prosecution continued to press Constable Robinson for the details of the cover-up story and what he was told and when, the trial judge Mr Justice MacDermott made it clear that was not the issue the court had to decide: "I am not in this case conducting an inquiry into why the officers who advised, instructed or constrained the accused acted as they did. Neither the police, as such, nor those officers in particular are represented in these proceedings or charged with anything. My task throughout has been to decide whether or not the accused is guilty as charged."[33]

That is an attitude which some might find regretable, especially those who regard a criminal trial as being dedicated to the pursuit of truth. The question mark that hangs over this case is why it was better to tell lies, until they were discovered, in the hope that they would be believed, and not tell the truth at the very outset. The issue of protecting the identity of an informer was simply a smokescreen, for December 1982 marked the mid-point in the so called strategy of terrorist conversion, or more accurately the recruitment of accomplices as informers. Between 1981 and the end of 1983 twenty-five people had emerged from terrorist organisations and agreed to give evidence against their erstwhile colleagues.[34] Of these "supergrasses" fifteen were connected with the Provisional IRA, five with INLA, and five with the loyalist terrorist group the Ulster Volunteer Force, so that the existence of informers and the need to guard against their activities must have been very apparent to Dominic McGlinchey who was a leading figure in INLA.

It should not be thought that the "supergrass" cases in the 1980s was a new and innovative approach to the gathering of evidence to obtain convictions. Informers had been giving evidence in return for immunity from prosecution or early release from a prison sentence and subsequent resettlement since at least 1978. The Secretary of State for Northern Ireland told the House of Commons on 26 February 1985: "The total direct expenditure on the protection of individuals who gave evidence against former accomplices in terrorist organisations in the *last seven years* [emphasis added] amounted to just over 1. 3 million pounds."[35]

On 3 April 1982 Constable Robinson was acquitted of the murder of Seamus Grew. After the verdict Mr Seamus Mallon, the deputy leader of the Social Democratic and Labour Party in Northern Ireland and Member of Parliament for the area in which the killings had taken place said that the case was a "deadly body blow to the hope that justice will ever be fairly administered in Northern Ireland." He wanted to know if the RUC Chief Constable intended to take any action against the officers named in court as part of cover-up allegations.[36]

There was an inquiry carried out initially by John Stalker, the Deputy Chief Constable of the Greater Manchester Police, and completed by Colin Sampson, the Chief Constable of West Yorkshire, into the the cover-up disclosed at the Robinson trial. It was thought at the time that the inquiry would not get anywhere and it didn't. On 25 January 1988 the Attorney General, Sir Patrick Mayhew Q.C., announced in the House of Commons that "in the public interest" no prosecutions against members of the RUC will take place. He failed to say why the public interest was so served by such a decision.

Others may take a different view of the refusal to prosecute those who took part in a conspiracy to falsify and fabricate evidence and to otherwise obstruct the course of justice. According to the journalist Matthew Parris in the television programme *Week-End World*, " . . . at least one officer who could face charges has threatened to reveal embarrassing details of RUC and security forces' operations dating back many years. His revelations might draw in not only former senior RUC men but also British politicians who, he says have condoned politically sensitive and dubious operations including some across the Irish border."

Was that threat effective enough to persuade the politicians to stifle any prosecution for offences which were so clearly committed? In the last analysis, the politicians can always be relied upon to save themselves and allow truth to be the first casualty to conceal what has been done. While such an attitude persists, the violence will continue in Northern Ireland.

Postscript

On 3 December 1992 Sir John May's Second Report on the Maguire case was published. He states: "As a result of all the time which I have spent considering the case both before and since preparing my interim report in 1990, I have reached the conclusion that the Maguire Seven were the victims of a serious miscarriage of justice. Further, if the Attorney General had been aware in 1975 of the matters of which I am now aware affecting the reliability and credibility of the scientists upon whose evidence the prosecution case depended, I do not think he would have granted even the limited fiats which he did."[1]

With that conclusion I completely agree.

However, on one material matter of detail I profoundly disagree with Sir John May: on 17 January 1975 Mr Eliot Michael Hill was instructed as Counsel for the prosecution in the case, and accordingly it became his responsibility to draft a Statement of Facts to be submitted to the Attorney General seeking the grant of his Fiat – or leave – to proceed with the prosecution against the Maguires. He did a first draft prior to 7 February 1975 on which date he, Sir Michael Havers, Mr Paul Oliver Purnell and Mr Philip Havers, accompanied three Surrey police officers and five staff members from the DPP's office to RARDE to see a demonstration of the TLC procedure. After that date he amended the first draft, and the Statement of Facts were submitted to the Attorney General.

On 17 February 1975 the Attorney General wrote a minute to his Legal Secretary commenting on the Statement of Facts:

"The evidence against the others seems to be confined to the nitroglycerine traces under fingernails and on plastic gloves. Counsel's theory is that they had been breaking up explosive material and disposing of it as they feared a police raid. If this is correct, as it may well be, it is likely to have taken place after the arrival of Patrick Conlon at about 1 p.m. – 3 p.m. on 3 December, since swabs taken during the night of 3 December showed NG traces on all of them, including Patrick Conlon, who therefore seems to have arrived in time for the disposal process – possibly to warn the others to dispose of any explosive. But the police found no explosive when they searched. They found black tape identical with that used in the Talbot bomb, but that is the only connection with the Talbot bomb – or with any other bomb except through the statements of the four Guildford bombers who implicate Anne Maguire; but their statements are not evidence."

Patrick Conlon, Gerard's father, was generally known as Guiseppe, but his real name was in fact Patrick Joseph Conlon.

Of much greater importance was the fact that first, the description of the Guildford Four as "bombers" by the leading Law Officer of the Crown may come as a somewhat rude shock to those who believe in the presumption of innocence, i.e. that a suspect is deemed to be innocent until proved guilty in a court of competent jurisdiction. Second, it may be that what was not fully appreciated at this early stage of the case was the importance of the nitroglycerine traces under the fingernails which led to the scientists maintaining not just contact with NG, but with kneading it. The reason for this may not be hard to find, for Sir John May says[2] that he discovered no mention of the kneading hypothesis in the statements that had been prepared for the proposed prosecution in the Maguire case at the time of the visit to RARDE on 7 February 1975. Indeed it was only on the day before the committal, which began on 20 March 1975, that Mr Elliott prepared a further – third statement – in which he said: "It is my opinion that traces of nitroglycerine detected under the fingernails indicate that an explosive substance containing nitroglycerine has been handled and manipulated rather than merely touched."

The committal proceedings before the magistrates' court, at which the Crown had to make out a case for the seven defendants to answer and commit them for trial on indictment, were conducted by Mr Eliot Michael Hill. In spite of what Sir John May says about the absence of any reference in the witness statements prior to 7 February, it is a fact that Mr Hill knew of this hypothesis prior to that date, because he made express reference to it in paragraph 13 of the Statement of Facts: "Each of the person listed above had nitroglycerine under his fingernails and the officers taking the tests noted that the Maguire family had short bitten nails. The expert evidence will be that to get nitroglycerine under the fingernails it is necessary to 'knead' and that its presence under the nails is indicative of breaking sticks of explosives into smaller pieces, of inserting a detonator, of moulding the explosive into a convenient shape, of dismantling an already constructed bomb or some such 'intimate' act. *This will be the more so if the nails are short and bitten.*" (The emphasis in italics were added to the revised Statement after the visit to RARDE.) How Mr Hill acquired this knowledge at the time he wrote paragraph 13, without its source being reduced to writing, is not known.

Whatever the state of the Attorney General's knowledge on this point at the date of his minute it might have been changed on 18 February 1975, when there was the conference between the Attorney General and the prosecution team. This was clearly an important conference, and Sir

John May considers[3] what weight which may or may not have been given on that date to inadmissible evidence or to improper speculation.

It is necessary here to consider the perfected Statement of Facts drafted by Mr Eliot Michael Hill and sent by the Director of Public Prosecutions to the Attorney General on 14 February 1975. The words in italics show the revisions to the first draft.

"Whilst Anne Maguire had been implicated by Hill, Conlon, Richardson and Armstrong in the preparations for and the execution of the Guildford bombings, she and her family had no reason to suppose that they had been implicated in the bombing campaign since nothing that had been published about the police investigations seemed to point to them."

Sir John May passes over this part of the Statement without comment. Several are called for: first, was it seriously suggested that terrorists scan the newspapers for details of police investigations into crimes they have committed, and if the newspapers fail to make any reference, direct or indirect, which may lead the police to those terrorists then they need do nothing? Further, the point, certainly in so far as it concerned Patrick Armstrong and Carole Richardson, was wrong, for as Sir John May notes[4], Carole Richardson and Patrick Armstrong were arrested in Kilburn, North London on 3 December 1974. Miss Richardson was arrested shortly after 6:30 p.m. at her step-father's house in Iverson Road. Anne Maguire was arrested at her home at about 8:45 that same evening. Carole said nothing to the police about Mrs Maguire during those times. Patrick Armstrong was arrested in a squat at 14, Algernon Road, at 9:25 p.m. and thus he could not have said anything about Mrs Maguire prior to her arrest, because she was under arrest before he was. It must follow, therefore, that at the time Mrs Maguire was arrested she had not been implicated by . . . Richardson and Armstrong in the preparations for and the execution of the Guildford bombings . . . " as the Statement of Facts may seem to allege.

The Statement goes on: "However *the Talbot bombing took place on 30 November and since one bomb did not explode, they will have feared that examination of that bomb might lead to them*, and in the early hours of 3 December 1974, Patrick Joseph Conlon (Gerard Conlon's father) crossed from Belfast to Heysham, told the security services at Heysham that he had crossed to collect a heavy goods vehicle from Tunbridge Wells, and travelled directly to the Maguire home at 43 Third Avenue, Harlesden. He appears to have arrived unannounced at some time between 1:00 p.m. and 3:00 p.m. that afternoon, although there is a suggestion that he first sent a telegram to Patrick Maguire senior (Anne Maguire's husband) in advance of his arrival. If at any stage he did, it is clear from the interview with the members of the Maguire family and others present at the house that afternoon and evening that Patrick Maguire senior had not divulged Patrick Conlon's expected arrival to anyone. Enquiries are proceedings to see if any such telegram was sent and received; no trace of it was found in the house. Patrick Conlon's explanation to the security services at Heysham was a lie and can be proved to be such. Living at the Maguire house at that time were Patrick Maguire senior, Anne Maguire, their four children – Vincent John Patrick, aged 16, John Patrick Thomas, aged 15, Patrick Joseph Paul, aged 13, and Anne Marie, aged 8 – and Anne Maguire's brother, William John Smyth. Smyth appears to have arrived home about 5:00 p.m. that evening." Sir John May points out that this is incorrect; Mr Smyth did not return from work until about 6:30 p.m.

"At 7. 00 p.m. that evening, two officers of the Metropolitan Police Bomb Squad commenced observations on 43 Third Avenue and saw four men and one woman in the front room. They are able to identify the woman as Anne Maguire and one of the men as Sean Liam Tully of London W9. Soon after they arrived, Tully left 43 Third Avenue in a Ford Escort motor car which was followed for a short distance by the observing officers who recorded the number of the car and returned to continue their observation of the house. At 7:45 p.m. Patrick Maguire senior, Patrick Conlon, Smyth and a man called Patrick O'Neill left the house and went to the nearby Royal Lancer public house – again followed by the two observing officers who then returned to the house. At 8:45 p.m. they were joined by other officers and the police then entered the house immediately behind Vincent Maguire who appeared to be returning to the house at that time. Present in the house when the police entered were Anne Maguire, her children Vincent, John and Anne Marie, and two children of Patrick O'Neill. With some obstruction from John Maguire, Patrick Maguire senior, Patrick Conlon, Smyth and O'Neill were identified in the Royal Lancer and detained. During the course of that night, hand swab tests were carried out on those four men and on Anne Maguire and her three sons The tests on the four men and on Vincent and Patrick (junior) Maguire proved to be positive as follows: (The positive finding were then set out.)

"The test on Anne Maguire was negative, as were the tests carried out then and subsequently on the house and its contents save for 39 clear plastic gloves, of the kind used in laboratories and hospitals which showed clear traces of nitroglycerine on the outer surfaces. Anne Maguire has stated, and this has been confirmed, that she suffers from a skin disease on her hands which necessitates the application of ointment and that she wears these plastic gloves when doing housework, etc. She and the other members of her family have stated that the plastic gloves recovered from the house were hers and that she was the only person to use them.

"A pair of ordinary household rubber gloves recovered from the house were hers and tests on them proved negative for explosives. Also found in the house was a quantify of 1" black plastic adhesive tape, similar in all respects with the tape used to bind the unexploded Talbot bomb. Differing stories were told about the source and use of that tape. Forensic tests have revealed no mechanical match between the tape recovered at the house and the tape on the Talbot bomb. Investigations are still proceeding, at the Metropolitan Police Forensic Science Laboratory to see whether threads found adhering to the Talbot bomb can be connected with any of the many items of clothing taken from 43 Third Avenue."

Before looking at some of the detailed matters referred to in paragraph 10 of the Statement of Facts, mention should be made of the note dated 4 March 1975 written by Roger Maitland about the conference held on 18 February 1975 between the Attorney General, Sir Michael Havers, Mr Eliot Michael Hill and others. Mr Maitland was the lawyer in the Attorney General's Department who had reservations about the RARDE scientists' work methods and results. He recorded this: "The A.G. was informed that Mrs Maguire's eighteen pairs of rubber gloves were found in a pile and that, due to a blunder by the police, cross-contamination was probable. The gloves had been tested as a batch and traces of nitroglycerine were found."

There are some who may find this observation astonishing, since the only evidence against Mrs Maguire was the traces on the gloves, and here at the outset of the case, before she was even committed for trial some unidentified person was telling the chief Law Officer of the Crown that the gloves were not possibly, but probably, cross-contaminated. Why didn't the person or persons who told Mr Sam Silkin that fact also tell the trial judge and jury at the Old Bailey who had made the blunder, what form it took, and how the cross-contamination came about? Why, in the light of that information, not only what had probably been done, but who had done it, did the Attorney General sign the consent form for the prosecution to proceed against Mrs Maguire?

Was it because it was alleged that Mrs Maguire was a vital cog in the IRA and, accordingly, the decision to press on with the charge against was made, even though there was no evidence to connect her with that organisation? It would have looked odd also to allege that her two sons, aged 16 and 13 were possessing nitroglycerine in the family home, yet she was not. As set out previously, in the event on 24 February 1975 the

236

murder charges against Mrs Maguire were withdrawn in the magistrates court on the application of the Director of Public Prosecutions. On that same day, six days after the decision was made to proceed against them, Vincent and Patrick Maguire were charged with unlawfully possessing nitroglycerine. So far as I know, it was not until Sir John May published Mr Maitland's note of 4 March that there had been public disclosure of the fact that, due to a blunder by the police – and what that was has still not been revealed – Mrs Maguire's gloves were probably cross-contaminated. If the prosecution knew this fact, did they tell the lawyers defending Mrs Anne Maguire? If they did not, then why not?

Turning to the Statement of Facts, there is the reference to the Talbot bombing. On 30 November 1974, at about 10 p.m., two bombs were thrown at the window of the Talbot Arms public house in Little Chester Street, Belgravia in London. One bomb rebounded from the window frame and exploded outside the premises, injuring five customers inside the pub. The other bomb failed to explode and was recovered.

The bomb was wrapped in one-inch matt black PVC tape. Two sets of fingerprints were found on the bomb: they belonged to Joseph O'Connell and Brendan Dowd, both members of an active service unit of the Provisional IRA. They were part of the units responsible for the bombings of the public houses in Guildford and Woolwich. They had no connection in any way with either the Guildford Four or the Maguire Seven. Of course, as will be apparent, neither Paul Hill or Gerard Conlon could have been responsible for the Talbot Arms bombing, for both were under arrest and in custody at the time it was carried out.

What is surprising about the Statement of Facts is the certainty of language expressing the supposed reactions of the Maguires: "*However, the Talbot bombing took place on 30 November and, since one bomb did not explode, they will have feared that examination of that bomb might lead to them* . . . " Note that it says "they will have feared", and not "they might have feared".

On what basis that proposition is advanced is not known. If their reaction was fear, why would they wait until 3 December to do anything about disposing of explosives which they were alleged to have had in their possession? The unfortunate Patrick O'Neill – and his three children – arrived at 43, Third Avenue between 6:40 and 7 p.m., when the bomb squad officers took up observation; there was still, so the prosecution alleged, some bulk of explosive left at the house for him to knead and thus contaminate him-

The fingerprints on the Talbot bomb excluded not only the Guildford

Four but also the Maguires, and the police must have known that at the time Mr Eliot Michael Hill drafted the first (Unrevised) Statement of Facts that there was nothing whatever to connect Mrs Maguire or any of the others with that bomb. Nobody would be misled by the allegation that the quantity of 1" black plastic adhesive tape found on the bomb was similar in all respects to the tape found in 43 Third Avenue, for in the very next sentence Hill accepted that they did not match. That tape is of a kind in constant use in almost every house and workshop throughout the United Kingdom.

It is also a fact that on 20 December 1974 a time bomb was left by Joseph O'Connell at Aldershot railway station. It failed to explode. The assembly material featured one inch black matt PVC tape. That was seventeen days after the arrests at Third Avenue.

Mr Eliot Michael Hill seemed to have laid strong emphasis on the fact that Patrick (Guiseppe) Conlon had lied to the security services at Heysham and such a lie could be proved. It would have been an easy and indeed fundamental matter of security to check whether Mr Conlon held a license to drive a heavy goods vehicle, which he was supposed to have said he was to collect from Tunbridge Wells, and further to check his railway ticket to that destination. One wonders whether that was ever done, for Mr Conlon had been unable to work for the previous eleven years due to his health, and had been on a course of anti-TB drugs, and had extensive fibrosis and calcification of both lungs. He must have been a most unlikely looking heavy goods vehicle driver. Indeed his family doctor thought he was not fit enough to travel to London.

According to Grant McKee and Ros Franey, Mr Conlon's ticket was checked. It was a return. They state that prior to his departure from Belfast he informed the RUC at Springfield Road of his intention to travel to London. A letter from the RUC in 1981 proved the fact that he did so. There may not have been as much force in Mr Hill's point as he thought there was at the time he made it.

Mr Hill seems to have told the Attorney General in the Statement of Facts of the time of arrival at the Maguire house of Patrick O'Neill and the three children. He put it at between 6:00 p.m. and 7:00 p.m. He said: "O'Neill maintains that his presence at the house on 3 December was purely fortuitous and arose from the fact that his wife had been taken into hospital that day and that he had brought his two children to Harlesden, arriving at some time between 6:00 p.m. and 7:00 p.m."

There may be two errors here for there were three not two children, and in fact Mrs O'Neill had not been released from hospital as was expected, rather than admitted that day.

238

"He lives in Stockwell. Enquiries are still proceeding to establish the true position with regard to Mrs O'Neill and the need for O'Neill to visit Third Avenue with the children – the evidence presently available is that they had no night clothes or toilet articles with them."

In retrospect it would appear that a very simple check with the hospital at which Mrs O'Neill had been treated would show the date of her admission and departure. The record might also have shown the date of her intended departure and the reason for her non-release on December 3. Looking at the dates on which the Statement of Facts was drafted, it seems that the police were in great hurry to establish those facts, if they ever did. Mr O'Neill was released on bail and yet neither fled nor hid. He had been in the Maguire house for a very short period of time, but because of the forensic tests the prosecution could not have proceeded against the others if they discontinued the prosecution against him.

No one seems to have commented on the fact that only two police officers went to observe the "bomb factory" as 43, Third Avenue at 7:00 p.m. on the night of December 3, or since those officers could see four men and a woman in the house while they watched, that the lights must have been on and the room curtains open, so that anyone could look inside the house from outside, whilst the occupants of that house were supposedly breaking up explosives.

There is in addition something extremely odd about the conduct of these two officers who seemed to do everything as a pair, as if they were joined at the wrist. When Mr Tully, who was later arrested but never charged and completely exonerated, left the Maguire house, both officers followed his car for some distance. When the four men left the house and went to the Royal Lancer both officers followed and then both returned to the house. One might have expected that one officer would have in the latter instance stayed at or near the public house, whilst the other returned to observe 43, Third Avenue. The time of leaving the house was put by the officers at 7:45 p.m. whilst the four alleged it was about 8:15, fixing that time as being after a phone call – by Patrick O'Neill to his wife at the hospital.

That disputed half-hour assumed an significance at the trial, used of course to the advantage of the prosecution. In his summing up of the evidence to the jury, the trial judge Sir John Donaldson, quite improperly in my view, suggested that the reason for there being no bulk of nitroglycerine found in the Maguire house was that it might have been disposed of while the men were on their way to a nearby pub, while under police observation, without the disposal being observed by the police. In an Aide Memoire about the Guildford Four and Maguire

Cases sent to the Home Office in July 1987, the distinguished former Law Lord, Lord Scarman, described this suggestion as "absurd".

Prosecuting counsel also seemed to have some doubt about the existence of the telegram. If it did exist then it should have contained an indication of Mr Conlon's expected arrival. But a telegram was indeed sent to Patrick Maguire, not by Mr Conlon but by Nurse and Jones, the solicitors in Belfast. The telegram said nothing about Mr Conlon's intention to travel to London; it told Mr Maguire about the arrest of Gerard Conlon.

It is my view, in the light of this, that when Sir Michael Havers opened the case for the prosecution against the Maguire Seven he used extravagant and theatrical language and – contrary to Sir John May's view – I consider he indulged in improper speculation about the conduct and behaviour of the seven defendants in the case. Sir John May says[5]: "On the basis of the scientific evidence, counsel were starting from the premise that seven individuals had knowingly handled bulk NG. It was proper for them to consider why and in what circumstances such handling could have occurred. Gerard Conlon's arrest and his father's arrival were facts which could give rise to an inference that the handling occurred as a consequence. If one starts from the premise that there was explosives in or near the house, the arrest of a close relative for a bombing offence might well give rise to a desire to dispose of it."

This is not, in my view, in accordance with the position set out in the Statement of Facts. At the time that was drafted and revised the allegation was that when Hill, Conlon, Richardson and Armstrong were arrested Mrs Maguire and her family had no reason to suppose that they had been implicated in the bombing campaign. It was the fact that the bomb had failed to explode at the Talbot Arms in Belgravia on 30 November 30 that " . . . they will have feared that examination of that bomb might lead to them."

When Havers opened the case to the jury the position had substantially changed. It was the receipt of the telegram from Northern Ireland stating that a relative had been arrested there that started the "alarm bells ringing" and it was "all hands to the pumps" and there was "the gathering of the clans". "The Maguires had called "a hastily convened council of war." Indeed, when the trial judge summed up he said in terms, "The Crown say that the Guildford arrests would create panic amongst these people, that they were in possession of explosives, and they say there is some evidence of panic, or at least grave concern, in relation to the arrest of Gerry Conlon."

Whatever that evidence was it seems not to have been important enough to justify inclusion in the Statement of Facts nor was it identified in any other circumstance. I consider that there was substantial and unjustified speculation in the opening speech of Sir Michael Havers to the jury in the Maguire Seven trial, and some of the blame for the wrongful conviction of these seven innocent people can be attributed to that fact.

The bombing campaign carried out by the Provisional IRA continued long after the arrest of the Guildford Four and the Maguire Seven. Even whilst the jury were out considering their verdicts in the Maguire case there were three explosions in the London area.

The first was on a commuter train from Sevenoaks to Cannon Street; the second occurred in King Street, Covent Garden; the third in Tavistock Square in Bloomsbury. In July 1975 Brendan Dowd was arrested in Liverpool; Joseph O'Connell and others were arrested in Balcombe Street in London in December of the same year.

Then the bombings stopped, but the problems for the police and the lawyers began, for Dowd and O'Connell and others began confessing to bombing the public houses in Guildford – and one in Woolwich – offences in respect of the which the Guildford Four were serving sentences of life imprisonment. Gerard Conlon and Paul Hill were convicted of the Woolwich bombing. The struggle to establish the real truth involving the real terrorists was just about to begin.

Notes

Chapter 1
BLOODY SUNDAY– A JOLLY GOOD SHOW ?

1. *The Compton Report*: Report of the enquiry into allegations against the security forces of physical brutality in Northern Ireland arising out of events of the 9 August, 1971. Cmmd 4823, paras. 60 and 64

2. Ibid Para. 62

3. *The Widgery Report*: Report of The Tribunal appointed to inquire into events on Sunday, 30th January 1972, which led to loss of life in connection with the procession in Londonderry on that day by The Rt. Hon. Lord Widgery. H.L. 101, H.C. 220, para. 17.

4. Ibid.

5. Samuel Dash, *Justice Denied*, A Challenge to Lord Widgery's Report on "Bloody Sunday", The International League for the Rights of Man, in association with the National Council for Civil Liberties. 1972, page 13.

6. Simon Winchester, *In Holy Terror*, Faber and Faber, 1974, page 201.

7. Widgery para. 24.

8. Ibid.

9. Widgery para. 25.

10. Ibid. para. 36.

11. Raymond McClean, *The Road to Bloody Sunday*, Ward River Press, 1983, page 132.

12. Widgery para. 36.

13. Ibid.

14. Widgery para. 38.

15. Hansard H.C., Debates Vol. 830 para. 37.

16. Widgery, para. 31

17. Ibid para. 19.

18. Ibid para. 32.

19. Ibid para. 31.

20. Ibid para. 26.

21. Ibid.

22. Ibid. para 30.

23. Dash, page 22.

24. Widgery, para 27.

25. Dash, page 22.

26. Ibid.

27. Widgery, para. 27.

28. Dash, page 22.

29. Widgery, para. 95.

30. Dash, page 22.

31. Widgery, para.95.
32. Ibid para 62.
33. *The Times*, 1 February 1972.
34. Ibid.
35. Widgery, para.98.
36. Ibid, para. 43.
37. Ibid, para. 47.
38. Ibid.
39. Ibid para. 51(ii).
40. Ibid para. 41.
41. Ibid para. 70.
42. Ibid.
43. Dash, pages 32-33.
44. Widgery, para. 71.
45. Ibid para. 72.
46. Ibid para. 73.
47. McClean, page 185.
48. Widgery, para. 73.
49. Ibid para. 81.
50. Ibid para. 80.
51. Ibid para. 99.
52. Ibid para. 84.
53. Ibid.
54. McClean, page 186.
55. Ibid page 143.
56. Widgery, para. 85.
57. Ibid.
58. Ibid. para. 96.
59. Ibid. para. 97.
60. Ibid para. 101.
61. Ibid para. 87.
62. Dash, page 29.
63. Ibid.
64. Widgery, para. 87.
65. R -v- Foxford 1974 Northern Ireland Law Reports, page 189.
66. Winchester, page 201.
67. Widgery, para. 85.
68. Dash, page 13.
69. Widgery para 88.
70. Ibid.
71. Widgery, Conclusion No. 10.
72. R -v- Foxford page 189.

73. Professor Keith Simpson, *Forty Years of Murder*, Harraps, London 1978.

74. Ibid, page 137.

75. Widgery para 95.

76. Ibid, para 68.

77. Dash, page 35.

78. Widgery, para. 67.

79. Ibid para. 74.

80. Ibid para. 76.

81. Ibid. para. 78.

82. Ibid para. 81.

83. Ibid para. 82.

84. Dash, page 37.

85. Widgery, para. 91.

86. *Secret History*, Channel 4 Television.

87. Ibid.

88. Widgery, para 85.

89. McClean, pages 142 and 143.

90. Widgery, pages 1 and 2.

91. Winchester, page 210.

92. Liz Curtis, *Ireland and the Propaganda War*, Pluto Press, 1984.

93. Winchester, page 211.

94. Ibid page 200.

95. Robert J. Spjut, Criminal Statistics on Security in Northern Ireland, British Journal of Criminology, Vol 23 No 4.

96. *Troubled Times*, Fortnight Magazine, Blackstaff Press 1991.

97. Published by Methuen, 1985.

98. Hamill, page 89.

99. Ibid page 90.

100. Ibid.

101. *Secret History*, Channel 4 Television.

102. Dash, page 22.

103. Cashinella on Secret History.

104. Dash, page 22.

105. Ibid page 23.

106. *Secret History*, Channel 4.

107. Ibid.

108. Widgery, Summary of Conclusions, No.8.

109. Dash, page 27.

110. Widgery, para. 51(i).

111. *The Guardian.*, 8 March 1972.

112. Cited in the Law Officers' Department "Prosecutions in Northern Ireland, A study of Facts, H.M.S.O 1974.

113. 1974 Northern Ireland Law Reports at page 200.

114. Martin Dillon, The Dirty War, Hutchinson, 1990- The dates and details of this part of the work are drawn from that book.

115. Ibid, page 136

116. Ibid, page 150

Chapter 2
THE CASES OF THE MAGUIRE SEVEN AND THE GUILDFORD FOUR

1. Law Report, *The Independent*, 27 June 1991.

2. Ibid.

3. *The Independent*, 27 June 1991.

4. *The Guardian*, 27 June 1991.

5. Ibid.

6. *The Irish Times*, 27 June 1991.

7. *The Guardian*, 9 May 1991.

8. Ibid.

9. *The Guardian*, 27 June 1991.

10. Interim Report on the Maguire Case, by the Rt. Hon. Sir John May, London HMSO printed 12 July 1990 (The May Inquiry Report).

11. Robert Kee, Trial and Error, page 81 (Hamish Hamilton 1986).

12. The May Inquiry Report, para. 3. 17.

13. Ibid, para. 4.7

14. Ibid, para. 3.8.

15. *Trial and Error*, page 84. Mr Robert Kee is the man to whom the Maguire family and the Guildford Four owe an immense debt of gratitude for his unstinting efforts in the campaign on their behalf.

16. The May Inquiry Report, para. 4. 8.17. Ibid para. 4.6.

18. *The Times*, 15 January 1976.

19. Trial and Error p 88

20. *The Times*, 15 January 1976.

21. The May Inquiry Report, para 8. 5.

22. Ibid, para 7. 2.

23. Ibid para. 9. 3.

24. *The Times*, 15 January 1976.

25. The May Inquiry Report, para. I. 7.

26. Law Report, *The Independent*, 27 June 1991.

27. *Trial and Error*, page 114.

28. *Miscarriages of Justice*, Bob Woffinden, p. 271, Hodder and Stoughton, 1987.

29. *The Guardian*, 24 May 1991.

30. The May Inquiry Report, para. 7. 5.

31. *Miscarriages of Justice*, page 262.

32. (1982) 3 All E.R. page 480.

33. Ibid page 481.

34. May Inquiry Report, para. 7. 6.

35. Ibid, para. 7. 7.

36. *The Guardian*, 23 May 1991.

37. *The Times*, 23 May 1991

38. *The Guardian*, 23 May 1991.

39. *The Independent*, 2 June 1990.

40. The May Inquiry Report,para. 11. 13.

41. Ibid.

42. Ibid para. 11. 14.

43. Ibid.

44. Ibid para. 9. 3.

45. *The Independent*, 18 May 1991.

46. Law Report, *The Independent*, 27 June 1991.

47. *Trial and Error*, page 201.

48. *Time Bomb: Irish Bombers, English Justice and the Guildford Four*, Grant McKee & Ros Franey, page 318, Bloomsbury 1988.

49. Ibid.

50. Christopher Price was another most excellent and distinguished campaigner for the Maguires.

51. *The Guardian*, 11 June 1991.

52. *Time Bomb*, page 318.

53. The May Inquiry Report, pages 25-26.

54. *Who's Who*, 1990.

55. Published by the Tablet on 6 December 1986.

56. *Trial and Error* page 140.

57. Ibid. p 141

58. The May Inquiry Report, pages 13-14.

59. *Trial and Error*, page 84.

60. *Time Bomb*, page 138.

61. The May Inquiry Report, para. 5. 8.

62. The May Inquiry Report, para. 7.2.

63. *Trial and Error*, page 86.

64. The May Inquiry Report, para. 4. 4.

65. Ibid para. 4. 5.

66. Ibid para. 4. 4.

67. Ibid para. 4. 7.

68. *Trial and Error* p 86

69. Ibid page 87.

70. The May Inquiry Report, para. 3. 7.

71. Ibid para. 4. 5.

72. Ibid para. 4. 7.

73. Ibidpara. 3. 12.

74. Quoted in *The Times*, 5 May 1976.

75. The May Inquiry Report, para. 12. 1.

76. Ibid para 12. 3.

77. Ibid.

78. Ibid para. 12. 4.

79. Ibid para. 12. 3.

80. Ibid para. 12. 2

81. R -v- Bates (1911) 1 Kings Bench 964.

82. *The Guardian*, 10 September 1991.

83. *The Times*, 10 September 1991.

84. As he now is, former legal Secretary to the Attorney-General and then the Director of Public Prosecutions from 1977 to 1987.

85. *Irish Times*, 12 September 1991.

86. *Irish Times*, 11 September 1991.

87. *The Independent*, 13 September 1991.

88. Sir John May, Interim Report, para. 11. 3.

89. *The Independent*,7 June 1980.

90. The May Inquiry Report, para. 11. 20.

91. *The Independent*,12 June 1990.

92. The May Inquiry Report,para. 11. 21.

93. Ibid para. 11. 20.

94. *Trial and Error*, page 203.

95. *Miscarriages of Justice*, page 264.

96. The May Inquiry Report, para. 11. 30.

97. *Trial and Error*, page 210.

98. *The Irish Times*, 10 September 1991.

99. *Time Bomb*, page 131.

100. Ibid page 134.

101. *Proved Innocent*, Gerry Conlon, page 195, Hamish Hamilton 1990.

102. *Time Bomb*, page 320.

103. Ibid.

104. *Trial and Error*, page 255.

105. Cited by Robert Kee, page 204.

106. Miscarriages of Justice, pages 263/264.

107. Sir John May, Interim Report, para. 51.

108. *The Guardian*, 10 October 1991.

109. *Proved Innocent*, page 211.

110. (1946) 31 Criminal Appeal Reports 146.

111. *Financial Times*, 20 October 1989.

112. *The Times*, 18 September 1975.

113. *Financial Times*, 20 October 1989.

114. *Trial and Error*, page 222

115. *The Times*, 27 July 1990.

Chapter 3

THE HACKNEY ARMS TRIAL

1. *The Branch – History of the Metropolitan Police Special Branch, 1883-1983*, Nigel West, Secker & Warburg, 1983.

2. *Insight, The Sunday Times*, 18 June 1972.

3. *The Branch*, page 154.

4. *The Times*, 8 June 1972.

5. *The Times*, 13 June 1972.

6. *The Branch*, page 154.

7. Ibid.

8. Report of an Enquiry into allegations of ill-treatment in Northern Ireland, Amnesty International, 1972, page 24.

9. Ibid.

10. 18 June 1972

11. *The Times*, 8 June 1972.

12. *The Times*, 13 June 1972.

13. *Insight.*

14. Ibid.

15. Ibid.

16. Ibid.

17. *Reluctant Judas,* the life and death of the Special Branch Informer, Kenneth Lennon, Geoff Robertson, Maurice Temple Smith Ltd, 1976.

18. *Insight.*

19. Ibid.

20. Ibid.

21. *Reluctant Judas*, page 59.

22. Ibid page 60.

23. Ibid page 61.

24. *Insight.*

25. *The Times*, 13 June 1972.

26. *Reluctant Judas*, page 62.

27. Ibid page 63.

28. *Insight.*

29. *Reluctant Judas*, page 63.

30. *Insight.*

31. *Reluctant Judas*, page 64.

32. *The Times*, 17 June 1972.

33. *Reluctant Judas*, page 65.

34. Amnesty International Enquiry Report, page 24.

35. *Error of Judgement, The Truth about the Birmingham Bombings*, Chris Mullen, pages 94-95, Chatto & Windus, 1986.

36. *Fortnight* No. 294, page 34, April 1991.

37. *Reluctant Judas*, page 63

38. Part I of the Written Evidence of the Commissioner of Police of the Metropolis to the Royal Commission on Criminal Procedure, Scotland Yard, 1972.

Chapter 4
THE CASE OF EDWARD MANNING BROPHY AND THE LA MON HOUSE HOTEL

1. *Troubled Times*: Fortnight Magazine and the Troubles in Northern Ireland 1970-92, Blackstaff Press, 1991, page 180.

2. Ibid page 178.

3. Desmond Hamill, *Pig in the Middle – The army in Northern Ireland 1969-1986*, Methuen, 1986,page 221.

4. *Troubled Times*, page 176.

5. Merlyn Rees, *Northern Ireland, a personal perspective*, Methuen, 1985, page 276.

6. *Troubled Times*, page 178.

7. Ibid page 181.

8. Ibid.

9. Chris Ryder, *The RUC, A Force under fire*, Methuen, 1989, page 172.

10. Hamill, page 221.

11. Ibid page 220.

12. Ryder page 172.

13. Ibid page 174.

14. Hamill, page 223.

15. Ryder, page 174.

16. Patrick Bishop & Eamonn Mallie, *The Provisional IRA*, Heinemann, 1987, page 267.

17. Northern Ireland Judgement Bulletin, Incorporated Council of Law Reporting for Northern Ireland, page 5.

18. Ryder, page 175.

19. Hamill, page 223.

20. *Troubled Times*, page 184.

21. Ibid page 185.

22. Keith Kyle, *Mr O'Connor's story*, *The Listener*, 10 March 1977.

23. Peter Taylor, *Beating the Terrorists?*, Penguin, 1980, page 165.

24. Ibid page 167.

25. Ibid page 173.

26. Ibid pages 284/285.

27. Report of an Amnesty International Mission to Northern Ireland 28 November – 6 December 1977, page 10.

28. Northern Ireland Judgement Bulletin, page 2 and seq.

29. Practice Note (Judge's' Rules) 1964, 1 All England Law Reports 327.

30. R -v- Hale & Cooper (1893) XVII Cox's Criminal Law Cases 689 at 690.

31. Practice Note

32. H.H. Judge Bennett Q.C., Committee of inquiry into police interrogation procedures in Northern Ireland, 1973, Cmnd. 7497, page 26.

33. Ibid page 42.

34. Paragraph 87.

35. Northern Ireland Judgement Bulletin, page 10.

36. Ibid pages 12-13.

37. Ibid page 14.

38. Ibid page 18.

39. Ibid.

40. Ibid page 21.

41. Ibid page 19.

42. Ibid page 26.

43. Ibid page 20. Emphasis is in the transcript of the judgement.

44. Ibid page 21.

45. Ibid page 25.

46. At page 707 of the Report.

47. 1982 Criminal Law Review, page 194.

48. At page 471.

49. At page 701.

50. Page 30 of the judgement.

51. Ibid.

52. An offence contrary to section 19(i) (a) of the Northern Ireland (Emergency Provisions) Act 1973, as amended.

53. Page 34 of the judgement

54. Ibid page 40.

55. McIlkenny -v- Chief Constable of West Midlands Police Force & Anor, (1980) 2 All England Law Reports 227 at 234.

56. Ibid.

57. Page 231 of the Report.

58. Hunter -v- Chief Constable of West Midlands Police Force & Anor,(1981) 3 All England Law Reports 727 at 730.

59. *Irish Times*, 8 November 1991.

Chapter 5

SUFFER LITTLE CHILDREN – PART 1

THE KILLING OF MAJELLA O'HARE AND JOHN BOYLE

1. Father Raymond Murray, *The SAS in Ireland*, Mercier Press, 1990, pages 166/167.

2. Witness statement of Seamus Reavey dated 14 August 1976, taken by Father Murray.

3. Brigadier Peter Morton, *Emergency Tour – 3 Para in South Armag,* pages 210/211. The book was published on 30 January 1989 by William Kimber.

4. Ibid page 211.

5. Witness statement of a girl aged 16, dated 26 August 1976, taken by Father Denis Faul.

6. Ibid.

7. Witness statement of James O'Hare dated 26 August 1976, taken by Father Faul.

8. Witness statement of another girl aged 13, dated 26 August 1976, taken by Father Murray.

9. Statement of Nurse Alice Cambell, dated 26 August 1976, taken by Father Faul.

10. Morton, page 211.

11. Witness statement dated 26 August 1976, taken by Father Murray.

12. Nurse Cambell's statement.

13. Witness statement of James O'Hare, dated 26 August 1976, taken by Father Faul.

14. Witness statement of Mary O'Hare, dated 26 August 1976, taken by Father Murray.

15. Morton, page 211

16. Patsy McArdle, *The Secret War*, Mercier Press 1984, page 19.

17. Liz Curtis, *Ireland the Progaganda War*, Pluto Press, 1984, page71.

18. McArdle, page 20.

19. Morton, page 210.

20. Ibid.

21. Ibid.

22. Ibid. page 213.

23. Ibid.

24. McArdle, page 20.

25. Father Murray, page 226.

26. Desmond Hamill, *Pig in the Middle – The Army in Northern Ireland 1969-1985*, Methuen, 1986, page 229.

27. Tony Geraghty, *Who Dares Wins – The story of the SAS 1950-1980*, Fontana Collins, 1981, page 206

28. Adams & Ors, *The War between the SAS and the IRA*, Pan Books, 1988, pages 97-98.

29. Ibid page 206.

30. Ibid page 98.

31. Northern Ireland Judgment Bulletin 1979 No. 5, page 2.

32. Adam & Ors, page 98.

33. Hamill page 229.

34. N. I. J. B. page 4.

35. Ibid page 6.

36. *Newsletter*, 12 July 1978.

37. Ibid.

38. Quoted in Curtis, page 36.

39. *Newsletter*, 12 July 1978.

40. Ibid.

41. Ibid.

42. Father Murray, page 227.

43. N. I. J. B. page 15.

44. Ibid.

45. Ibid page 14.

46. Ibid.

47. Ibid page 5.

48. Ibid.

49. Ibid page 4.

50. Ibid page 13.

51. Ibid page 14.

52. Father Murray, page 228.

53. Adams & Ors, page 98.

54. Hamill, page 230.

55. Father Murray, page 228.

56. Geraghty, page 208.

57. Father Murray, page 228.

58. N. I. J. B. page 9.

59. Ibid.

60. Ibid page 4.

61. Ibid page 9.

62. Father Murray, page 231.

63. N. I. J. B. page 6.

64. Kader Asmal, *Shoot to Kill – International Lawyers' inquiry in to the lethal use of firearms by the Security Forces in Northern Ireland*, Mercier Press, 1985, page 35.

65. (1976) 2 All England Law Reports, page 945.

66. Ibid page 946.

67. These courts were so named because they had been set up following His Lordship's report into procedures to deal with terrorist activity in Northern Ireland. The writer understands that this practice caused Lord Diplock, who was immensely proud of his achievements in the field of human rights in International Law, much personal sadness that his name should be associated with courts in which the fundamental right of trial by jury had been abolished.

68. (1976) 3 All England Law Reports, page 947.

69. Kader Asmal, page 86.

70. Ibid page 36.

71. Ibid.

72. Hansard, vol. 954, paragraphs 223 and 224.

73. Ibid. paragraph 224.

74. Ibid.

75. Hansard, vol. 955, paragraphs 508 and 509.

76. Hansard, vol. 962, paragraphs 28 and 29.

77. N. I. J. B. page 7.

78. Ibid page 9.

79. Ibid.

80. Ibid page 6.

81. Ibid page 11.

82. *Ambush*, page 100.

83. N. I. J. B. page 12.

84. Ibid. page 16.

85. Geraghty, *Who Dares Wins*, page 207.

86. Ibid, page 212.

87. Mark Urban, *Big Boys' Rules*, Faber & Faber, 1992, page 66.

88. Geraghty, page 213.

Chapter 6
SUFFER LITTLE CHILDREN – PART II
THE CASE OF STEPHEN PAUL MCCAUL

1. Page 35 of the transcript of the trial

2. H.H. Judge Bennett: Report of the Committee of inquiry into police interrogation procedures in Northern Ireland, Cmnd. 7497, page 19.

3. Page 37 of the transcript

4. Miranda -v- Arizona 384 U.S- 436 (1966)

5. Page 39 of the transcript.

6. Ibid page 20.

7. *The Evidence of Children*, J.R. Spencer and Rhona Flin, Blackstone, 1990, pages 238-239.

8. Rule IV(d).

9. Page 35 of the transcript.

10. Ibid pages 58-59.

11. Ibid pages 51-52.

12. Ibid pages 14-15.

13. Ibid page 52.

14. Ibid page 41.

15. Ibid page 42.

16. Ibid.

17. Ibid page 45.

18. Ibid page 60.

19. Ibid page 62.

20. Northern Ireland Judgement Bulletin 1980 No. 9.

Chapter 7
DEATH IN THE DARKNESS
THE KILLING OF SEAMUS GREW AND RODERICK CARROLL

1. Statement of Mrs Maureen Grew.

2. *The Guardian*, 26 January 1985.

3. *The Times*, 20 April 1990.

4. *The Guardian*, 26 January 1985.

5. *War without Honour*, Fred Hoyroyd, The Medium Publishing Company, 1989, page 73.

6. Ibid.

7. Ibid page 74.

8. Statement to Father Raymond Murray dated 23 December 1982.

9. Ibid.

10. Ibid.

11. Statement of Mrs Maureen Grew.

12. Ibid.

13. Report of autopsy carried out at Craigavon Area Hospital, 1:30 p.m., 13 December 1982.

14. Report of autopsy carried out at Craigavon Area Hospital, 3:30 p.m., 13 December 1982.

15. *Stalker*, John Stalker, Harrap Ltd, 1988, page 40.

16. Produced as exhibit 42 at the trial R -v- Robinson.

17. Northern Ireland Judgement Bulletin, 1984, No. 4, page 5.

18. Ibid.

19. Ibid pages 12-13.

20. Ibid page 5.

21. Statement to Father Raymond Murray dated 14 December 1982.

22. N.I.J.B. page 10.

23. Statement to Father Raymond Murray dated 17 December 1982.

24. N.I.J.B. page 3.

25. Section 21 Northern Ireland (Emergency Provisions) Act 1978.

26. Statutory Instrument 1979 No. 745.

27. N. I. J. B. page 3.

28. Ibid pages 3-4.

29. Stalker, pages 52-53.

30. Ibid page 53.

31. N. I. J. B. page 9.

32. Ibid page 5.

33. Ibid page 6.

34. For a list to the end of 1983 of these twenty-five supergrasses see Gifford, *Supergrasses: the use of accomplice evidence in Northern Ireland*, Cobden Trust, 1984.

35. Hansard, House of Commons debates Vol. 74 col. 124.

36. *The Times*, 4 April 1984.

Postscript

1. Sir John May's Second Report – HC 296, page 47.

2. Ibid page 38.

3. Ibid page 44.

4. Sir John May's Interim Report, page 11.

5. Sir John May's Second Report – HC 296, page 45.